Technical English 3

Teacher's Book

Celia Bingham

With additional material by David Bonamy

Pearson Education Limited

Edinburgh Gate
Harlow
Essex CM20 2JE
England

and Associated Companies throughout the world.

www.pearsonelt.com

© Pearson Education Limited 2011

The right of Celia Bingham to be identified as author of this Work has been asserted by her in accordance with the Copyright, Designs and Patents Act 1988.

First published 2011
Sixth impression 2017

ISBN: 978-1-4082-6805-6

Set in Adobe Type Library fonts
Printed by CPI UK

Acknowledgements

We would like to dedicate this book to the memory of David Riley, whose tireless professionalism contributed so much to its creation and success.

Illustrated by HL Studios, Long Hanborough.

Every effort has been made to trace the copyright holders and we apologise in advance for any unintentional omissions. We would be pleased to insert the appropriate acknowledgement in any subsequent edition of this publication.

Contents

Introduction   page 5

Unit 1 Systems   page 8

Unit 2 Processes   page 16

Review Unit A   page 24

Unit 3 Events   page 28

Unit 4 Careers   page 36

Review Unit B   page 44

Unit 5 Safety   page 48

Unit 6 Planning   page 56

Review Unit C   page 64

Unit 7 Reports   page 68

Unit 8 Projects   page 76

Review Unit D   page 84

Unit 9 Design   page 88

Unit 10 Disasters   page 96

Review Unit E   page 104

Unit 11 Materials   page 108

Unit 12 Opportunities   page 116

Review Unit F   page 124

Word list   page 128

Introduction

Technical English is a four-level course for students in technical or vocational education, and for company employees in training at work. It covers the core language and skills that students need to communicate successfully in all technical and industrial specialisations. *Level 1* is for students with a basic knowledge of general English who require an elementary course in English for specific purposes. This is benchmarked against CEF level A1. *Level 2* is for students who have completed Level 1, or have an elementary knowledge of general English, and now require a pre-intermediate course in English for specific purposes. This is benchmarked against CEF level A2. Level 3 is for students who have completed Level 2, or have a pre-intermediate level of general English and now require an intermediate course in English for specific purposes. This is benchmarked against CEF level B1. Level 4 is for students who have completed Level 3, or have an intermediate level of general English and now require an upper intermediate course in English for specific purposes. This is benchmarked against CEF level B2.

The course uses a multi-thread syllabus consisting mainly of communicative functions, notions, grammar, vocabulary and skills. The work-specific communicative functions (e.g. *giving instructions, making recommendations*) and technology-specific notions or concepts (e.g. *causation, resistance*) are selected on the basis of relevance to the needs of students in technical training and work contexts. Grammatical exponents of functions and notions are selected on the basis of frequency and relevance to needs. In Level 1 the grammar is sequenced; in Level 2 a more cyclical approach is taken, in which functions and notions reappear with more complex grammatical exponents. In Levels 3 and 4, the syllabus organisation is increasingly driven by topics, skills and genre or text type, within which appropriate grammar, vocabulary, functions and notions are introduced or recycled.

The vocabulary of the course is a selection of common-core lexical items that have a high frequency of use across a range of technical and industrial contexts. Many of these items can be found in general contexts, but have a greater frequency and often a more specific meaning in technical contexts. Many of them are the kind of words which a specialist in one field might use to explain technical concepts and specialised terms to the general public, or to specialists in other fields. For students who need additional exposure to a more specialised industry-specific vocabulary, it is recommended that *Technical English* be supplemented by a course book from the appropriate *Vocational English* series, also published by Pearson Education.

The methodology is transparent and straightforward, with a practical task-based approach. Activities are firmly rooted in shared meanings and clear contexts. The approach recognises that the students may have differing motivations towards learning English, but assumes that they have a knowledge of, and interest in, technology and wish to develop their careers and technical skills. The topics and texts reflect current and future developments in technology, and are designed to stimulate students' interest and motivation to find out more about them. From the beginning of the course, students are encouraged to use their technical knowledge and problem-solving skills. The approach also takes into account the fact that most teachers of technical English will have no training (though most will have a keen interest) in technology. As much background information as possible about each topic is therefore provided both in the teaching material itself and in the Teacher's Book.

Course Book 3

The Course Book contains twelve core units and six review units. Each core unit is divided into three sections. Each section (corresponding approximately to a 60–90 minute lesson) is contained on two facing pages, unified by a single theme, which may be a function, a concept, a topic, or a genre, such as a report. There is a four-page review unit after every two core units.

Core units

Start here

This is a warm-up activity which begins each double-page section. It is often a question (such as *How do you think this works?*) based on a photograph or diagram, which pairs or groups discuss before they begin a reading or listening activity. The warmer is intended to activate students' existing knowledge about the topic of the unit and stimulate their interest in finding out more.

Listening

Listening skills are developed through a variety of activities using audio texts set in both work and training contexts. The listening activity requires students to carry out a practical task during or after listening, such as completing a specification chart, filling in a form, or labelling a spidergram. Audio texts set in work contexts include radio and TV interviews, news items and reports on technology, instructions, job interviews, investigative interviews, phone conversations, meetings, discussions, brainstorming sessions, descriptions of visuals, progress reports, work procedures, test reports, radio phone-in by technical experts, and product descriptions. Audio texts set in a training context include extended passages in monologue form such as lectures, presentations and technical demonstrations. Students listen for the main idea, specific information and discourse markers.

Speaking

Speaking activities at this level aim to equip students with the skills to communicate effectively with fellow professionals, colleagues, trainers, contractors, clients and customers. The tasks reflect real-world situations such as investigative interviews, collaborative team discussion, group training sessions, arguing or defending a point of view, group decision-making, explaining plans, projects and schedules, preparing group presentations, group problem-solving, speculating or hypothesising about causes, brainstorming, work discussions and formal meetings.

At this level, students are guided towards preparing and giving longer talks and presentations based on notes and diagrams. Speaking activities are conducted in pairs, small groups or individually to the class. In addition, there are speaking activities in the *Task* section (see below).

Reading

The written texts that technologists have to process in real life can vary enormously in length, complexity and genre. Readers' purposes vary from in-depth understanding to following instructions or searching for technical details. The reading texts in Course Book 3 reflect real-life texts and purposes, and are all based on authentic sources. These sources include descriptions of systems, explanations of process, technical descriptions, investigative reports, operating manuals, user guides, articles from technical journals, safety rules and procedures, memos from work colleagues, product reviews, transcripts of interviews with technologists, technical fact sheets and specifications, covering letters between clients and contractors, technical blogs and websites. Labelled diagrams and photographs are liberally provided to aid comprehension of technical data, and students are always given some background information or asked to think about a topic (often in the *Start here* activity) before they start reading, so that they are using the texts actively. For example they may be asked to look at a diagram of a device and discuss how it might work using their own knowledge *before* reading about how the device works. The texts use carefully controlled language and are accompanied by simple and practical tasks such as checking information, labelling a diagram, correcting details or completing a specification chart. Awareness of cohesive devices and discourse markers is further developed at this level.

Scanning

The skill of scanning a text at speed for information is further developed. In every unit there is a scanning activity which consists of questions asking for short, factual information. Students find this information in a timed activity by scanning quickly through a number of texts on the *Speed search* pages (see below) at the back of the book. In these activities it is important to set the questions and start the timer (for example the stopwatch function of a mobile phone) *before* the students open the book at the *Speed search* pages.

Writing

Writing skills are developed through a variety of tasks in realistic contexts, reflecting a more advanced range of text types which students might have to produce in a work context or as part of their technical training. Writing activities include operating manuals, user guides, process explanations, longer reports, product descriptions, covering letters for job applications, CVs, sets of instructions, rules and procedures, emails containing technical data and questions, reports on work done, design proposals, investigative reports, memos outlining decisions of a meeting and explanations of how things work. Peer-correction of written work is developed at this level, as well as collaborative group work leading to individual writing. Where such writing tasks are set as homework, it is important to allow time in class for the group work to be completed.

Task

The *Task* feature provides students with opportunities to combine and use their language, skills and technical knowledge to communicate in contexts that reflect real-life work or training situations. Tasks require different combinations of skill, knowledge and procedure. Some are in fact problem-solving or cognitive exercises designed to activate their background knowledge to help them in a reading, writing, listening or speaking activity. Others combine one or more skills, for example discussing with a partner how to improve a product, writing a design proposal for their new or modified design, and finally presenting their proposal jointly to the rest of the class and answering questions. Some tasks can be done individually, but most are done using pair work, group discussion, brainstorming and collaborative problem-solving leading to a joint output, for instance when groups meet to discuss a case study of an engineering failure, decide what went wrong and what should have been done to avoid the disaster, present the group's conclusions to the class and then, working individually, write a short report on their group's decisions.

Language

The language box draws students' attention to the key grammar of a lesson. The grammar is presented in a simple, straightforward manner and gives only the basic minimum of information necessary. The box is intended for reference or study only, and normally follows a reading or listening activity in which the student has understood the grammar point in context. Where necessary, the language box is accompanied by a short language practice exercise. If students need more information about grammar, or for revision, they can refer to the *Language summary* at the back of the course book.

Vocabulary

Vocabulary activities develop students' knowledge and use of common-core technical or sub-technical vocabulary. Many activities use visuals to clarify the meanings of core technical terms such as *extrusion* or *injection*. Others deal with lexical sets (e.g. physical properties) and word families and affixes (e.g. *stabilise*, *stabiliser, stabilisation*. Students are made aware of words used across several specialisms and everyday words that take on special meanings in technical contexts (e.g. *eject* in plastics processing and aviation). Everyday words are presented alongside their more technical Graeco-Latin synonyms (e.g. *twisting/torsion*).

Reference

Language summary

This gives more information about all the language points dealt with in the core units. It can be used as a reference during a lesson, or for revision.

Reference section

This section at the back of the book includes useful reference material for the student, for example units of measurement and their abbreviations, how to say mathematical symbols and operations, how to say internet symbols and British and American English.

Extra material

This contains the materials needed by one side of a pair of students, or members of a group, to enable them to carry out the communication activities in the *Task* sections.

Audio script

This is a complete transcript of all the listening material in the Course Book. It can be used in different ways according to the levels and needs of your students. Students can use it to check their answers after they have completed a listening task.

Speed search

This is a double-page spread which contains a number of reading texts of different styles, topics and formats. The texts do not show any reference to the pages or units they are related to. Students are given a short time to scan quickly through the two pages to find the specified information. (See *Scanning* above)

Review units

Each Review Unit revises and practises material from the preceding two core units. In addition it contains a *Project* section, which gives the students opportunities to do some simple further research into topics linked to the topics of the core units. They are encouraged to use the internet or a library to carry out the research as homework, and present the results to the class either individually or as group tasks.

Teacher's Book 3

Unit summary

The first page of each core unit in the Teacher's Book sets out the key objectives of the core unit of the Course Book.

Briefing

Each core unit in the Teacher's Book has a briefing which gives background information about the technical topics in the core units, and highlights the key vocabulary which needs special attention in the unit. It also lists some Web sites which give more in-depth information about the topics.

Teaching notes

Each double-page spread in the teaching notes corresponds to a double-page section in the Course Book. Each main unit of the Teacher's Book contains procedural notes for each activity in the Course Book, ideas for extra activities if appropriate, answer keys and audio scripts. Every review unit contains answer keys for the review units in the Course Book plus a photocopiable *Quick test* of the preceding two main units, to test lexis, grammar, functions, reading and writing.

Word list

This is at the end of the Teacher's Book. It contains all the key words used in the Course Book. It is sorted into alphabetical order with references to the unit where each word appears.

TestMaster CD-ROM

This contains entry and exit tests, progress tests and individual unit tests which can be downloaded and edited as required. Test can be customised for specific purposes and institutions. The TestMaster CD-ROM is enclosed with the Teacher's Book.

Additional support

Course Book CD This contains all the recordings for the listening exercises in the Course Book.

Workbook with Audio CD This provides additional material based on the Course Book, which can be set as class revision or homework. It also contains a unit-by-unit word list.

Companion Website The Companion Website contains supplementary teaching activities and industry-specific material to support the Course Book and the Workbook.

David Bonamy

1 | Systems

Contents

1 Rescue

Objectives

In this section students will …

- listen to a news report about an air-sea rescue
- read an incident report and complete an incident report form
- study and practise using cohesion
- revise asking and answering questions in the past simple
- learn vocabulary for safety equipment and telecommunications

2 Transmission

Objectives

In this section students will …

- read and complete a text about how an emergency beacon works in a rescue situation
- listen to a recording about a rescue
- describe a system
- revise and practise non-defining relative pronouns
- practise saying figures and measurements in specifications
- learn vocabulary for telecommunications and satellites

3 Operation

Objectives

In this section students will …

- answer questions about a diagram
- practise writing an operating manual
- revise and practise the imperative for giving instructions
- learn instruction verbs and vocabulary for mechanical and marine engineering

Briefing

This Unit looks at **systems**, in particular the components of **search and rescue (SAR)** systems: satellites, emergency beacons, self-activating devices, automatic and manual release mechanisms.

Section 1 deals with the events surrounding a search and rescue operation (based on a real-life incident) and the equipment and technology used in **locating** (discovering the exact position of) the survivors of a boat that has sunk in the open sea. The reading text on page 5 gives the facts, the main point being that the only way the survivors can alert the rescue team is by means of their **emergency beacon**. This is an **EPIRB**, or **Emergency Position Indicating Radio Beacon**, which automatically **detaches** itself (frees itself) from the boat as it sinks, floats to the surface, **activates** itself (switches on) automatically and automatically transmits an emergency signal, including its exact location, on the **406 MHz (megahertz)** radio channel, via the international **Cospas-Sarsat** satellite system, to the coastguard, who then organise the rescue. The important point about the EPIRB is that all its functions (mentioned above) are automatic, so that even if the survivors are badly injured and unable to operate a hand-held beacon, the EPIRB will continue to operate independently.

Section 2 describes the Cospas-Sarsat satellite system in more detail. The diagram in Exercise 1 on page 6 shows three types of beacon being used: the EPIRB (see previous paragraph) from the shipwreck has already been described. The crashed aircraft has an **ELT** (**Emergency Locator Transmitter**), which is hard-wired into the aircraft and activates automatically on impact. The survivor is carrying a **Personal Locator Beacon (PLB)** which is activated manually. All three types are connected to the Cospas-Sarsat system. The data from the beacon transmission goes via the satellite first to a **ground station**, then to a **national centre** and finally to the nearest **rescue centre**. The Cospas-Sarsat system was originally set up by the USA, the former Soviet Union, France and Canada. *Sarsat* is an acronym of Search and Rescue Satellite-Aided Tracking. *Cospas* is a Russian acronym with a similar meaning. As of 2010, there are 26 countries participating in the system. The system uses two satellite sub-systems. The first consists of **GEOSAR** (Geostationary Search and Rescue) satellites, which are at a higher altitude and **geostationary** (their position remains fixed relative to the Earth). The second consists of **LEOSAR** (Low-altitude Earth Orbit Search and Rescue) satellites, which orbit the Earth at low altitudes around the North and South Poles. LEOSAR has narrower coverage of the Earth because of its low altitude, but can calculate precise locations because it moves relative to the Earth. GEOSAR has wider coverage because of its greater altitude, but cannot provide locations. Each sub-system has strengths and weaknesses, which is why two types of satellites are needed, working together to provide full coverage and precise location of signals. More detailed information on the satellite systems can be found on the Cospas-Sarsat website (see below).

Section 3 describes the self-activating, free-floating beacon (EPIRB) in some detail, and in particular its **release mechanism** which enables it to detach itself from a sinking ship or boat, float free and then activate itself. The key mechanism is the **hydrostatic release unit** (HRU), a mechanism, operated by water pressure, that releases the beacon when the water surrounding it reaches a specific pressure. When the HRU in a sinking ship reaches a depth of 4 metres, the pressure of the water at that depth pushes a knife through a rod (see diagram on page 8) which releases a spring and lever arm. The arm pushes the beacon away from a magnet, which causes the beacon transmitter and light to switch on. The beacon then floats on the surface, continuing to transmit to the satellite system. In addition to this self-activating mode, it is possible to activate the beacon manually, which is illustrated in the diagram on page 9.

The Cospas-Sarsat satellite search-and-rescue system: Find the **Cospas-Sarsat** web site.

Emergency beacons: Find the **Beacons NZ** (New Zealand) website and search for 'Air', 'Land' and 'Sea'.

Two commercial websites providing factsheets, manuals and user guides for emergency beacons are **CM Hammar** and **McMurdo**. Search for 'EPIRB'.

Teacher's notes

1 Rescue

Start here

> **Extra activity**
>
> As a warmer, ask students to keep their books closed and tell them that they are in a boat in the middle of the ocean. There has been an accident and the boat is sinking. Ask them to decide amongst themselves what equipment they need to have in the boat in order to get rescued.

1 Ask students to open their Course Books and focus their attention on the diagram and the photo on the right. Tell them to compare the diagram about the rescue with their ideas in the warmer but do not go into too much detail at this stage, as they will listen to a recording about the rescue in 2. Go through the named labels in the diagram with the class, making sure students pronounce the words correctly, particularly *winch*. Pre-teach some of the vocabulary that they will be using in this section: *fire* (a flare), *inflate*, *sink* (*sink–sank–sunk*), *strike* (an object; *strike–struck–struck*), *rescue*, *a signal*, *a satellite*). Then put students into pairs to answer the questions.

1 C life jacket, D life raft

2 A flare, E beacon, F radio

3 B winch

> **Extra activity**
>
> Put students into pairs to test each other on the named labels from the diagram. They take it in turns to cover up one of the labels and ask the other student what the device is, e.g. *What is E? It's a beacon.*

Listening

2 ▶ 🔘 02

Explain to students that they are going to listen to a news report about an air-sea rescue. They will need to put the devices from the illustration into the order that the reporter mentions them. Play the recording. Allow students to compare answers, then go through the answers with the class.

1 B   **2** F   **3** D   **4** C   **5** E   **6** A

▶ 🔘 02

A dramatic air-sea rescue took place at 11 a.m. this morning in the Indian Ocean. Two sailors were pulled up from the sea into a helicopter using a powerful winch, in very rough seas and a high wind.

The sailors were in a small boat, the *Tiger*, about 77 kilometres from land. Suddenly their boat struck an object, and it sank almost immediately.

The sailors wanted to send an emergency signal by radio, but the boat went down too quickly, and the radio sank with the boat. So the men did the best thing to save their lives – they inflated their life raft and jumped in. They were already wearing their life jackets, of course. But their problem was how to call for help 77 kilometres from land.

Fortunately, the boat had a free-floating beacon, which activated when the boat sank to four metres. The beacon detached itself from the boat, floated to the surface of the sea and switched on automatically. Then it transmitted a signal to the rescue satellites.

The rescue team received the emergency signal, and raced in their helicopter to the two men in the life raft.

When the helicopter came close to the life raft, the sailors fired two flares. The pilot saw the flares and brought the helicopter over the life raft. Then the sailors were winched up.

The whole rescue operation, from the moment the *Tiger* sank, took only 90 minutes, thanks to the automatic beacon and the satellite system it was linked to.

3 Ask students to read through the statements. They could then discuss in pairs the order in which they think the events actually happened. Then play the recording once more for them to check.

1 C   **2** E   **3** B   **4** G   **5** F   **6** D   **7** H   **8** A

Reading

4 ▶ 🔊 03

Ask students to read the news article about the air-sea rescue. When they have finished, ask them to find the words in 4 in the text and underline them. To help them find the people or things the words refer to, tell students to read the sentence (or words) before the words they underlined.

Then ask students to look at the words in the box. Play the recording for students to hear the words. Play it again for students to repeat. Drill the words chorally. Then ask individual students to say the words, checking their pronunciation as they do so.

▶ 🔊 03

kilometres

flares

visible

emergency

signal

coastguard

beacon

free-floating

satellite

automatically

megahertz

wavelength

> **1** the two sailors
> **2** the signal
> **3** the beacon
> **4** the beacon
> **5** on the surface
> **6** in an air-sea rescue

Extra activity

Draw a table of four columns on the board with the headings 1–4. Then write the words below next to the table (but not the answer key in brackets). Tell students to copy the table and put the words in the correct column according to the number of syllables in each word.

beacon (2); coastguard (2); emergency (4); kilometres (4); megahertz (3) satellite (3); signal (2); visible (3); wavelength (2)

---

5 Ask students to use information from the news article in 4 to complete the incident report. Allow students to compare answers. Then go through the answers with the class.

> **Incident report form**
> Name of rescue helicopter pilot: *Ricardo Moussa*
> Date of rescue: *18 July*
> Name of boat: *Tiger*
> Distance of boat from land: *77 km*
> Number of people rescued: *2*
> Time of first emergency signal: *09.30*
> Type of emergency beacon: *406 MHz free-floating beacon*
> Time of rescue: *11.00*
> Method of rescue: *winch (into helicopter)*

Speaking

6 First, remind students how to form questions using the past simple: *I carried out the rescue on 18 July.* → *When did you carry out the rescue?* The verb *be* is different: *The vessel was in the Indian Ocean.* → *Where was the vessel?*

Put students into pairs. Allow them some preparation time to write questions for the safety officer, based on the form in 5. Then ask them to take turns to be the rescue pilot and the safety officer, using the questions they prepared. Tell students not to read out the questions they wrote but to try and remember the questions from memory. While they are doing the activity, go round the class monitoring the students. Go through any errors with the class at the end of the activity. When they have finished, you could ask a couple of pairs to perform their roleplay in front of the class.

> *Possible interview questions:*
> What's your name?
> When did the rescue take place?/When did you carry out the rescue?/What was the date of the rescue?
> What was the name of the boat?
> How far was the boat from the land?/What was the distance of the boat from the land?
> How many people did your team rescue?/How many people were rescued?
> What time was the first emergency signal?
> What type of emergency beacon did the boat have?
> What time did your team carry out the rescue?
> How did they do/carry out the rescue?

2 Transmission

Start here

1 Allow students a few minutes to look at the illustration. Then tell them to read through the description, ignoring the gaps, to find out what happens in a rescue. Ask one or two stronger students for feedback. Students complete the text with the words in the box, and then compare answers. Do not correct answers yet as students will be checking their answers with the recording in 2.

Listening

2 ▶ 🎧 04

Tell students that they are going to listen to a dialogue about how the system in the diagram in 1 works. Play the recording once for students to follow the process in the diagram. Play the recording a second time for students to check their answers in 1.

1 activate
2 detaches
3 transmits
4 receive
5 converts
6 locates
7 carries out

▶ 🎧 04

A: So how does the rescue service work? What happens after your plane crashes, or your ship starts sinking?

B: Well the first thing you do, if you're a survivor of a plane crash or a sinking ship is to activate your personal emergency beacon manually.

A: OK, but what happens if I can't locate my personal beacon, or it sinks with my ship?

B: Well, most planes and ships today are fitted with automatic beacons. So when the plane hits the ground or the ship starts to sink, the beacon detaches itself and activates itself automatically.

A: Right, so let's assume my beacon is activated. What happens next?

B: Well, the beacon then transmits a radio signal, and one or more satellites receive the signal and …

A: … and the satellites then send the signal to the rescue team?

B: No, they can't do that, not directly. First they send the signal to their ground station. And the ground station then processes the signal, in other words it converts or changes the signal into useful data.

A: Right, I see. And what happens next?

B: Well, the ground station then passes this data on to a national centre. And the national centre then forwards the data to the rescue centre which is nearest to the location of the crashed plane or sinking ship.

A: I see. And the rescue centre sends out the rescue team?

B: Yes, that's right. First it locates the beacon, in other words, it finds out its exact position and marks it on a map. Then it sends out the rescue team.

A: And the rescue team carries out the rescue?

B: That's right. The team searches for the survivors, finds them, winches them into the helicopter and then takes them back to the rescue centre or straight to hospital.

Reading

3 Draw students' attention to the shaded glossary box. Read through the explanation of *geo-* with the class. Explain that *geo-* is a prefix that means *Earth*.

Ask students to look at the text and the illustration. Explain that some of the information in the text is incomplete. Ask students to read through the text and the missing phrases. Then tell students to complete the text with phrases A–G in the correct order. Allow students to compare answers. Then go through the answers with the class.

| 1 D | 2 F | 3 E | 4 B | 5 G | 6 C | 7 A | |

Language

Relative pronouns

Go through the Language box with the class. Read through the first line of the examples in the box with the class. Explain that that second sentence of the pair gives extra information about the first sentence. We can join the two sentences using a relative pronoun, and in non-defining relative clauses we separate the two clauses using a comma. For more information on relative pronouns, refer students to page 103 at the back of the Course Book.

4 Ask students to work individually or in pairs to join the sentences by replacing the words in italics with a relative pronoun. Allow students to compare answers before checking the answers as a class.

1 The beacon sends a signal to the satellite, from where the signal is transmitted to the ground station.
2 The rescue centre contacts the helicopter pilot, who then carries out the rescue.
3 The sailor activated his beacon, which sent a 406 MHz signal to the satellite.
4 The sailors were winched into the helicopter, where they were given blankets and hot drinks.
5 The sailors were taken by helicopter to the rescue centre, from where they were driven by ambulance to the nearest hospital.
6 Hundreds of survivors are saved every year by the Cospas-Sarsat system, which was first launched in 1982.

Speaking

5 Focus students' attention on the table and on the items a–h. Go through the example with them and ask them to read each of these items in this column out loud. Then check with the whole class by asking individual students to read out the items.

a (from) two to five kilograms
b two hundred and sixty millimetres high, by one hundred and two millimetres wide, by eighty-three millimetres deep
c GME–two–oh/zero–three–double–F–one–eight–seven–five–six
d thirty-five thousand kilometres
e four–oh/zero–six–megahertz
f (from) minus forty degrees Celsius to (plus) forty degrees Celsius
g five watts
h oh/zero point five seconds every fifty seconds

Task

6 Refer students back to the table in 5 and ask them to match 1–8 with the correct items a–h. They can then check their answers in pairs.

1 e   **2** g   **3** h   **4** b   **5** a   **6** f   **7** c   **8** d

Scanning

7 Treat the Speed search as a competition. Go through the questions with the class first. Then ask students to turn to pages 116–117 and find the text on the Cospas-Sarsat system. Tell them to read the text as quickly as they can and find the answers to the three questions. Explain that they do not need to read every word in the text, just look for the information to answer the questions. Ask students to put up their hand when they have finished. Allow the majority of students to finish. Then check the answers with the first person to put up their hand to see if they were correct and are the winner of the competition.

1 1982
2 US, Canada, France, Soviet Union (Russia)
3 at least 29

3 Operation

Start here

1 Put students into small groups of three and focus their attention on the diagram of the free-floating emergency beacon and the glossary box at the bottom left. Ask them to study the information and discuss the questions. Note that *HRU* is an abbreviation for *Hydrostatic Release Unit*.

When students have finished, get feedback from the class on question 1 but do not go over question 2 at this point as students will learn the answer in the next task.

> **1** because manual beacons may be lost, or the crew may be injured or unable to activate them manually; so the beacon will operate even if the crew is unable to activate it

Vocabulary

2 Students work in their groups to match the synonyms in a–e with the words and phrases in italics in 1–5.

> **1** c   **2** a   **3** e   **4** b   **5** d

> **Extra activity**
>
> When students have finished, check their pronunciation of the words in 1–5, especially *submerged*, *ejected* and *range*. You could also check their pronunciation of *signal* and *magnet* at this stage. Get them to say: *out of range of the magnet*.

Task

3 Ask students to work in groups to match questions 1–5 with their answers a–e. When they have finished, choose one student from the class to read out the questions and another to answer them.

> **1** c   **2** e   **3** a   **4** d   **5** b

> **Mixed-ability classes**
>
> With stronger classes you could set this up as a competition. Ask the group that finishes first to put their hands up. When all groups have finished, ask students from the group who finished first to give their answers. Ask students in the other groups if they agree with the answers or not.

Writing

4 Focus students' attention on the extracts from the operating manual. Explain that they describe how the beacon in the diagram on page 8 works. Each strip 1–7 refers to a different stage in the diagram. Go through the instructions for stage 1 from the manual and explain that stages 2–6 are incomplete. In their groups, students should each complete a different stage using the information from the diagrams.

When they have finished, allow students to compare work and suggest improvements before they produce a single copy.

Mixed-ability classes

For stronger students, allow them to remain in the same groups they were in for 1–3 and ask each group member to work on two stages. For weaker students, have groups join together with another group so each student has one stage to complete.

Note that in the illustration on the first page of this unit, the beacon is shown attached by a line or cable to the life raft. This is not mentioned in the model answer or other exercises, which focus on how the appliance works rather than the survivors' actions. However, if possible, the survivors should attach the beacon to the life raft.

Model answer:
Free-floating emergency beacon for Cospas-Sarsat rescue system
How it works
1 If the boat sinks, and the beacon is submerged below four metres of water, the water pressure activates the HRU (hydrostatic release unit) automatically.
2 The water pressure inside the HRU pushes the knife downwards and cuts the (breakable) rod.
3 This releases the lever arm, which allows the spring to push the lever arm and the beacon away.
4 The lever arm then ejects the cover from the beacon and the beacon floats away.
5 The beacon then moves out of range of the magnet.
6 As a result, the beacon automatically activates itself (or switches on).
7 When it reaches the surface, the beacon transmits its signal and a light switches on.

Vocabulary

5 Focus students' attention on the first illustration on how to activate a beacon manually. Allow them time to study the information in it. Then ask them to look at the incomplete instructions below. Ask them to complete the instructions using the words from the box.

1 Pull
2 Remove
3 Tear off
4 Push; slide
5 Place; ensure
6 touch

Extra activity

To revise the words in the box, you could mime one of them (apart from *ensure*) for students to guess the word. The student who guessed correctly mimes the next word, and so on. Then ask them what *ensure* means.

Writing

6 Tell students that they are now going to produce an operating manual for a device of their choice. Go through the instructions first to make sure that they all know what to do before asking them to choose their device. If necessary, brainstorm some ideas for devices, depending on students' specialisms. For example, students in telecoms or electronics might choose a TV satellite dish, a wi-fi modem or a CB radio as their device.

Tell students to work in their groups and use the language in 4 and 5 to help them write the manual. When they have finished, allow students to compare work in their groups. Explain that as well as checking thoroughly for any mistakes in grammar, it is important to make sure that their work is very clear so that the reader of the manual can understand it easily.

2 | Processes

Contents

1 | Future shapes

Objectives

In this section students will …

- talk about products made from plastics
- listen and match news reports to photos
- read and identify predictions in a report on plastics in aerospace engineering
- revise and practise *will* for predictions
- talk about degrees of certainty using noun phrases and adverbs
- learn vocabulary for plastics applications

2 | Solid shapes

Objectives

In this section students will …

- describe the process of injection moulding of plastic using diagrams
- study and practise using the present simple passive
- read a text describing the metal-rolling process and rewrite it using the passive form
- use sequence words to describe a process

3 | Hollow shapes

Objectives

In this section students will …

- learn about the extrusion and blow moulding process and the pressure die-casting process to shape plastic
- study a diagram to put the notes in the correct order
- listen to a talk on the extrusion and blow moulding process
- practise using verbs to refer to a visual
- complete a table with different parts of speech to expand vocabulary
- practise writing full sentences from notes using active and passive tenses
- write an explanation of the pressure die-casting process using a diagram and notes
- explain a process using a diagram

Briefing

This Unit looks at **processes**, and in particular some of the processes involved in shaping plastics and metals.

Section 1 deals with current and future applications using plastics (or **polymers**) in innovative ways. Current developments include the bridge in the photograph on page 10. This is Europe's first **all-plastic bridge**, near Friedberg, Hesse, Germany (see also Review Unit A, page 18). The deck of the bridge was made of a single piece of FRP (fibreglass-reinforced polymer), 27 metres long. No screws, rivets or other fasteners were used in the deck. It was **pre-fabricated** (built in one piece beforehand) and transported as a single unit to the construction site, where it was attached to two steel supports. The total installation took less than one day. There is also rapid progress towards the **all-plastic car**. The photo on page 10 is of the Chevrolet Volt, which has a **body** made of **composite** (a combination of plastic with a fibre). It has transparent plastic **panels** all around the car. Eventually all parts, excluding the engine and the rigid frame, could be made of plastic composites. Progress is also being made towards building a passenger aircraft with an all-plastic **fuselage** (body). The aircraft in the photo is of the Boeing 787 *Dreamliner*, which has a fuselage mainly made of carbon-fibre-reinforced plastic, assembled without the 50,000 fasteners normally used in aircraft building, and is lighter and stronger than an aluminium one.

Section 2 deals with one of the main processes used in shaping plastic products: **injection moulding**, which combines **forming** and **casting**. In forming, the shape of a solid material is changed by applying pressure, with or without heat, to the material. In casting, the material is melted to liquid form and the **cavity** (space) inside a **mould** (AmE **mold**) is filled with the liquid, which then solidifies in the shape of the cavity. In injection moulding, **pellets** (pieces) of raw plastic are pushed along a **cylinder** by a rotating **screw**, and heated until the plastic becomes softer. Then the plastic is forced by a **ram** through a **nozzle** and **injected** into the cavity between the two halves of a mould (see diagram on page 12). When the plastic inside the mould is cool and hard, the mould opens and the shaped plastic is **ejected** from the mould. The **metal-rolling** process is a method of making a metal plate thinner. The metal is heated (but not melted) to soften it, and then forced by the pressure of two rollers into a thinner sheet. It is also possible to **cold-roll** some metals, where the pressure alone, minus the heat, is enough to compress the metal into a new shape.

Section 3 deals with **blow-moulding**, the most commonly-used method for making hollow plastic objects such as plastic bottles and bags. In fact, blow-moulding consists of two processes: the first, **extrusion** (squeezing out), is similar to the first part of injection moulding. The soft molten plastic is **extruded** (forced out) through the nozzle of a **die** (see Figure 1 on page 14), a metal block with a hole running through it. When the plastic is forced through the hole, it emerges as a long cylindrical tube called a **parison**. The parison is then enclosed by the two halves of a mould. When the two halves are together, they form the required shape, in this case a plastic bottle. Now the blow-moulding takes place (Figures 2 and 3). An **air hose** blows air into the parison, and the air pressure forces the soft plastic outwards against the sides of the mould. The mould is then cooled and opened, and the plastic bottle is ejected. Exercise 7 on page 15 deals with **pressure-die casting**, a process used for shaping metals. Here the metal is melted into liquid form, and poured into a **chamber** where a **piston** pushes the molten metal into the cavity of a mould. When the metal has **solidified**, the two halves of the mould open and the metal component is ejected.

> Current and future uses of plastics: Find the **Plastics Europe** website and search for 'Innovations'.
>
> Information on casting and forming of plastics and metals: Find the **Open University Learning Space** website and search for 'Engineering and technology' then the 'T173_2: Manufacturing' course page and find 'Casting / Forming'.
>
> More on plastics: Find the **British Plastics Federation** (BPF) website and search for 'Plastics processes'.

Teacher's notes

1 Future shapes

Start here

1   As a warmer, tell students to close their books. Ask them to work in pairs and name as many objects as they can that are made of plastic. Give them a time limit of two to three minutes. Find out which pair has the most objects.

Put students in pairs. Ask them to look at photos A–D and discuss the questions with a partner. Then ask the class for their ideas. Accept all answers but do not confirm them yet as the listening and reading texts to follow will provide them.

> The plastic bridge and ice rink exist now; part-plastic car bodies and plane fuselages have been designed and are planned for manufacture soon; fully plastic bodies and fuselages are expected in the next 25 years; plastic engines are unlikely for the foreseeable future.

Listening

2   ▶ 🔘 05

Tell students that they are going to listen to five news reports. They should match the photos A–D in 1 with the news reports. They then tell you what the other report was about.

> **A** 4   **B** 2   **C** 1   **D** 5
> The other report is about plastic packaging of the future that will be able to detect changes in temperature or the freshness of food, and give information to the customer.

▶ 🔘 05

1   Engineers in Germany have constructed Europe's first plastic road bridge. The bridge comes without nails and screws. Instead, the complete deck of the bridge is made of a composite plastic called fibreglass-reinforced polymer.
The whole deck was glued onto two steel columns. The bridge is 27 metres long and it can be used for cars, lorries and pedestrians, just like an ordinary bridge.
2   A major aircraft manufacturer has announced that it has designed a new type of aircraft with a plastic body. The company will start to manufacture the plane at the end of next year. More than fifty percent of the fuselage, or body, of the plane will be made of a composite plastic material.
This is a big step towards making a one hundred percent plastic fuselage.

3   Plastics packaging material is going to be smart, even intelligent, in the near future. A futurologist working for a major plastics manufacturing company has made a prediction for the next ten to fifteen years. He expects that we will see plastic packaging that can detect changes and give information to the customer. For example, the plastic packaging around food will contain very thin electronic chips. These chips will be able to detect changes in temperature, or changes in the freshness of the food. The plastic food package will then communicate this information to the customer.
4   A futurologist who works for a big international plastics manufacturing company has made an important prediction. He believes that by the year 2035 most cars and other land vehicles will have bodies made completely of plastic composites. However, he says, it is unlikely that cars, including their engines, will be completely made of plastics by that date.
5   Plastic ice is spreading over Scandinavia! Sweden now has more than nine ice skating rinks which are made … not of ice … but of plastics. Engineers in a major plastics company have designed and manufactured a new kind of plastic composite which feels just like ice. It has exactly the same friction and slipperiness as real ice, and the skates cut into the plastic to exactly the same depth as in real ice.

3   Focus students' attention on the table and the three headings. Tell them that they are going to hear the news reports again and that they should put the report number under the correct heading. After you have checked their answers, have a class discussion on products made from plastics in the future, e.g. ask them what advantages plastic bodies on cars would have, and if there are any disadvantages.

> designed but not yet manufactured: 2
> already manufactured and in use now: 1, 5
> planned or expected in the future: 3, 4

Scanning

4   Go through the instructions with the students. Then ask them to turn to pages 116–117 and find the text on plastics. Remind them that they do not need to read every word in the text, just look for the information which answers the questions. Ask students to put up their hand when they have finished. Allow the majority of students to finish, but check the answers with the first person to put up their hand to see if they were correct and are the winner.

> **1** polycarbonate
> **2** fibreglass
> **3** polyester

Reading

5 Focus students' attention on the heading of the article. Ask them what they know about plastics in aerospace engineering and what they think the article will say about the future of plastics in this industry. Then ask students to read the article individually and write the letter of the paragraph next to the appropriate time frame. Check the answers as a class and then ask students if any of their predictions were mentioned in the article.

> **1** A, B and C   **2** F   **3** E   **4** D

6 Make sure students understand that *likely* means the same as *probable*. Ask students to work in pairs to read through the predictions and tick the ones that were mentioned in the article in 5. Then ask them to read the article again and write the correct letter of the paragraph for its prediction. Ask them to discuss their answers in pairs before they check with the class.

> Students should tick predictions 2, 4 and 6 (they mean the same as the ones in the article).
> The paragraphs the predictions are in are: 2 B, 4 C, 6 C.

Language

Will for predictions

Go through the Language box with the students. Explain that these are ways to express certainty about the future. Point out that you can use *likely* in the expression *It's likely that they will make …* but you cannot say ~~They will likely make~~ … . Also point out that *certainly* and *probably* always come after *will* and before *not*, e.g. *They **will** probably **not** make …* .

7 Students can work in pairs to rephrase the predictions in 6, making sure that the meaning stays the same. Tell them to look back at the Language box to help them. Check answers by asking individual students to say a prediction that they have rephrased.

Possible answers:
1 They'll possibly build a plastic engine in the future.
2 They'll probably construct a plastic wing before 2035.
3 It's likely that they won't (*or* It's unlikely that they will) make a plastic engine before 2035.
4 It's certain that they won't manufacture a plastic engine before 2035.
5 It's possible that they'll make a plastic fuselage before 2035.
6 It's likely that they won't (*or* It's unlikely that they will) build a plastic engine in the future.

> **Mixed-ability classes**
>
> You can ask weaker students to write a few questions using this structure about anything in the future. This could be used as preparation for the speaking activity to follow.

Speaking

8 Tell students that they are now going to make their own predictions about the future. The predictions can be about aerospace or about the future in general, depending on the strength of the class. Read through the example with the class. Then ask the class to mingle and tell each other their predictions. If students wrote preparation questions in the optional activity above, they should not look at them during this exercise. When they have finished, ask students to tell the class about some of the predictions they heard from other students.

> **Extra activity**
>
> Students could write short news reports like the ones in the listening in 2 about two or three of their predictions they discussed in 8 for homework. They could then read them out to the class at the beginning of the next lesson.

2 Solid shapes

Start here

1 Focus students' attention on the title of this section. Ask them what *solid* means. Then focus students' attention on the diagram, which shows the process of injection moulding of plastic and ask them to look at the photos below. Allow students to study the diagram for a couple of minutes and help with any vocabulary. Pre-teach *screw* by giving examples from real life and ask them to find it in Figure 1. Then focus their attention on the pellets in the diagram and ask them to describe what a *pellet* is (a small piece of plastic). Ask them to find *mould* and elicit its meaning (a hollow form used for shaping fluid or plastic material). Finally, tell them to look at the photos and ask them which photo shows a *drain pipe*, and which photo shows a *bumper*.

Put students in pairs and ask them to discuss the questions. Go around the class, making sure students are using the named parts in the diagram in their discussion. Do not check their answers yet. The answers are given in 3 below.

Reading

2 Tell students that they are going to read about the process of injection moulding of plastic. Explain that the sentences are not in the correct order. Ask students to work individually to read the sentences and put them in the correct order according to the diagram in 1. They can then compare their answers with a partner before you check the order with the class.

> **1** C   **2** E   **3** B   **4** D   **5** G   **6** F   **7** A

3 Check students' answers to the three questions in 1 as a class.

> **1** to soften the plastic pellets
> **2** The screw turns and moves the pellets and then the plastic fluid along the cylinder towards the nozzle.
> **3** all the items except 2 (bottle) and 6 (bag) can probably be made using this process because they are *solid* objects which can be moulded in a cavity like the one in the diagram in 1. The bag and the bottle are probably made using blow-moulding, as shown in the next section; the telephone handset would be made in two parts.

Vocabulary

4 Ask students to look through the sentences in 2 and quickly find the words which mean *thrown out* and *pushed in*. Tell them to put their hands up when they find the words. Ask the first student to put their hand up to tell you their answer. Then check students' pronunciation of these words.

> ejected – thrown out
> injected – pushed in

> **Mixed-ability classes**
> Ask students what the opposites of these words are:
> cool (v) (heat)
> push (pull)
> raise (lower)
> soft (hard)
> thin (thick)

Language

Present simple passive

Go through the Language box with the students. Here students are presented with the present simple active and passive for describing a process. Focus students' attention on the second box and point out that you form the passive with the verb *be* + past participle. Point out that you use *by* before the agent.

Tell students that you can use both forms for describing a process but explain that the passive is usually preferred in technical language because it helps the reader focus on what happens to things rather than the agent. Point out that sometimes the agent needs to be mentioned, as in the example sentence, but often it is not necessary.

Tell students that they can find more information about the passive used in technical writing in the Language summary on page 100.

5 Ask students to refer back to the diagram in 1 to help them complete the sentences with the appropriate active or passive form of the verbs in brackets. Students could do this activity in pairs if you think they might struggle.

1 are stored
2 are transferred
3 is propelled
4 raise
5 flows
6 is forced

Writing

6 Focus students' attention on the diagram about the metal-rolling process. Ask them to describe the process shown in the diagram. Ask one or two stronger students, then ask the rest of the class to add anything that might have been missed out. Explain that in some places in the text, the active form of the verbs has been used where a passive form would be more appropriate. Read through the question with the class and check students understand what they have to do. Then ask students to rewrite the text individually.

First, the gap between the rollers is adjusted to the correct width. Next, the motor is switched on, and the heavy rollers begin to rotate in opposite directions. Now the metal plate is heated and then (the hot metal plate is) pushed through the gap between the rollers. As the hot metal moves between the rollers, it is compressed (by the rollers) to a thinner shape. Finally, the metal comes out from the rollers in the form of a metal sheet, and (it) is then cooled/which is then cooled.

3 Hollow shapes

Start here

1 Ask students to look at the main photo and ask them what *hollow* means. Then ask them to point at any hollow-shaped objects that they can see in the room.

Quickly revise and pre-teach some words for this section. Ask the students to look at the two small photos on the right. Ask them what is being done to the toothpaste (it is being squeezed onto the toothbrush), and what the man is doing to the balloon (he is inflating/blowing up the balloon).

Explain that students are going to discuss with their partner how the items in the photo were shaped. Put students in pairs. Before they start their discussion, tell them that there is a clue about how they are shaped in the two small photos on the right. During feedback, do not discuss their answers too much at this stage. A full explanation can be found in the listening exercise in 3.

> They were shaped by blowing air into hot molten (melted) plastic.

Listening

2 Focus students' attention on the diagram. Tell them that it illustrates two different processes of shaping plastic: Figure 1 illustrates the extrusion process and Figures 2 and 3 illustrate the blow moulding process.

Draw students' attention to the definitions of *polymer* and *molten* in the glossary box under the notes for Figure 1. Then allow them a couple of minutes to study the diagram and help them with any other vocabulary. For example, ask them to label the hopper and cylinder in Figure 1. Then ask them what the die does (it is used to cut and shape semi-soft solids). Ask them what the extruder does (it is a device that forces semi-soft solids through a die opening). Finally, ask them for another word for *molten* (melted).

Now ask students to look at the notes in the two boxes below the diagram and explain that they are not in the correct order. Tell them to work individually to put the sentences in the correct order. Then ask them to compare with a partner but do not confirm the students' answers yet as they have to check their own work in the listening exercise in 3.

The extrusion process

1 transfer of polymer pellets from hopper to cylinder of extruder
2 rotation of screw
3 movement of cold polymer pellets along cylinder
4 heating and melting of polymer pellets
5 movement of warm, soft molten polymer along cylinder
6 extrusion of molten polymer into mould

The blow moulding process

7 closure of two halves of mould with molten polymer inside
8 blowing of compressed air into molten polymer
9 inflation of molten polymer by compressed air
10 expansion of polymer to fit shape of mould
11 cooling of plastic bottle shape
12 ejection of plastic bottle from open mould

3 ▶ 🎧 06

Tell students that they are going to listen to a talk about the two processes in 2. Ask them to listen carefully in order to check the order of their notes.

See answers in 2.

▶ 🎧 06

Good morning everyone, and thanks for coming. This is the fourth short talk in our series of talks about the plastics industry. Last week we looked at the process of *injection moulding*. Today, I'm going to explain how *extrusion blow moulding* works.

Extrusion blow moulding is a method of making a hollow shape out of a thermoplastic. This shaping method is very useful for making things such as plastic bottles, petrol containers, jerry cans and so on.

As its name suggests, extrusion blow moulding consists of two separate processes.

The first one is the *extrusion* process. This is very similar to the injection moulding process we looked at last week. During extrusion, solid pellets, or small pieces, of plastic are heated, melted, pushed along a cylinder and extruded, or pushed out, into a mould.

The second process, *blow moulding*, takes place inside the mould, where compressed air blows into the centre of the molten plastic and expands it into a hollow shape such as a bottle.

Let's look at the first process, the extrusion of molten plastic into the mould.

As you can see in Figure 1, there is an extruder at the top left of the diagram. This operates like the injection moulding cylinder we saw last week.

As I'm sure you will remember, first of all, pellets of raw plastic are fed from a hopper into a large horizontal cylinder. Inside this cylinder, a large screw rotates. This rotation pushes the cold polymer pellets along the cylinder towards the right. There are heaters all along the sides of the cylinder. These heaters heat up the polymer pellets and melt them. The screw continues to push the soft, melted polymer along the cylinder.

As can be seen in Figure 1, there is a ninety-degree angle at the right-hand end of the cylinder. This angle, or bend, is inside the die in the top right-hand section of Figure 1. Now the molten plastic flows downwards through the die, and is extruded, or pushed out, into the mould.

So that's the end of the first part of my talk, about the *extrusion* process. Let's turn now to the second part, which is about the *blow moulding* process.

Blow-moulding consists of three stages. I will now describe each of the three stages in turn.

Let's look at the first stage. As Figure 1 shows, the hot, soft plastic is extruded down between the two halves of the open mould. The plastic is in the form of a long, hollow tube, called a parison. Then, as Figure 2 illustrates, the two halves of the mould close. Now the parison is inside the mould.

The second stage is illustrated in Figure 2, as well. In this stage, compressed air is blown through the nozzle into the molten polymer parison. The air inflates the parison, and as a result, the soft plastic expands to fit the shape of the mould. The plastic is cooled by the cold surfaces of the mould. This sudden cooling causes it to harden quickly in the shape of, in this case, a bottle.

The third and final stage is shown in Figure 3. Here, after a cooling period, the two halves of the mould open, and the bottle is ejected from the mould onto a conveyor belt.

4 Ask students to listen to the recording again and complete the sentences with the words and phrases in the box.

1 can see
2 can be seen
3 shows
4 illustrates
5 is illustrated
6 is shown

Vocabulary

5 Focus students' attention on the table and the example. Ask them to look back at the notes in the two boxes in 2 and find the example noun in the first note. Explain that they have to continue making a list of nouns and verbs as in the table in 5, using the first noun from the notes in the boxes and writing the verb form.

movement – move, extrusion – extrude, heating – heat, melting – melt, transfer – transfer, rotation – rotate, cooling – cool, expansion – expand, blowing – blow, ejection – eject, inflation – inflate, closure – close

Language

6 Ask students to look back at the notes in 2. Tell them that they must write the notes as full sentences. Go through the first example with the class and ask them to find the related note in the box.

Ask students to rewrite the sentences (in the correct order) using the verbs from their table 5 in the appropriate active or passive form. Then ask them to work in pairs to check their sentences.

The extrusion process
1 The polymer pellets are transferred from the hopper to the cylinder.
2 The screw rotates.
3 The cold polymer pellets are moved along the cylinder.
4 The polymer pellets are heated and melted.
5 The warm, soft molten polymer moves along the cylinder.
6 The molten polymer is extruded into the mould.

The blow moulding process
7 The two halves of the mould close/are closed with the molten polymer inside.
8 Compressed air is blown into the molten polymer.
9 The molten polymer is inflated by the compressed air.
10 The polymer expands/is expanded to fit the shape of the mould.
11 The plastic bottle shape cools/is cooled.
12 The plastic bottle is ejected from the open mould.

Writing

7 Focus students' attention on the diagram and explain that this diagram describes the process of pressure-die casting. Explain the difference between *cavity* and *chamber*. Allow students a couple of minutes to study the diagram. Tell them that they are going to write an explanation of the pressure-die casting process, using the passive where appropriate. They should also use *first*, *then*, *next* and *finally*.

Model answer:
Pressure-die casting
First, some metal is heated until it melts. Next the molten metal is poured into a chamber. Then a piston moves along the chamber. The molten metal is pushed (by the piston) under pressure into the cavity between the two halves of a mould and fills the cavity. When the metal cools and becomes solid, the mould is opened and the solid metal component is ejected from it/the mould.

Speaking

8 Tell students that they are going to explain the process in 7 to the class without using their notes. Allow students a few minutes to look through their notes and try to memorise the process. Then get individual students to explain the process, referring to the diagram where appropriate. Weaker or shyer students could present the process to their partner or in small groups of three.

Review Unit A

Answer key

1
1 When did you transmit the message?
2 Where did the accident take place?
3 How did you activate the beacon?
4 When did the boat strike the rock?
5 Why did you inflate the life raft?
6 When did the aircraft take off?

2 *Possible answers:*
When did ATC receive the emergency signal from the pilot?
Where was the plane at the time of the signal?
When did ATC lose radio contact with the plane?
How long did the radio silence last (for)?
Who did ATC contact?
Why did ATC contact the coastguard?
Where did the distress signal come from?
What data did the signal provide?/How did the signal help the rescue team find the plane?
What time did the rescue team catch sight of the plane?
When did they find the life rafts?
How many passengers survived?

3
1	detached	6	picked up/received
2	floated	7	send/transmit
3	activated	8	converted
4	transmitted/sent	9	locate
5	receive/pick up	10	found out

4
1 who 2 where 3 which 4 where 5 which
6 who

5
1 Turn the bike over and place it upside down on the ground.
2 Loosen the nuts that hold the wheel to the frame.
3 Take the wheel out of the frame.
4 Deflate the inner tube completely by pressing down on the inner part of the valve.
5 Use two tyre levers.
6 Push one lever in gently between the edge of the tyre and the rim of the wheel.
7 Pull the edge of the tyre out over the rim.
8 Leave this lever in position, and push the second lever between the tyre and the wheel rim.
9 Slide this second lever around the wheel rim under the tyre edge.
10 Detach the tyre and the inner tube from the wheel rim.

6 *Possible answer:*
First, the cause of the puncture is located. The inner tube is submerged in water to locate the hole. Next a small amount of air is pumped into the tube to look for bubbles from the hole. The location of the hole is then marked, and the tube is deflated completely. Now the area around the hole is rubbed with some rough material and a thin layer of glue is spread around the hole. The plastic backing is torn off from the patch, and the sticky side of the patch is placed firmly on the tube. Finally, the tube is slid back into the tyre, the tyre and tube are pushed into the wheel rim, and the tyre is re-inflated.

8
1	will use	6	pre-fabricated
2	are happening	7	transported
3	are designing	8	fastened
4	has already constructed	9	took
		10	will last
5	installed	11	will not/won't/does not corrode

9
1	have you done	8	haven't made
2	designed	9	is making
3	have already constructed	10	will probably finish
		11	will you transport
4	are you doing	12	will take
5	is/are pre-fabricating	13	will carry
6	will be	14	will attach
7	have you manufactured		

10
1 Engineers will probably not invent a time machine in the future.
2 They'll definitely manufacture an all-plastic car body some day.
3 It's unlikely that astronauts will be able to reach Mars in the next 20 years.
4 Sea levels will probably rise at least 0.2 metres in the next 50 years.
5 It's certain that Beijing won't make another Olympic bid in the next 20 years.
6 It's probable that an asteroid won't strike the Earth in the next 100 years.

11
1 How aluminium sheet is extruded.
2 How diesel oil is injected into the engine cylinder.
3 How land vehicles are propelled by the wind.
4 How boat propellers rotate in turbulent seas.
5 How pilots are ejected from damaged planes.
6 How survivors are transferred from the sea to the hospital.
7 How steel beams expand at high temperatures.
8 How agricultural sensors are inserted into the ground.

12 *Model answer:*
Stage 1: Input
The waste material is carried to the top of the hopper by a conveyor belt. It is then poured into the hopper, where it sinks down towards the cutter.
Stage 2: Reduction
The material moves between a roller and a cutter, where it is cut into very small pieces, and the volume is reduced.
Stage 3: Sterilisation
Now the waste is sprayed and sterilised. It moves down through a cylinder and falls into a rotating kill tank. Here the waste is mixed with the sterilising fluid and gases escape. The gases pass through a filter which cleans them.
Stage 4: Removal
Finally, the sterilised material is removed from the kill tank and taken to a recycling plant.

Project

15 At the end of every Review Unit is a project. Students can do their research on the internet. Then they should produce a document describing a process from their own technical field, which includes flow charts and diagrams to illustrate the process, and a user guide to explain how to operate the equipment and controls. Ask students to check their work thoroughly when they have finished for any mistakes in grammar, spelling or punctuation. They could also ask a partner to check through their work as well and suggest any improvements.

Quick test answer key

Part 1: Vocabulary and grammar

1
1 transmitted 2 located 3 converted 4 activated
5 ensured

2
1 winch 2 out of range 3 propel
4 submerge 5 release

3
1 pull 2 Remove 3 touch 4 Tear off
5 Slide 6 Place

4
1 blow 2 closure 3 expand 4 extrusion
5 inflate

5
1 which 2 where 3 who 4 from where

6
1 They inspected the new factory yesterday, where they build aircraft fuselages.
2 Khalid wanted the operating manual, which explained how the beacon worked.
3 I spoke to your boss yesterday, who explained the metal-rolling process.
4 They climbed to the top of the hill, from where they could see the coast.

7
1 Don't touch 2 Pull 3 Pour 4 Don't enter

8
1 It's probable that they'll make a new engine next year.
2 They certainly won't use a plastic engine in their aircraft.
3 It's certain that the ship won't sink.
4 It's possible that they'll be late for the meeting.

9
1 The emergency beacon is activated manually.
2 The sailors are winched out of the life raft.
3 The plastic is cooled by the mould.
4 The solid metal component is ejected from the mould.

Part 2: Reading and writing

Reading

1 d 2 b 3 a 4 c

Writing

Model answer:
First, a solid wooden pattern of the component is made. The pattern is pushed into sand inside a moulding box, and more sand is pressed around it. Then the model is removed, which leaves a cavity in the sand. Molten metal is then poured into the cavity through the runner. The molten metal fills the cavity, and excess molten metal rises up the riser. To make a hollow shape, a core is inserted into the mould. When the casting is cold and solid, it is removed. The mould is then destroyed and the runners and risers are cut away from the casting.

Review Unit A Quick test

Part 1: Vocabulary and grammar

1 Replace the words in *italics* with a word from the box.

> activated converted ensured
> located transmitted

1 The beacon *sent* an emergency signal to the satellite.
2 They *found* the survivors in a life raft in the sea.
3 The ground station *changed* the signals into data.
4 The sailor *switched on* the beacon manually.
5 They *made sure* that the beacon was on a flat surface.

(5 marks)

2 Write the words for these definitions.

1 w_____ a piece of equipment that uses a rope or a chain to pull people out of the sea
2 o____ o____ r_____ a phrase to mean that you are not within the distance to see or hear something
3 p_____ to move something forward
4 s_____ to sink under water
5 r_____ to free something

(5 marks)

3 Choose the correct option to complete the sentences.

1 First **pull/push** the clip towards you.
2 **Remove/Ensure** the cover of the beacon.
3 Do not **touch/tear off** the antenna.
4 **Tear off/Push** the tab.
5 **Pull/Slide** the switch to the left.
6 **Place/Ensure** the beacon in an upright position.

(6 marks)

4 Complete the table.

Verb	Noun
1 _____	blowing
close	2 _____
3 _____	expansion
extrude	4 _____
5 _____	inflation

(5 marks)

5 Choose the correct relative pronoun in these sentences.

1 The rod breaks, **which/where** releases the cover of the beacon.

2 The survivors were taken to hospital, **where/which** they were given medical assistance.
3 The rescue team found the passengers, **which/who** were in a life raft.
4 They drove to the station, **which/from where** they continued their journey by train.

(4 marks)

6 Join these pairs of sentences into single sentences. Use *which, where, from where* and *who*.

1 They inspected the new factory yesterday. Here they build aircraft fuselages.

_____

2 Khalid wanted the operating manual. The manual explained how the beacon worked.

_____

3 I spoke to your boss yesterday. He explained the metal-rolling process.

_____

4 They climbed to the top of the hill. From there they could see the coast.

_____

(4 marks)

7 Complete the sentences in the imperative, using the affirmative or negative form of the words in the box.

> enter pour pull touch

1 _____ the antenna while it is transmitting.
2 _____ the red lever down to work the machine.
3 _____ the molten metal into the chamber.
4 _____ the building without wearing goggles.

(4 marks)

8 Rewrite these sentences so the meaning is the same.

1 They'll probably make a new engine next year.
It _____.
2 It's certain that they won't use a plastic engine in their aircraft.
They _____.
3 The ship definitely won't sink.
It's _____.
4 They'll possibly be late for the meeting.

_____

(4 marks)

  PHOTOCOPIABLE

9 **Rewrite these sentences using the passive form. Use _by_ only when necessary.**

1 Someone activates the emergency beacon manually.

_____

2 The helicopter winches the sailors out of the life raft.

_____

3 The mould cools the plastic.

_____

4 They eject the solid metal component from the mould.

_____

(4 marks)

Part 2: Reading and writing

Reading

Complete the text with the phrases below.

Locating black boxes

When there is a plane crash, safety investigators immediately start searching for the aircraft's black boxes, (1) _____ immediately preceding the accident. Black boxes are attached to the aircraft's tail section, (2) _____. Although they are called 'black boxes', they are in fact bright orange. This, along with strips of reflective tape, is especially useful for the divers (3) _____ if a plane crashes into the sea. In addition, the black boxes are equipped with an underwater locator beacon. If a plane crashes in water, the beacon transmits an ultrasonic pulse, (4) _____.

Once the beacon sounds, it continues to transmit a signal once every second for 30 days.

a) who are trying to locate the boxes
b) where they have more chance of surviving impact
c) which can be detected by sonar and acoustic equipment
d) which provide details of what happened

(4 marks)

Writing

Study the diagrams and read the notes below. Then write an explanation of sand casting. Use _First_, _Then_, _Next_ and _Finally_, and the passive where appropriate.

Sand casting

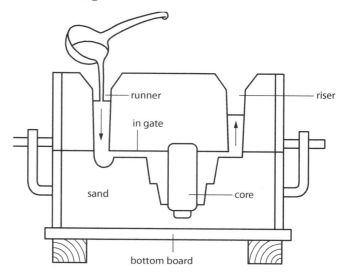

runner — riser
in gate
sand — core
bottom board

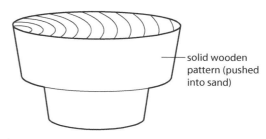

solid wooden pattern (pushed into sand)

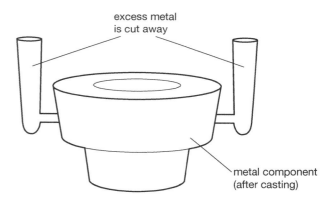

excess metal is cut away

metal component (after casting)

- make solid wooden pattern of component
- push pattern into sand inside moulding box
- press more sand around it
- remove model – this leaves a cavity in the sand
- pour molten metal into cavity through runner
- molten metal fills cavity
- excess molten metal rises up risers
- to make a hollow shape, insert core into mould
- when casting is cold, remove it
- destroy mould and cut away risers from casting

(10 marks)

3 Events

Contents

1 Conditions

Objectives

In this section students will …

- listen to a radio news report from the future about a new safety system and complete a text
- revise and practise the present perfect versus the past simple
- listen to a slide presentation and complete information
- revise the first conditional, and study and practise using the second conditional
- learn vocabulary for aerospace and mechanics

2 Sequence (1)

Objectives

In this section students will …

- talk about a sequence of events in a diagram and make notes
- listen to a presentation to match parts of a spacecraft to their functions
- practise asking and answering questions using the second conditional
- read a text and put events in the correct order
- study and practise using time clauses with the present perfect or present participle after *once*, *after*, *when* and *as soon as*

3 Sequence (2)

Objectives

In this section students will …

- talk about a sequence of events and put illustrations in the correct order
- exchange information with a partner to complete a chart with missing information
- work in a group to design a new product and write a description explaining how it works
- present a design to the class
- learn noun suffixes and semi-technical vocabulary

Briefing

This unit looks at chains of **events**, particularly in the operation of ejection systems for the crews of aircraft and spaceships.

Section 1 describes the NASA **launch abort system** (**LAS**), currently being tested for the Orion space **capsule** of the Ares Moon **rocket**. The LAS allows an **astronaut crew** to escape safely if a rocket **launch** has to be **aborted** (stopped) soon after it has started. Ares rockets were originally intended to replace **space shuttles** in 2015, but the Ares programme was cancelled in 2010. However, the Orion space capsule, with its launch abort system, has been retained for use as an **escape pod** for the International Space Station. The 'crash' of the Ares rocket (audio 7) is an imaginary event set in the future, 2020.

Section 2 gives a more detailed look at the LAS components, and the operation of the LAS system (see diagram on page 22) during a launch emergency. The LAS and the crew capsule to which it is attached (by means of **explosive bolts**) together form a single **unit** at the **tip** (or **nose**) of the rocket. If an emergency occurs during the first 100,000 metres of the launch, the **abort engine** is automatically activated (Figure 2) and pushes the unit (LAS + capsule) away from the rocket with great force. Once the unit is safely free of the rocket, two additional sets of engines are activated: first the **attitude-control engine** (Figure 3) adjusts its **attitude** or **orientation** (the direction in which it is pointing in three-dimensional space) and **stabilises** the unit (makes it **stable**). Then the **jettison engine** (Figure 4) **jettisons** (or discards) the LAS: assisted by the explosive bolts which **detonate** at the same moment, this engine pushes the LAS away from the crew capsule, which now begins to fall to Earth. Finally, **parachutes** (Figure 5) are **deployed** (put into action) to allow the capsule to float safely to Earth. Other components (see page 22) are the **tank** containing solid **propellant** (fuel) and the **protective cover** over the crew capsule.

Section 3 deals with the operation of an aircraft **ejection** (or **ejector**) **seat**. When a pilot pulls the ejection seat handle, this sets off a chain of events that propels the **canopy** (the transparent cover on top of the **cockpit**) away from the aircraft and thrusts the pilot safely out of and away from the plane. Here is an outline of what happens during the ejection (for more detail, read Student B's material on page 115, followed by Student A's material on page 111; also see the illustrations on page 24): 1 The pilot pulls the handle. 2 The explosive bolts on the canopy detonate and release the canopy. 3 The canopy is detached from the cockpit and flies away. 4 The gun of the **catapult** (the **launch mechanism**) fires. 5 The catapult pushes the seat upwards on its **rollers** along the **guide rails**. 6 Leg **restraints** (straps) automatically tighten around the pilot's legs to stop them moving. 7 The seat leaves the rails and exits the cockpit. 8 The **rocket** below the seat fires, and lifts the seat into the air well above the aircraft. 9 The rocket motor burns out. 10 A metal **pellet** (ball) is fired upwards out of the parachute **pack** on the pilot's back. 11 The pellet pulls out a small parachute, called a **drogue**, which opens up. 12 The drogue pulls out the main **parachute**, which opens up. 13 At the same time the seat and leg restraints are released and the seat falls away, allowing the pilot to float down to Earth supported by the parachutes.

Orion capsule and Launch Abort System: Find the **NASA** website and search for 'Orion' and 'LAS'. Also find the **Popular Science** magazine website and search for 'Launch abort system'.

Ejection seats: Find the **How Stuff Works** website and search for 'How Ejection Seats Work'.

Teacher's notes

1 Conditions

Start here

1 Focus students' attention on the photo on the right. Then put them in pairs to discuss the question. Ask them for their ideas in a feedback session. Do not discuss their answers in detail yet as the information will be found in the listening and reading exercises that follow.

Pre-teach some vocabulary that they will be using in this section (*abort, activate, crash, eject, float down, launch, capsule, rocket, parachute*).

Listening

2 ▶ 💿 07

Tell students that they are going to listen to a news report from the year 2020, which discusses a new system for rocket launches. Ask them to read through the questions before you play the recording. Tell them that *LAS* means *Launch Abort System*. Then elicit ideas about what the Launch Abort System might be. You could also ask students to identify the capsule in the photo and ask them what it is for. See the Briefing section at the beginning of the unit in the Teacher's Book for more information.

> 1 to eject the crew capsule from the rocket if something goes wrong in the first 100,000 metres of the ascent
> 2 The capsule, which the LAS is attached to, is ejected from the rocket; then it detaches itself from the LAS; finally, three sets of parachutes open and the capsule floats down to Earth.

▶ 💿 07

[R = Reporter; TC = Technology Correspondent]

R: This is the six o'clock news for today, the 14th of April, 2020.
First, the news in brief. The new Ares moon rocket has failed to launch. The rocket has crashed into the Indian Ocean. The crew capsule containing the six astronauts has landed safely in the ocean. Rescue helicopters have taken the astronauts to hospital, where they are recovering. The director of the space program has resigned.
Now the news in detail. Six astronauts escaped death early this morning when their Orion crew capsule detached itself safely from their Ares space rocket. The Ares rocket was launched at 5.05 this morning but after only a few seconds it was obvious that something was seriously wrong.
At first the rocket flew straight upwards, but then it turned and moved almost horizontally before starting to fall back towards Earth. The rocket then crashed into the ocean and disappeared from sight.
For more details about the ejection system on the Ares rocket, we can now turn to our technology correspondent, Jeff Walker, who is at the recovery site.

TC: Luckily for the crew, the Ares rocket was fitted with the new Launch Abort System. If something goes wrong within the first 100,000 metres of the rocket's ascent, the Launch Abort System, or LAS, is activated and carries the crew capsule away to safety, just like the ejection seat system in an aeroplane.
The LAS is at the nose, or tip, of the rocket, and contains an abort engine and a supply of solid fuel. It is attached to the crew capsule.
As soon as the launch failed, and the Ares rocket changed course, the LAS was automatically activated. The abort engine fired with a massive 180,000 kilograms of thrust, and the LAS, attached to the Orion crew capsule, was ejected and shot upwards at high speed and away from the rocket. It reached a speed of 725 kph in less than three seconds.
When the solid fuel burnt out, the crew capsule detached itself from the LAS. Three sets of parachutes then opened up, and the crew capsule floated down and landed safely in the ocean.
Helicopters reached the capsule within a few minutes, and took the six astronauts to hospital at their base to recover. All six are well and in good spirits. Sarah.

R: Thanks, Jeff.

3 Ask students to read the first part of the news report they just heard and complete it with the correct form of the verbs in brackets. Then ask them to check their answers against the audio script on page 119.

> 1 has failed
> 2 has crashed
> 3 has landed
> 4 escaped
> 5 detached
> 6 was launched

Language

Present perfect v past simple

In the next two sections students will be revising the difference between the present perfect and the past simple. This is an area that many students have problems with. When they have done the exercises, tell them that they will find more information about the present perfect and the past simple in the Language summary on pages 100–101.

4 Ask students to look at the examples in the Language box and go through the report in 3 in pairs before checking answers with the class.

> Verbs 1–3 are present perfect and 4–6 are past simple. The present perfect shows that no specific time is mentioned or implied; the past simple either mentions or implies a specific time in the past.

5 Tell students that they are going to complete some more news stories. Explain that each story (1–4) is reported twice – the first in brief (B), and the second in detail (D). You could ask students to complete the stories in pairs.

1 have landed, touched
2 have collided, flew
3 has struck, (has) sunk, ran, sank
4 has burnt down, caught, collapsed

Listening

6 ▶ 🎧 08

Tell students that they are now going to listen to a talk from 2010 about the invention of the LAS system and that they are going to complete some sentences about the system. Focus their attention on the two slides and go through the information with them. Ask students to read through the sentences below so that they know what information they need to listen out for. Then play the recording for students to complete the sentences.

Slide 1: activates; will eject
Slide 2: activated; would eject

▶ 🎧 08

… as the Challenger disaster showed.

So now I'd like to tell you about our dream for the future of space travel, a future that will make safety a reality for our astronauts. I'm talking about an ejection system for astronauts!

If you look at the first slide, this describes the reality we have today. We have ejection seats today, but only for aircraft.

If an aircraft fails in some way, the pilot will activate the ejection system. And if the pilot activates the ejection system, the system will immediately eject the ejection seat, with the pilot, from the plane.

So let's turn to the second slide, which describes our dream for the future. We don't have ejection capsules yet for spacecraft, but one day soon, with the LAS system, our new invention, we will.

Let me describe what would happen if we had an LAS system in our spacecraft today.

If a spacecraft failed in some way, the computer would activate the LAS system. And if the computer activated the LAS system, the system would eject the capsule, with the crew, from the spacecraft.

Now, as Figure 1 here illustrates, the ejection system for aircraft …

Language

First and second conditional

Point out to students that the first sentence they completed in 6 is in the first conditional and the second sentence is in the second conditional. Tell them that in the next two exercises they will be practising using the second conditional for imagined or impossible situations. Go through the Language box with the students in order to revise the first and second conditionals. Ask students to identify the tenses used in the two conditional sentences. For the first conditional we use the present simple in the condition clause and *will* + infinitive in the

result clause. In 6, the inventor uses the first conditional because she is talking about a situation which is possible.

For the second conditional we use the past simple in the condition clause and *would* + infinitive in the result clause.

Also point out the use of the comma to separate the condition clause from the result clause.

Tell students that they can find more information about the first and second conditionals in the Language summary on pages 102–103.

7 Ask students to read through the statements. You could then put them in pairs to complete them, using the second conditional. Make sure they understand that some gaps require two words.

1 had, would have
2 ejected, would open
3 opened, would float
4 worked, would land

8 Ask students to complete the dialogue using the second conditional. Put weaker students in pairs to do this activity.

When checking answers, you could ask two students (who are not sitting next to each other) to take the part of A and B and read out their answers. Ask the rest of the class to listen carefully to see if they agree or not with their answers.

1 were
2 would your research priorities be
3 ran
4 would you do
5 would develop
6 would you focus
7 was/were
8 would send
9 found
10 would build

Speaking

9 Put students in pairs to practise the dialogue in 8.

> **Extra activity**
>
> If you think students need more practise on the second conditional, you could write these sentence beginnings on the board and ask students to complete them. Then ask the class for their ideas.

If I worked for NASA, …
If I was an inventor, …
If I passed all my English exams, …
If I could buy any car, …

2 Sequence (1)

Start here

1 Focus students' attention on the diagram, which shows how the Launch Abort System (LAS) works. Put students in pairs or groups of three to discuss the questions about the diagram. Tell them to make brief notes as they go along. Go around the class, monitoring the students and making sure they are referring to all the named parts in the diagram. Do not check their answers yet as the answers are given in the listening and reading texts.

See the Briefing section at the beginning of the unit in the Teacher's Book for more information on the Launch Abort System (LAS).

Listening

2 ▶ 🔘 09

Tell students that they are now going to listen to a presentation about the Launch Abort System (LAS). Play the recording once for students to follow the information in the diagram and check their notes.

▶ 🔘 09

I'd like to spend a few minutes now describing the main parts of the LAS, or Launch Abort System, of the Ares space rocket. As you can see in Figure 1, on the left-hand side of the illustration, the Launch Abort System is right at the nose, or tip, of the rocket. It's shaped like a dart, or a pawn on a chessboard. The job of the LAS is to lift the astronauts to safety if something goes wrong during the rocket launch.

Now let's look at the LAS in more detail. As can be seen in Figure 2, the cone-shaped structure attached to the bottom of the LAS is the Orion crew capsule. This is where the four to six astronauts live and work.

As you can see, a protective cover surrounds the Orion crew capsule and shields it from the hot engine exhaust.

Inside the LAS, the abort engine provides the power to lift the complete LAS and crew capsule at high speed away from the falling rocket. The exhaust from this engine escapes through nozzles in front of the engine.

Below the abort engine in the LAS you can see the solid propellant. This is the fuel for the abort engine. All two thousand one hundred kilos of fuel in the abort engine burn in less than three seconds.

Right at the tip, or nose, of the LAS, as Figure 3 shows, there is a ring or circle of four small nozzles. These are the nozzles of the attitude-control engine. When these nozzles fire, they spin the LAS around to stabilise it and orient it.

Just above the crew capsule, as Figure 4 illustrates, there is a third engine, called the jettison engine. When this engine fires, it pushes the crew capsule away from the LAS.

And finally, in Figure 5, you can see the parachutes. When the capsule reaches a safe altitude, the parachutes open up and bring the crew back to Earth.

3 ▶ 🔘 10

Ask students to work on their own to match the parts with their function. You could check answers by asking one student to name a part and another student to say the function.

Then play the recording to check students' pronunciation of the parts. Make sure that they are pronouncing the sound in *engine* correctly.

1 b   2 c   3 a   4 d

▶ 🔘 10

jettison engine
protective cover
attitude-control engine
abort engine
launch abort system
crew capsule
stabilise
stabilisation
orient
orientation
explosive bolts
parachute

Speaking

4 Focus students' attention on Figures 1 and 2 in the diagram and read out the example questions. Elicit a couple of answers. Put students in pairs to practise asking and answering questions about the diagram in 1 and the table in 3, using the second conditional. While they are doing the activity, go around the class, monitoring students and making sure they are using the second conditional.

Possible questions and answers:
If the crew capsule didn't have a protective cover, what would happen?
Hot exhaust would burn the capsule and the crew.

What would happen if the jettison engine didn't work?
The crew capsule would remain attached to the LAS.

What would the crew do if the jettison engine didn't work?
(I don't know but) they would (probably) try to activate it manually.

If the attitude-control engine stopped working, what would happen?
The LAS would point in the wrong direction/would not be stabilised.

What would happen if only one of the parachutes opened?
The crew capsule would fall to Earth too quickly.

What would happen if the abort engine didn't fire?
The LAS wouldn't be ejected from the spacecraft.

Scanning

5 Draw students' attention to the glossary box at the bottom of the page and explain that *G* is the measurement of the force of the Earth's gravity. For more information on measurements, refer students to the Reference section on page 107.

Go through the instructions with the students. Then ask them to turn to pages 116–117 and find the table with facts about the Launch Abort System. Remind them that they do not need to read every word in the text, just look for the information which answers the questions. Ask students to put up their hand when they have finished. Allow the majority of students to finish but check the answers with the first person to put up their hand to see if they were correct and are the winner.

> **1** 13.36
> **2** 2.64
> **3** 3
> **4** 11

Reading

6 Tell students that they are going to read a text about how the launch abort system works and put the events A–H in the correct order. Read the events as a class and then put students in pairs to complete the task.

> **1** H   **2** F   **3** E   **4** G   **5** C   **6** D   **7** B   **8** A

Language

Time clauses

Go through the Language box with the students. Focus their attention on the first table. Explain that they can join the two sentences to form one, beginning with the words *after*, *once*, *when* and *as soon as*. In these examples we use the present perfect and present simple to show that one action finishes before another starts.

Focus students' attention on the second table. Read the two sentences and explain that we can use *after* + gerund and that we can omit the subject in the first action clause when it is the same as in the second. Also point out the use of the comma to separate the two clauses.

7 Ask students to scan the text to find and underline examples of the form as quickly as they can. Then ask them whether the example sentences follow the form shown in the first or the second table in the Language box.

> After detecting the fault, the rocket's computer system activates the abort engine.
> When the abort engine has burnt out, the LAS continues to move away from the falling rocket.
> As soon as the LAS has reached the correct orientation, the explosive bolts detonate.
> Once the capsule has reached a safe altitude, parachutes open up and allow the capsule to float down into the ocean.

8 Ask students to make full sentences from the notes. Point out that they should use the forms from both tables in the Language box. Weaker students could do this activity in pairs.

> *Possible answers:*
> **1** After checking all systems, the computer begins the countdown.
> **2** As soon as the countdown has ended/ends, the rocket is launched.
> **3** Once the computer has activated/activates the abort engine, the LAS is ejected.
> **4** After firing for three seconds, the abort engine burns out.
> **5** When the crew capsule has separated/separates from the LAS, the parachutes open.
> **6** After opening, the parachutes lower the capsule gently into the sea.

3 Sequence (2)

Start here

1 Ask students to look at the photo. Put students in pairs or small groups to discuss the questions. Then ask the pairs or groups to share their ideas with the class in a feedback session.

> **1** A pilot has just activated the ejection seat in his/her plane.
> **2** Perhaps there was an engine failure and the plane was about to crash.
> **3** A parachute will open up from the pilot's backpack, and he/she will (hopefully) descend safely to the ground.

Task

2 Put students in pairs. Ask them to look at illustrations A–H and discuss the best order to explain how the ejection seat system works, using the named parts in the illustrations. Then ask the whole class for their ideas in a feedback session. Check their pronunciation of all the named parts in the illustrations.

> **1** H   **2** C   **3** B   **4** E   **5** A   **6** D   **7** G   **8** F

Vocabulary

3 Ask students to work individually and match the phrases 1–6 with the same or similar meanings a–f. When checking answers, ask one student to read out one of the phrases and another student to say which phrase has the same or a similar meaning.

> **1** d   **2** c   **3** e   **4** a   **5** b   **6** f

4 Students work individually to complete the nouns with the correct endings in the box. Tell them it may help to say the words so that they can hear whether it sounds correct or not. They can then check their answers in pairs before you check with the class.

> **1** deployment
> **2** ejection
> **3** stabilisation
> **4** orientation
> **5** activation
> **6** restraint

> **Extra activity**
>
> Ask students to underline the stressed syllable in the words in 4. Do an example on the board with them first. Tell students to say the words out loud as they underline the stressed syllable. After checking answers, explain that in words ending in -ion, the stress usually falls on the syllable immediately before it.

> **1** de<u>ploy</u>ment
> **2** e<u>jec</u>tion
> **3** stabili<u>sa</u>tion
> **4** orien<u>ta</u>tion
> **5** acti<u>va</u>tion
> **6** re<u>straint</u>

Task

5 Put students in A and B pairs. Tell them that they are going to complete a chart about the ejection sequence. Student A in each pair should look at the chart on page 25 and Student B should look at the chart on page 109. The information to complete the charts is at the back of the Course Book. Student A reads the text on page 111 and Student B reads the text on page 115. Using the information from the texts, students then take turns to ask and answer questions to complete their chart.

Student A's answers:
1 handle
2 explode; canopy
3 canopy; cockpit/plane
4 catapult gun; seat
5 guide rails
6 restraints
7 clears/leaves
8 up and away

Student A should ask questions like this to get the answers above:
1 How is the ejection seat system activated? What do you pull?
2 What do the bolts do? What does this release? What is released by this action?
3 What flies away? Where does it fly away from?
4 After this, what is fired? Why is it fired?
5 What do the rollers of the seat move along?
6 What prevents your legs from moving away from the seat?
7 What does the seat do before the rocket engine fires?
8 What happens to the seat after the rocket engine has fired? Where is the seat propelled?

Student B's answers:
1 30–60; burns out
2 timer; pellet
3 (top of the) seat; pellet
4 opens (up)
5 drogue (small) parachute; parachute
6 restraints
7 pulls you out of your seat
8 float to Earth

Student B should ask questions like this to get the answers above:
1 How high does the rocket lift the seat? What happens to the rocket then?
2 What activates the drogue gun? What does it fire?
3 Where does the small parachute come out of? What pulls it out?
4 What does the small parachute do once it is out of the seat?
5 What comes out at 14,500–11,500 metres? What pulls it out?
6 What is/are released after this?
7 What does the main parachute do after it opens?
8 What happens then? What do you do then?

Writing

6 Ask students to read the article. Then elicit some problems that might cause problems for the system for racing cars. Put students in small groups. Go through the instructions with them and make sure that they know what to do. Remind them to use the language in 5 to help them with the task. Tell them to appoint one person to take brief notes as they go along. When they have finished, they should go through the notes to make sure that they have covered everything.

7 Students now write the completed version of their system. They should make sure that they organise their description into clear stages. Remind them to look back at 5 to help them with the organisation of the description.

Speaking

8 Ask students to appoint one person to read out their group's description on the design to the rest of the class or to another group. At the end you could have a class vote on the best description.

Mixed-ability classes

Tell the students from other groups to listen carefully to the description and make notes of any questions about the design they would like to ask the group, which they can ask when the group has finished presenting their design.

---

4 Careers

Contents

1 Engineer

Objectives

In this section students will ...

- discuss blogs with a partner
- listen to a radio interview with an engineer talking about his job and answer questions
- complete an error correction task
- revise and practise the present simple, the present continuous and *going to*
- learn and practise using vocabulary for writing a CV
- write a covering letter for a job application

2 Inventor

Objectives

In this section students will ...

- compare two diagrams and answer questions
- read an extract from a technical article to complete a chart
- study synonyms and antonyms for semi-technical and bio-medical language
- revise and practise using comparatives and conjunctions
- make questions from answers about the gene gun
- role-play an interview

3 Interview

Objectives

In this section students will ...

- categorise advice for a job interview
- listen to a job interview and complete the interviewer's notes
- learn vocabulary for employment
- revise and practise using the present perfect v past simple with *for*, *since* and *ago*
- write a short CV
- role-play a job interview

Briefing

This unit looks at **careers** and **career paths** in engineering, job-seeking and job interviews.

Section 1 deals with a typical career path from **apprentice**, to **technician** and finally **graduate engineer**. Hans Fischer leaves school at 16 and joins a pharmaceutical company as an apprentice technician doing electronics maintenance work on the **packing line** for three years while attending a **vocational school** part-time, finally gaining a **certificate** from the school. He continues working at the same company as a technician for a further three years (a total **work experience** of six years), before joining a **degree course** at a nearby university of applied sciences. Four years later, he gains a **bachelor of engineering** degree (**B.Eng.**) in **mechatronics** (a subject which combines **mechanical engineering**, **electronic engineering**, and **software engineering**). He then returns to his original pharmaceutical company with the new **job title** of Robotics Engineer and a **job description** to design and build robots. Since leaving university he has invented a robotic device, which he is currently **piloting** (trialling and testing) on one of the packing lines. He plans to take further **qualifications**, starting with a **master's degree** (**M.Eng.**) by **distance learning**. As his **CV** (**curriculum vitae**) shows, he also has personal **competences** such as social and organisational **skills**.

Section 2 deals with a real-life person, John O'Brien, a laboratory technician who became a well-regarded **inventor** of a highly accurate modification of a **gene gun**, a device for inserting genetic information into brain cells. The text on page 28 provides full information about his invention, and the way in which he discovered how to make the gene gun more precise. John had a **eureka moment** when he suddenly understood that small holes in the **barrel** of the gene gun, like the ones in a machine-gun barrel, would allow gases to escape and reduce **recoil** (powerful backwards movement), increasing the accuracy of the 'shot' and reducing tissue damage. John's story may help to motivate technical students in their studies, since John invented his **prototype** while still working as a technician. The moral of the story is that you don't need to have a degree in order to be creative (although it helps, of course, as in Hans Fischer's case).

Section 3 deals with job interviews and provides some guidelines on what to do and what to avoid doing when preparing for an interview and while being interviewed. Reme Gomez is lower down the **career ladder** than Hans. She is currently a **junior technician** at a plastics processing company, where she has worked for seven years (including three years as an apprentice). She is currently studying part-time for a **Technician Diploma** at her local technical college for two days a week. She already has a **Certificate of Technical Competence** for which she studied part-time while she was an apprentice: this qualification teaches basic skills such as **measuring**, **marking out**, **technical drawing**, **fitting**, **bench work** and so on. She has learned **CADCAM** (**computer-aided design** and **computer-aided manufacture**: computer software used to design and manufacture products). Although young and with only a small amount of work experience, Reme is quite a successful interviewee, following the interview guidelines very well.

> New Scientist magazine article on John O'Brien: Find the **New Scientist** (paywall) and search for 'Life as a lab technician'.
>
> Advice for job-seekers and a template and examples for the Europass CV: Find the Europass website.
>
> For information about specific career paths, find web sites of engineering institutions, such as the **Institution of Mechanical Engineers**, the **Institute of Electrical and Electronic Engineers** and the **Institution of Civil Engineers**.

Teacher's notes

1 Engineer

Start here

1 Put students in pairs and ask them to discuss the questions.

> **Extra activity**
>
> Ask students their opinions of blogs in general and of ones they have seen on the internet. Ask them what makes a good blog.

2 Direct students' attention to the blog. Ask them what they think of it. Ask them to complete the mini-profile under the blog with information from the photo captions.

> FULL NAME: Hans Fischer
> OCCUPATION: engineer
> EMPLOYER: Farmakon
> LEISURE ACTIVITY: scuba diving

Listening

3 ▶ 🎧 11

Tell students that they are going to listen to an interview with Hans. Ask them to read through the questions first so that they know what information to listen out for. Explain that they should not try to look for the answers in the profile below as some of the information is incorrect. After listening, students compare answers in pairs before checking with the class.

> **1** Germany
> **2** Farmakon International
> **3** for eight years
> **4** He designs, builds and tests robots for the packing lines. He works with robots every day.

▶ 🎧 11

[I = Interviewer; HF = Hans Fischer]

I: I'm talking to Hans Fischer today. Hans is a young German engineer who is currently working at Farmakon International, a large German pharmaceutical company. He also happens to be an inventor in his spare time. Good morning, Hans.

HF: Good morning.

I: You've become famous because of your latest invention. But you're not really an inventor, are you? Or at least, inventor is not your job designation.

HF: That's correct. My actual job title is Robotics Engineer.

I: So, what is your job description? What do you actually do every day?

HF: I design and build robots for the packing lines. Then I test them. I work with robots every day.

I: And how long have you worked at Farmakon?

HF: Well, I've worked here as an engineer for the last two years. Before that I was at university for four years, and

before that I worked at Farmakon for six years. So I've worked at Farmakon for eight years altogether.

I: I see. So how old were you when you first started work at Farmakon?

HF: I was sixteen. I left secondary school and then I joined Farmakon as an apprentice technician.

I: And how long was your apprenticeship?

HF: It lasted for three years. During my apprenticeship, I studied part-time at vocational school.

I: And then after your apprenticeship ended, you became a technician at Farmakon. Is that right?

HF: Yes, that's correct. After my apprenticeship ended, I worked here as a technician for three more years while I studied part-time for university entrance. Then I went to study full-time at the University of Applied Sciences in Munich.

I: What course did you do there?

HF: A Bachelor of Engineering degree in Mechatronics. My main subject was Robotics. I got my degree two years ago.

I: Congratulations!

HF: Thanks.

I: And then after university did you come straight back to work at Farmakon?

HF: Yes, that's right. That's when I became a Robotics Engineer here.

I: And did you have your idea for an invention soon after returning to Farmakon, after your degree?

HF: Yes, that's right.

I: So tell me about your invention. What is it?

HF: Well, I've designed a robot that can work safely with a human worker.

I: That's very interesting. Can you use it at Farmakon?

HF: Oh yes, I'm piloting it now on one of the packing lines. I'm trying it out and testing it.

I: And what's your next step? What do you intend to do next?

HF: Well, next month, if the pilot is successful, I'm going to build another robot for a different packing line.

I: Excellent. And what are your plans for your career from now on?

HF: I'm doing a Masters degree next year. It's a distance-learning course. I've already been given a place on the course.

I: That's great. Well, Hans Fischer, it's been very interesting hearing about your achievements and your plans. Good luck with your future career. Thank you very much.

4 Focus students' attention on Han's profile. Explain that there are five mistakes in it. Tell them that they are going to listen to the recording again and that they should correct the mistakes. Ask them to check their answers with a partner. If necessary, play the recording again before checking answers with the class.

> *Five mistakes:*
> He joined Farmakon at *16*.
> He was apprentice for *three* years.
> His current job title is *Robotics Engineer*.
> Length of time in current post is *two* years.
> He has a degree in *Mechatronics*.

Language

Present continuous for present and future; *going to*

Go through the Language box with the students. As an alternative, to revise these forms, ask students to close their books, then write the examples in one column on the board and in another column write the uses in a different order. Then ask the students to match the example sentences to their uses. Finally, ask them to identify the tenses used.

Tell students that they can find more information about these tenses in the Language summary on page 100.

Speaking

5 Put students in pairs. Students take it in turns to ask and answer the questions. Tell them to make notes of their partner's answers. Then, in a feedback session, ask individual students to tell the class about their partner.

Reading

6 ▶ 🔘 12

Go through the information in the CV with the students. Explain that the word for CV in American English is *resume*. Ask them if the layout of CVs in their country is similar to this one. If not, ask them what the differences are. Ask students how long they think the ideal CV should be. (In the UK employers like CVs to be no longer than two pages and if possible, just one page.)

Put students in pairs and ask them to complete the CV with the words in the box. When they have finished, ask them to check their answers with the audio script on page 120.

Focus students' attention on the words in the box. Play the recording once through. Then play it again, pausing after each word, for students to practise saying them. You could then ask them to listen again and underline the main stressed syllable in each word.

▶ 🔘 12

apprentice	responsibilities
technician	employer
robotics	business
mechatronics	qualification
pharmaceutical	institution
curriculum vitae	competences
CV	

1 Robotics Engineer
2 I design, build and test/pilot robots for packing lines.
3 Farmakon International GmbH
4 Pharmaceutical manufacturing
5 Bachelor of Engineering in Mechatronics
6 Robotics
7 University of Applied Sciences, Munich, Germany
8 Apprentice technician

Writing

7 Go through the instructions with the class. Ask students to read through the advertisement. Ask them if they think Hans has the right qualifications for this job and what makes him a good candidate. Ask them what information they think he should include in his covering letter. Go through conventions of writing a formal letter first. You can use the model letter below as a guide. Revise the features of a formal letter on the board (i.e. the position of the address, paragraph structure, greeting and ending of the letter, etc.) Write some standard phrases on the board, e.g. *I am currently ..., I look forward to hearing from you, I would like to apply for ..., Yours sincerely, I am writing in application for ..., Please find my curriculum vitae enclosed/attached* (for an email).

Ask students where in a letter you would find these phrases (at the beginning, middle or end). Then explain that we use *Yours sincerely* when we know the name of the person we are writing to and *Yours faithfully* when we do not know the name. Explain that we can also use *Yours truly* instead of *Yours sincerely*.

Students write a draft covering letter either in class or for homework. When they have finished or at the beginning of the next lesson, they can check their work with a partner for grammar, spelling and punctuation mistakes. Emphasise that this is very important, particularly when applying for a job. They can also suggest other improvements to their partner's letter.

Model answer:
80246 Munich
Georgenstrasse 35
Germany

Mr John Wells
Personnel Manager
RoboDesigns
PO Box 499
London W8 2FZ
UK

28 May 2014

Dear Mr Wells,

I would like to apply for the position of Graduate Mechatronics Engineer, advertised in this month's *Robotics* magazine. Please find my curriculum vitae enclosed.

I have a Bachelor of Engineering degree from the University of Applied Sciences in Munich, and I have more than six years of industrial experience in the field of mechatronics and robotics. I am applying for this job as I would like to have the opportunity to obtain more experience in design and development in mechanical and electro-mechanical products.

I look forward to hearing from you.

Yours sincerely,

[signature]

Hans Fischer

2 Inventor

Start here

1 Focus students' attention on the diagram. Pre-teach the word *gene* (a sequence of chemicals within a cell which carries information about characteristics and is passed from parent to child). Tell students that the diagram shows two types of gene gun. Put students in pairs and ask them to study the diagram and answer the questions. Tell them to make notes of their answers but do not go over them until the students have checked their own answers in the reading text in 2. If they are struggling, you could explain the word *spread* (move outwards in all directions).

Reading

2 Ask students to read the article and check their answers in 1. Tell them to ignore the words in bold for now. Do not go over any vocabulary for now as they are just reading for gist. Students will be studying vocabulary from the text in 4 and 5.

1 They're used for inserting genetic material into cells.
2 In the modified gene gun (new design) the external barrel is narrower and it is straight, not conical. This means it can fire the DNA with greater accuracy.
The modified design has small holes in the barrel.
The barrel of the modified gene gun has no spacer.
3 The standard design was not accurate enough, was too wide and so could cause tissue damage.

3 Ask students to look at the chart. Explain that they have to complete it with information from the article in 2. Tell them to look back at the article, quickly read through it and underline the relevant information about the two types of gene gun. Then ask them to complete the table with the information. When they have finished, they can check their answers in pairs before you check with the class.

Key differences between the standard and modified gene gun

	Standard	Modified
Diameter of barrel	40 mm	5 mm
Spacer?	yes	no
Holes in barrel?	no	yes
Shape of barrel	conical	straight
Recoil	high	reduced

Vocabulary

4 Ask students to look at the synonyms in bold in the article in 2. Read the words as a class and check students' pronunciation, particularly of *roughly*. Remind students that words in English are sometimes spelt differently to how they are pronounced, such as words that contain the letters *ough*. Then ask students to match the synonyms in bold to the phrases (1–8). Weaker students could do this activity in pairs.

1 recoil	**5** optimum
2 modified	**6** roughly
3 pulse	**7** external
4 breakthrough	**8** membrane

5 Now ask students to match the words listed with their opposites in the text.

1 minimum
2 reduce
3 inaccurate
4 difference
5 insert
6 prevents

> **Mixed-ability classes**
>
> Stronger students could try to write the opposites of the words first and then check their answers in the article in 2. Note that students may produce words that are not in the text but may still be correct.

Language

Comparative; conjunctions

Go through the examples in the Language box with the students to revise the comparative form.

Explain to students that we use comparatives to compare two different things. To make comparisons with short adjectives, we add *-r* or *-er* to the adjective. We use *more/less* before adjectives or nouns.

In the third example, explain that to emphasise the difference when comparing facts between two things, we can use the conjunctions *but*, *while* and *whereas* to join two sentences. We generally use *but* in spoken and informal written English, and *while* or *whereas* in formal written English.

Also point out that when a sentence is joined by *and* or *but*, and a subject is repeated in the second clause, we tend to leave the subject out, e.g. *It is more accurate and has less recoil. The standard gun works but is inaccurate.* You can also use *one* instead of repeating the subject.

6 Go through the example sentences with the class. Ask students to look back at the table they completed in 3 and work individually to write similar sentences. Students then read their answers out to the class.

> *Possible answers:*
> The modified design has a narrower barrel than the standard one.
> The standard one has a spacer, whereas the modified one does not.
> The modified design has holes along the side of the barrel, while the standard one does not.
> The shape of the modified barrel is straight, but the standard one is conical (in shape).
> The modified design has much less recoil than the standard one.

Speaking

7 Ask students to look back at the text in 2 once more for the information listed 1–8. Tell them to prepare questions for the answers. Then put students in pairs to take turns asking and answering the questions.

> *Possible questions:*
> **1** What's the gene gun for?
> **2** How large is the gun?
> **3** How is it powered?
> **4** What's the barrel of the modified gun made of?
> **5** How wide is it?
> **6** Why are there small holes along the side of the barrel?
> **7** How does the width of the barrel compare with the standard barrel?
> **8** What's the difference in shape between the two barrels?

8 Put students in pairs. Go through the instructions so that they know what to do. They then take it in turns to be the reporter and the inventor. While they are role-playing the interview, go round monitoring and helping them. Make a note of any mistakes in language that you could go over in a feedback session.

3 Interview

Start here

Warmer

Ask students to brainstorm job titles for their industry. When they have finished, ask them to choose four of the jobs each and explain what the person does using relative clauses, e.g. *A lab technician is someone who tests, records and analyses the results of experiments in a laboratory.*

1 Focus students' attention on the photo and elicit what the situation is. Ask them how they feel about job interviews and what advice they would give someone attending an interview. Accept all reasonable answers at this stage. Then ask students to look at the table and complete it with the advice listed below under the correct headings.

Ask students what the difference between *interviewee* and *interviewer* is. Check pronunciation of both these words.

> Before the interview DO: 2, 5, 8, 10
> During the interview DON'T: 3, 4, 6
> During the interview DO: 1, 7, 9

Listening

2 ▶ 🎧 **13**

Tell students that they are going to listen to part of a job interview. Explain that they should listen carefully and tick the advice in 1 that the interviewee follows.

> Reme follows 1, 7, 9.
> She also probably followed 2, 5, 10 before the interview.

▶ 🎧 **13**

[I = Interviewer; RG = Reme Gomez]

I: ... So, Ms Gomez, can I check a few details from your CV? When did you complete your school education?
RG: I left school just over seven years ago.
I: And now you're a technician?
RG: Yes, that's right. I'm a junior technician at MultiPlastics.
I: I see. And how long have you worked there?
RG: Erm, I went there straight from school so I've been there for seven years. I started as an apprentice.
I: How long did your apprenticeship last?
RG: For three years.
I: And after your apprenticeship ended, they promoted you to junior technician. Is that correct?
RG: Yes, that's right. I've been a junior technician there for the last four years.
I: And you're currently studying part-time for a technician's diploma, are you?
RG: Yes, I am. I go to the technical college twice a week.
I: And how long have you been a part-time student?
RG: For two years now. I started the diploma course just over two years ago.
I: And you already have your Certificate of Technical Competence, of course?
RG: Yes, I studied part-time for my certificate while I was an apprentice. My employer gave me time off work, to help me. I got my certificate five years ago.

I: Right, thank you, I think the details are clear now. So, Ms Gomez, why would you like to work with us?
RG: Well, you're one of the leading companies in your field. I'd like to broaden my experience.
I: And why should we offer you this job? What technical skills do you have?
RG: Well, my benchwork is very accurate. And I've learned CADCAM.
I: And what about your personal skills?
RG: Well, I work hard, I'm punctual and my present employer says I'm very reliable.
I: What about interpersonal skills? Do you like working with others?
RG: Yes, I'm willing to learn and I think I'm a good team worker.
I: Good. So now, do you have any questions to ask us?
RG: Yes, I would like to know a bit more about the salary and benefits ... that come with the job.

3 Play the recording again for students to complete the interviewer's notes on the interview. Allow students to compare answers before checking the answers as a class. For weaker classes, play the recording again for students to check answers.

> Name – Reme Gomez
> Present job – junior technician
> Years in present job – four
> Years in apprenticeship – three
> Qualification – Certificate of Technical Competence
> When gained qualification – five years ago
> Studying for diploma (part-time) now
> Technical skills – (1) accurate benchwork (2) CAD/CAM
> Personal skills – works hard, punctual and reliable
> Interpersonal skills – willing to learn, and good team worker

Vocabulary

4 Students match the words and phrases 1–8 with the same or similar meanings a–h. When checking answers, choose one student to call out a word from 1–8 for another student to give the answer a–h.

> **1** f   **2** g   **3** c   **4** a   **5** h   **6** d   **7** e   **8** b

5 Explain that students are going to complete the five interview questions using some of the words (1–8) from 4. Explain that they will need to change the form of the word in some cases and add other words in order to complete the question. Ask them to look at the answers to the questions first and then complete the questions.

> **Extra activity**
>
> After completing the questions in 5, students work in pairs to take turns asking and answering the interview questions.

1 qualifications
2 your employer
3 is your job title
4 competences do you have/are you competent at doing
5 benefits do you get/are there

Language

Present perfect v past simple; *for, since, ago*

Go through the time expressions and examples in the Language box with the students. Remind them that we use *for* to talk about a period of time and *since* to talk about an exact time when something started. *For* and *since* are often used with the present perfect. We can also use *for* with the past simple, but not *since*. Point out that we use *ago* with the past simple to mean *before now*.

We use *from ... until (now)* with the present perfect or past simple to talk about the exact time period from when something started up to the present or the time it finished. Point out that we can use *to* instead of *until*, but with the past simple only.

6 Explain to students that they are going to complete interview questions for Reme's answers. Tell them to read the answer first and then complete the question. Weaker students could do this activity in pairs. If they have any difficulty, refer them back to the Language box.

> 1 have you been a junior technician
> 2 did you become an apprentice
> 3 were you an apprentice
> 4 have you worked for MultiPlastics
> 5 did you study for your certificate
> 6 did you receive your certificate
> 7 have you been a (part-time) diploma student
> 8 has MultiPlastics been in business

Speaking

7 Put students in pairs to take turns to be Hans and the interviewer. Tell them to look back at Hans' CV on page 27. Before the activity, elicit some interview questions from the class and allow them to make notes. Explain that they can also use the questions in 6 for ideas. During the activity, go round the class, monitoring the students. Go through any errors with the class at the end of the activity in a feedback session.

> *Possible questions and answers:*
> 1 Where are you working at the moment?
>   I'm working at Farmakon International.
> 2 How long have you worked for Farmakon International?
>   I've worked there for ... years.
> 3 What type of business does Farmakon International do?
>   It's a pharmaceutical manufacturer.
> 4 What is your current position in the company?
>   I am a robotics engineer.
> 5 What do you do in your job?
>   I design, build and test/pilot robots for packing lines.
> 6 What qualifications do you have?
>   I have a degree in engineering.
> 7 When and from where did you receive your degree?
>   I received my degree in [year] at the University of Applied Sciences in Munich.
> 8 How long did you study for your degree?
>   I studied for four years.

Scanning

8 Go through the instructions with the students. Then ask them to turn to pages 116–117 and find the advertisement for the job of Electrical Design Manager. Remind them that they do not need to read every word in the text, just look for the information which answers the questions. Ask students to put up their hand when they have finished. Allow the majority of students to finish but check the answers with the first person to put up their hand to see if they were correct and are the winner.

> 1 Higher National Diploma (HND) in Electrical Engineering or equivalent
> 2 AutoCAD
> 3 Europe and the Middle East
> 4 47–50K

Task

9 Tell students to imagine themselves as ten years older than they actually are. Ask them to imagine the kind of work experience and jobs they would have. Tell them to write a new CV for themselves in ten years' time and that they should make sure the CV is no more than one page long. Point out that they should check their CV carefully for grammar, spelling and punctuation mistakes when they have finished. Emphasise that this is very important. Allow students to compare CVs at the end of the activity and offer each other feedback.

10 Ask students to write down some details of a job they would like to apply for in ten years' time.

11 Students now prepare for their job interview. Ask them to write notes to answer the questions referring to their CV.

> **Mixed-ability classes**
> You could ask stronger students to write three more typical interview questions.

12 Put students in groups of three or four. They should take it in turns to be interviewed by a panel of two or three interviewers. If possible, arrange tables as you would have them in an interview situation. When it comes to their turn, each interviewee hands their CV over to the interview panel. Allow interviewers some time to read it before they start asking their questions. While they are role-playing the interviews, go round monitoring. Take notes on any mistakes they make with the time expressions they have studied in this section and correct them in a feedback session. Give students examples of any good answers to questions that you heard and write them on the board.

> **Mixed-ability classes**
> Stronger groups could ask their extra questions from 11.

Review Unit B

Answer key

2
1 burnt out
2 burnt out
3 is activating
4 will detonate
5 have detonated
6 detonated
7 is firing
8 will separate

4
1 has destroyed; struck
2 has hit; reached
3 has taken off; took off

5
1 After sounding the fire alarm, the computer closes all the fire doors.
2 As soon as the explosive bolts have detonated, they break apart.
3 After opening, the drogue parachute pulls the main parachute out of the pilot's backpack.
4 As soon as the fuel in the cylinder has ignited, the burning gas expands rapidly.
5 Once the drill bit has passed 350 metres, it cuts into oil-bearing rock.
6 After detecting a temperature change, the sensor sends the data to the thermostat.

6
Solution (in this order):
1 Break the windows at the back to reduce the weight.
2 Break two windows at the front, hold one gang member upside down out of the window to deflate the front tyres and stabilise the vehicle.
3 Drain the rear fuel tank through an access panel at the bottom of the bus.
4 Gang members leave one by one from the front, collecting stones to replace their weight.
5 Keep adding stones until someone can safely go to the rear to retrieve the gold.

8
1 deployment
2 stabilisation
3 descent
4 propulsion
5 detonation
6 restraint

9
1 do you do
2 work
3 modify
4 are you modifying
5 am/'m working
6 am/'m trying
7 Are you going
8 am/'m presenting

10
Possible answers:
What shape is it?
How high is it? How wide is it?
How many containers does it have?
What does the structure do?/What is it for?/What is its purpose/function?
How does the structure operate/work?
How much energy is used in operating it?
Why does it use so little energy?
How much weight can it lift?
What's the maximum weight that it can lift/raise?
What's the diameter of the two arms of the structure?
How long does it take for a container to go from one level to the other?

12 1 c   2 h   3 e   4 b   5 a   6 g   7 d   8 f

13
Possible answer:
The Durban stadium has a slightly larger capacity than the Cape Town one. It held about 2,000 more spectators during the World Cup, and about 3,000 more afterwards. The roof of the Cape Town stadium is five metres higher than Durban's roof, but the Durban stadium has an arch 106 metres in height above the roof, so the total height of the Durban stadium is much greater. The Durban stadium is longer and wider than the Cape Town stadium.

14
1 do you work
2 have you worked
3 I've been
4 did you work
5 was
6 did you leave
7 wanted
8 have you finished
9 did you complete

Project

15 At the end of every Review Unit is a project. Go through the list of instructions with the students. Tell them to find an advert for a job they are interested in and to research the company on the internet. At the end of the task, they could ask another student to check through their letter of application for grammar, spelling and punctuation errors and suggest any improvements to the letter. Students can also role-play the interview for practice.

Quick test answer key

Part 1: Vocabulary and grammar

1
1 eject
2 external
3 ascend
4 difference
5 prevents

2
1 activation
2 ejection
3 employment
4 deployment
5 movement
6 obstruction
7 orientation
8 qualification

3
1 c   2 d   3 e   4 b   5 a

4
1 experience
2 apprentice
3 qualification
4 interview

5
1 exploded
2 have/'ve worked
3 have you flown
4 collided

6
1 since
2 ago
3 for
4 from

7
1 fails, will
2 worked, would
3 were, would
4 send/will

8 *Possible answers:*
1 As soon as you start falling from the plane, position yourself so you face the ground.
2 Once you are facing the ground, arch your back and move your head back.
3 When you have arched your back, stretch out your arms and legs and bend your knees.
4 After following this procedure, you can look for a safe place to land. Then activate the parachute.

9
1 lower than the salary for the job in Cambridge
2 less experience than the job in London
3 temporary whereas/while the job in Cambridge is permanent

10
1 am/'m having
2 is looking for
3 check; maintain
4 am/'m going to ask

Part 2: Reading and writing

Reading

1 the crew shut down the nuclear reactors and the submarine runs on battery power
2 the submarine
3 the DSRV
4 the crew
5 the vehicle/the DSRV

Writing

Dear Mr Jones

I would like to apply for the position of Electronics Systems Engineer, as advertised on your website.

I have a Bachelor of Science degree from Leeds University and five years' experience working for Renault as an engineer for their F1 team.

As you can see from the attached CV, I have knowledge of digital signal processing and the latest design methodologies. I have recently taken a course in Kinetic Energy Recovery Systems (KERS).

I am confident and have good problem-solving skills. I speak German, French and English and I am also willing and able to travel globally.

I look forward to hearing from you.

Yours sincerely

Andy Smith

Review Unit B Quick test

Total _____ /55

Part 1: Vocabulary and grammar

1 Complete the opposites.

1 insert   e_____
2 internal   e_____
3 descend   a_____
4 similarity   d_____
5 allows   p_____

(5 marks)

2 Write the noun form of these verbs.

1 activate _____   5 move   _____
2 eject   _____   6 obstruct _____
3 employ   _____   7 orient   _____
4 deploy   _____   8 qualify _____

(8 marks)

3 Match the words with their meanings.

1 recoil   **a)** approximately
2 optimum   **b)** changed and improved
3 breakthrough **c)** powerful backward movement
4 modified   **d)** the best
5 roughly   **e)** sudden new idea

(5 marks)

4 Complete the sentence with the words in the box.

apprentice   experience   interview   qualification

1 Do you have any _____ in mechanical engineering?
2 After school, I joined the company as a(n) _____ technician.
3 I have a(n) _____ in Applied Sciences.
4 I am available for a(n) _____ for the job.

(4 marks)

5 Complete the sentences with the words in brackets. Use the past simple or present perfect.

1 The rig _____ on 15 July 2010. (explode)
2 I _____ at this company for eight years now. I'd like a change. (worked)
3 How long _____ for this airline? (you / fly)
4 Two jet fighters _____ near the M40 motorway yesterday. (collide)

(4 marks)

6 Complete the sentences with *for*, *since*, *ago* or *from*.

1 I've worked for this company _____ 2008.
2 They activated the abort engine five minutes _____.
3 They've been in the automotive business _____ twelve years.
4 Angela studied engineering at university _____ 2007 until 2010.

(4 marks)

7 Choose the correct option to complete these sentences.

1 If the engine **will fail/fails**, the pilot **will/would** escape using the new ejection system.
2 If the machine **works/worked**, we **will/would** finish the job by this evening.
3 If I **were/would** be you, I **will/would** take an engineering degree.
4 The deadline is tomorrow. If I **send/sent** my application off now, they **will/would** get it in time.

(4 marks)

8 Rewrite these sentences so the meaning is the same. Use the words below once only.

after   as soon as   once   when

How to skydive from a plane

1 You start falling from the plane. Position yourself so you face the ground.

   _____

2 You are facing the ground. Then arch your back and move your head back.

   _____

3 You have arched your back. Then stretch out your arms and legs.

   _____

4 You have followed this procedure. Then you can look for a safe place to land.

   _____

   Then activate the parachute.

(4 marks)

9 **Read the two job adverts. Then complete the sentences below to compare the two jobs.**

JOB A
Electronic Design Engineer, Cambridge
(1) Salary: £30,000
(2) Design experience: two years
(3) Terms of employment: permanent

Job B
Electronic Design Engineer, London
(1) Salary: £16,000
(2) Design experience: three years
(3) Terms of employment: temporary

1 The salary for the job in London is ______________.
2 The job in Cambridge requires ________________.
3 The job in London is ______________________.

(3 marks)

10 **Complete the sentences with the words in brackets. Use the present simple, present continuous or *going to*.**

1 I ________ an interview for a job next week. (have)
2 The company ________ someone with experience in the oil industry. (look for)
3 Currently I ________ and ________ the equipment on the rigs. (check / maintain)
4 I ________ them about training courses at the interview. (ask)

(4 marks)

Part 2: Reading and writing

Reading

Read the text. Explain what the words below refer to.

Submarine rescue operations

If there was an explosion on a submarine, or it had a collision, the crew would transmit a distress signal. If the accident is serious, then rescue attempts to save the crew must be made within 48 hours of the accident. The crew would shut down the nuclear reactors and the submarine would run on battery power. If this happened, then oxygen levels would be reduced and carbon dioxide levels would rise. If the battery stopped working, then the heating systems would fail and the temperature of the submarine would drop. The submarine would also be in danger of flooding. The success of any operation to rescue the vessel would depend on the depth of the submarine below the surface, the position it is in, the currents around the submarine and the condition of the seabed.

In the event of the sinking of a submarine, a DSRV (Deep-Submergence Rescue Vehicle), which is a mini-submarine, is sent down to rescue the crew. It can rescue up to 24 of them at a time. When the vehicle reaches the submarine, it attaches itself onto the escape hatch and then creates an airtight seal so that the hatch can be opened.

1 this (line 6)
2 it (line 14)
3 It (line 19)
4 them (line 19)
5 itself (line 20)

(5 marks)

Writing

Read the job advert and the application letter. Rewrite the letter, dividing the long paragraph into the five paragraphs according to the sections below.

Electronics Systems Engineer – F1
Excellent opportunity for an experienced engineer to join our team.
Interested?
Click here

Dear Mr Jones

I would like to apply for the position of Electronics Systems Engineer, as advertised on your website. I have a Bachelor of Science degree from Leeds University and five years experience working for Renault as an engineer for their F1 team. As you can see from the attached CV, I have experience in digital signal processing and design methodologies. I have recently taken a course in Kinetic Energy Recovery Systems (KERS). I am confident and have good problem-solving skills. I speak German, French and English and I am also willing and able to travel globally. I look forward to hearing from you.

Yours sincerely

Andy Smith

Paragraph sections for a covering letter

1 Reason for writing
2 Factual information
3 Reference to CV
4 Skills you have for the job
5 Closing comment

(5 marks)

5 Safety

Contents

1 Warnings

Objectives

In this section students will …

- brainstorm safety systems with the whole class
- read an article about a car warning system and answer questions
- listen to a phone conversation about a meeting and answer questions
- study and practise using discussion markers
- have a class discussion on car safety
- learn vocabulary for control and warning systems

2 Instructions

Objectives

In this section students will …

- match safety signs to their instructions
- label a diagram and listen to a dialogue to check answers
- study and practise using active and passive modals for necessity and obligation
- read a maintenance manual and answer true/false questions
- write a set of instructions for maintaining a machine or device
- learn vocabulary for car maintenance

3 Rules

Objectives

In this section students will …

- discuss a potential incident in a photo and devise a rule to prevent it
- read and understand a set of rules
- study and practise using the present participle for giving advice
- study and practise using *only … if* and *don't … unless*
- brainstorm a potentially dangerous situation in groups and present ideas for a preventative rule to the class
- write a rule for an activity, procedure, sport or game
- learn vocabulary for flight navigation and air traffic

Briefing

This unit looks at aspects of **safety**, including warning systems and safety rules and procedures.

Section 1 deals with **Lane Keeping Assist** (**LKA**), a **lane departure warning system**, which warns a driver when his or her vehicle begins to move out of its **lane**. Most systems give a warning which is **audible** (heard), **visible** (seen) or **tactile** (felt, such as a vibrating steering wheel), while others take **remedial** (**corrective**) action such as applying the brakes or **counter-steering** (turning the **steering column** in the opposite direction). The system uses cameras acting as **sensors** that **monitor** the **lane markings** and send data to the vehicle's **controller** (central computer). Tom (audio 15) believes that automatic safety devices are dangerous, because they make drivers feel safer than they really are. He prefers systems that give **feedback**, for example, seats that vibrate when a car starts to go off the road.

Section 2 deals with safety instructions. In the **ISO** (**International Organization for Standardization**) system, blue safety signs communicate **mandatory** instructions ('you *must* do this'), and the black ones with red circles are **prohibitive** ('you must *not* do this'). In a **disc brake** (see diagram on page 38), the **calliper** (AmE **caliper**) has two **jaws** that move together and squeeze the **disc** (AmE **rotor**) to stop it rotating. The system is based on **hydraulics** (how liquid in motion transmits energy). The **brake line** (pipe), **master cylinder** and **brake cylinder** are filled with oil (**hydraulic fluid**), which resists compression. As a result, when the pedal is **depressed** (pushed down), the energy of that motion is transmitted to the **piston**, which pushes one **pad** (attached to a calliper jaw) towards the disc and squeezes it against the other pad. If a brake pedal feels **spongy** (soft), air may have entered the brake lines: since air can be compressed (unlike hydraulic fluid), it will not transmit all the energy from the brake pedal to the piston.

Section 3 deals with '**rules of the air**' for aircraft pilots, designed to keep aircraft separated from each other and prevent mid-air **collisions**. The rules are based on **Free Flight** (see reference below), which allows pilots to decide their speed, **heading** (direction) and altitude without assistance from air traffic controllers.

Rules of the Air (Part 1) on page 40 specify the correct altitude for an aircraft travelling in a particular direction. A vertical distance of at least 1000 feet (304.8 metres) must be kept between two aircraft flying in different directions. Altitude is measured in flight levels: one **flight level (FL)** equals 100 feet. (Note that the aviation industry still uses feet rather than metres.) Draw the face of a magnetic compass on the blackboard. Write the **bearings** (compass directions) N (north), NE (north east), E (east) and so on clockwise around the compass face. Then next to N write 0° / 360°, next to NE write 45°, next to E write 90°, and so on around the whole face. (See Reference section, page 108.) Aircraft flying roughly to the *right-hand side* of the compass (0° to 179°) must fly at **odd-numbered** FLs such as 170 (17,000 feet), 190 and so on. Aircraft flying roughly to the *left-hand side* of the compass (180° to 359°) must fly at **even-numbered** FLs such as 160 (16,000 feet), 180 and so on. These rules only apply to aircraft when they are **cruising** (not changing altitude).

Rules of the Air (Part 2) on page 110 also apply to cruising aircraft. They state how to overtake or pass another aircraft. The diagrams are self-explanatory.

Rules of the Air (Part 3) on page 115 apply when two aircraft are at different **phases** of flight: **climbing**, **cruising** or **descending**. If an aircraft is cruising, it has priority over aircraft that are climbing or descending. If an aircraft is descending, it has priority over an aircraft that is climbing.

Lane Keeping Assist (LKA) systems: Find the **Auto Evolution** website and search for 'Lane keeping assist systems explained'.

Article 'Are cars too safe?' by Don Norman: Find the **Business Week** website and search for 'Are cars too safe?'.

How disc brakes work: Find the **How Stuff Works** website and search for 'Disc brakes'.

Principles of Free Flight: Find the website of the **National Aerospace Laboratory (NLR)**, Netherlands, and search for 'Free Flight'.

Teacher's notes

1 Warnings

Start here

1 Ask students if they own a car and what safety systems or features it has. Write their answers on the board. Ask students to add any more they might have left out. Then ask them to put these safety devices into the two categories in 1 – (a) and (b). Get feedback from the class.

Possible answers:
(a) ABS (Anti-lock Braking System), ESC (Electronic Stability Control), ACC (Adaptive or Autonomous Cruise Control), airbag technology
(b) CWS (Collision Warning Systems), LKA (Lane Keeping Assist systems – see reading text in next exercise), IPAS (Intelligent Parking Assist System)

Extra activity

For homework, you could ask students to search the internet under *automobile safety* for examples in addition to the ones given in the answer key above and the ones they mentioned.

Reading

2 Ask students to cover the text and focus their attention on the photo. Tell students that they are going to read about a car warning system. Ask them to look at the photo and say what they think the system is for. Ask them to read the text quickly and answer the questions below. Allow students to compare answers before you check with the class.

1 (a) beep, alarm (b) (flashing) light (c) vibration
2 Toyota
3 no action
4 (a) remedial (b) monitor (c) detect (d) intentionally (e) counter-steer (f) torque

Vocabulary

3 Focus student's attention on the table and go through the examples with them. Then ask them to read through the article again to find the phrases which complete the table. While going through the answers with them, check understanding of *drift* and *counter-steer* by asking them which action is deliberate and which is accidental.

remain in correct lane	leave the lane	go back into lane
stay in lane	drifts out of its lane	returns the car to its lane
keep their vehicle in its lane	departs from its lane	regains its position in the lane
maintains its position in the lane	is moving out of its lane	bring the vehicle back into the lane

Listening

4 ▶ 🎧 14

Tell students that they are going to listen to a phone conversation between two work colleagues. Play the recording for students to listen and answer the questions. Allow them to compare answers in pairs before you check with the class.

1 to invite Tom to a brainstorming meeting about a new warning system for drivers
2 Before: They discuss Tom's research project and Max's new product. After: Max invites Tom for lunch to talk about holiday plans.
3 Probably (c): they are very positive about each other, praising each other's work where appropriate and they make time for social chat (about holidays) over lunch. If their relationship is already very good, then (b) is also possible.

▶ 🎧 14

[T = Tom; M = Max]
T: Tom Redman.
M: Hi Tom, it's Max here.
T: Max! Good to hear from you. How are you?
M: Fine, thanks. How are things with you?
T: Great, thanks.
M: I hear your research project is going well.
T: Yes, I think we're making progress.
M: What is it you're looking into?
T: We're trying to find out whether car safety systems make people drive less safely.
M: That sounds very interesting.
T: Thanks. So how about your work? How is your latest product design coming along? Your last one was a big success.
M: Yes, it was very popular with the customers. And the new product is looking very good. Very good indeed. And that brings me to my reason for calling you.
T: Mm?
M: I'm planning to hold a brainstorming session next week with the rest of the design team. I thought that your ideas would be very useful. Would you have time to join us?
T: Of course. When are you meeting?
M: Hopefully next Tuesday at ten. If you're free then.
T: Yes, I think that's OK for me.
M: Great. See you next Tuesday then. I'll send you an email to confirm it.
T: Good.
M: And if you can join us for lunch afterwards, we can have a chat about holiday plans.
T: I'm looking forward to it. Bye.

5 ▶ 🎧 15

Tell students that they are now going to listen to the brainstorming meeting. Play the recording for students to answer the questions. Then elicit answers from the whole class.

▶ 🎧 15

[M = Max; T = Tom; A = Man; B = Woman]

M: We need to think about a new warning system to help drivers keep in their lane while driving. Any ideas?

A: Well, I think that we should have infra-red sensors under the bumpers. They can monitor the lane markings.

B: Or we could have cameras inside the windscreen. They can see further ahead.

A: Yes, I agree, you have a point there, cameras are probably better. They can detect the lane markings, then the controller can give a warning. For instance, you could have a flashing light or another visible warning. Or you could have an audible warning like a beeping sound.

B: I don't think that's a good idea. Beeps and lights are too annoying and distracting for the driver.

A: So why don't we have a SatNav voice telling the driver 'You're crossing into the next lane'?

B: No, drivers wouldn't like that. I mean, it would sound like an angry school teacher. Or your wife or husband criticising you. We shouldn't use a SatNav voice. By the way, I had a very bad experience with a SatNav last week …

M: Anyway, let's keep to our main discussion. If we don't have a voice, a beep, or a flashing light, what do you suggest?

B: Well, I think we should use normal feedback signals, in other words, signals from the real world.

M: What do you mean?

B: Well, for example, if you go too fast, or leave your lane unintentionally, the car could make you feel a little fear, let's say, for example, by tightening the seat belt a little.

A: That might be too frightening and make the driver over-react. It could make him take too much corrective action and press the brakes too hard. Alternatively, he might counter-steer too much, you know, steer too much in the opposite direction.

B: You have a point there. So let's make the feedback more gentle. If the car crosses the line, the warning system makes the steering wheel vibrate a little. Just enough vibration to make the driver feel something is wrong.

A: Yes, I like that.

M: That sounds good. I think we're on to something here. What do you think of all this, Tom? You've done research into how people drive when the car is full of safety devices.

T: I think the vibrating steering wheel is a good idea. You shouldn't have a system that takes control of the driving from the driver, for example by pressing the brakes automatically. That makes people drive more dangerously, because they think that the car is completely safe. Warnings, like the vibrating steering wheel, are much better. They make the driver stay alert and responsible for his own safety.

1 to think of a new warning system to keep drivers in the right lane
2 (a) cameras inside the windscreen (b) a gentle vibration of the steering wheel

6 Play the recording again for students to answer the questions. Elicit answers from the class.

1 infra-red sensors under the bumpers
2 a flashing light, a beeping sound, a SatNav voice giving a warning, a tightening seat belt
3 He thinks that they encourage drivers to drive more dangerously because they think the car is completely safe. He thinks warnings are better because they make the driver take responsibility for safety.

7 Ask students to read through the extracts from the discussion first and then complete them with the words and phrases listed. Do not provide answers yet as students will be checking their own answers in 8.

8 Play the recording again for students to check their answers to 7.

1 you have a point
2 For instance
3 By the way
4 Anyway
5 in other words
6 Alternatively

9 Ask students to look back at the words and phrases in 7 and match them with the language functions 1–6.

1 For instance
2 By the way
3 in other words
4 you have a point
5 Alternatively
6 Anyway

Speaking

10 Tell students that they are going to discuss the question *Are cars too safe?* and write the title on the board as a reminder. Put students in two groups (A and B) and ask them to read their role. Allow some time for students to discuss in their groups what points they will make and to take brief notes before they start. While they are preparing, go round monitoring and offer help where needed.

2 | Instructions

Start here

1 Ask students to look at the warning signs A–F and discuss what each one shows with the class. Students then match the signs with the instructions 1–6. When checking the students' answers, ask them which signs show that the action is (a) mandatory or (b) prohibited.

> **1** E   **2** F   **3** B   **4** C   **5** D   **6** A
> **(a)** the circular blue and white signs
> **(b)** the circular red and black signs

Listening

2 ▶ 🎧 16

Focus students' attention on the diagram. Ask them to identify what it shows (the car brake system). Then put students in pairs or small groups to label the diagram with the parts of the system in the box below. If they are unsure, they should try to make an educated guess. Do not check answers at this point as they are given in the listening in 3.

1 calliper	5 brake line
2 piston	6 hydraulic fluid
3 brake pads	7 master cylinder
4 disc	8 brake pedal

Now focus students' attention on the words in the box. Play the recording once through. Then play it again, pausing after each word for students to practise saying them. You could then ask them to listen again and underline the main stressed syllable in each word.

▶ 🎧 16

disc
piston
brake line
master cylinder
brake pedal
hydraulic fluid
brake pads
calliper

Listening

3 ▶ 🎧 17

Tell students that they are going to listen to a discussion in which a driver gets advice on checking their brake system. Tell students to listen to the recording and check their answers to 2.

▶ 🎧 17

A: You should check your car brake system at least once a year. And while you're driving, you should notice anything unusual with your brakes.

B: What sort of thing should I notice?

A: Well, if the brake pedal feels soft or spongy, or if you have to pump it up and down to stop the car, you must check the brakes.

B: What could be wrong?

A: Well, there could be air in the brake lines or air in the master cylinder. Or the brake fluid level could be too low.

B: What do you mean, air in the brake lines?

A: Well, just look at the diagram here. You can see the disc. You can also see the brake pads, and the calliper. The disc is that circular part mounted on the hub behind the wheel of the car. Above the disc in the diagram is the calliper. The calliper, shown in green in the diagram, fits over the top of the disc. On each end of the calliper are the brake pads, marked in dark blue. These are made of a softer material than the disc to prevent the disc from being scratched or damaged.
So, when you put your foot on the brake pedal and press it down, the brake pads are squeezed together onto the disc. The calliper and the pads are just like your finger and thumb holding a plate. If the pressure is hard enough, the pads will stop the disc from moving.

B: How is the energy from the brake pedal passed to the calliper?

A: Well, if you look again at the diagram, you can see a thin pipe running from the master cylinder to the piston in the calliper. This pipe, called a 'line', contains a hydraulic fluid, which is a special type of oil. It's shown in light blue in the diagram.
So, when you press the brake pedal with your foot, a piston compresses the brake fluid in the master cylinder. This causes the piston in the calliper to push the brake pads onto the disc. When the pads squeeze the disc tightly, the disc slows down and stops.

4 Ask students to read through the questions first, so that they know what to listen out for. Then play the recording again for students to answer the questions. They can check their answers in pairs before you check with the class.

> **1** check brake systems at least once a year; notice anything unusual with brakes while driving
> **2** check the brakes if the pedal feels spongy or if you have to pump it up and down
> **3** air in the lines, air in the master cylinder, low brake fluid
> **4** to prevent the disc from being scratched or damaged

Language

Active and passive modals

Go through the Language box with the students. Remind them that we use *must/mustn't*, *have to* and *need to* to say that something is necessary. We use *should* to give advice or a recommendation and *don't have to/need to* to say that something is unnecessary. These modals and semi-modals are often used with the passive in safety rules and procedures.

Tell students that they can find more information about modals and semi-modals followed by active or passive verbs in the Language summary on page 102.

5 Refer students back to warning sign A in 1 and read out the example sentence. Tell them that they are going to write similar instructions for the other signs using the modal verbs from the Language box and the passive where appropriate.

Possible answers:

A Hard hats/Safety helmets must be worn here/on this site.
B A safety harness needs to be worn/used here.
C Fires must not be extinguished with water here.
D This machine must not be oiled/cleaned when it is moving.
E You must not drink this fluid.
F Breathing equipment needs to be worn in this area.

> **Extra activity**
>
> For homework, you could ask students to find some more safety signs on the internet and write the instructions for them.

6 Read through the instruction and example with the class. Allow students to think about what recommendations for improvements could be made to their college or workplace. Tell them to write at least five sentences. You could then put students in groups and ask them to read out their sentences to decide on the five best recommendations. Groups then take it in turns to read out their recommendations to the class.

7 Students could work in small groups for this activity. Tell them that they are going to discuss rules and procedures which they consider unnecessary in their college, their workplace or their life in general. Go through the example with the students first and elicit a couple of other ideas from the class to get them started.

Reading

8 Tell students that they are going to read a car manual about the brake system. Ask them if they can tell you some things that are essential in order to maintain their brake system. Ask them to read through the manual quickly to see if it mentions these. Then, for each action 1–12, ask students to write *E* for actions which are essential, *R* for actions which are recommended or *U* for unnecessary actions. When they have finished, ask them to check in pairs before you check with the class.

1 R	**2** R	**3** R	**4** U	**5** E	**6** R	**7** E	**8** E
9 E	**10** E	**11** U	**12** R				

9 Ask students to read through the statements first, then read the article again to identify whether the statements are true or false.

1 T
2 F – air has entered the system, not escaped
3 T
4 F – a light squealing noise may not be serious

Vocabulary

10 Students work individually to match the verbs to do with car maintenance (1–8) with their meanings (a–h). When checking answers, you could ask one student to read out one of the verbs from the first column and another student to read out its meaning.

1 d	**2** h	**3** c	**4** g	**5** b	**6** e	**7** f	**8** a

Language

11 Go through the instructions with the class first. Make sure that they know that they should only change the odd-numbered instructions into the active form, and that they must begin each sentence with *You*. Ask them to find the first action in the text in 8 and read the example sentence. Ask them to rewrite the other odd-numbered sentences in a similar way. Tell them that, if possible, they should shorten the sentences if they think some of the information is not needed.

> **1** You should inspect the complete brake system at least once a year.
> **3** You should normally replace the brakes after 20,000–30,000 kilometres.
> **5** You must not use the brakes when the brake pads are below the minimum thickness.
> **7** You need to drain the brake lines and refill them with new brake fluid.
> **9** You must replace the pads and inspect the discs for damage.
> **11** You probably do not need to replace the pads.

Writing

12 Elicit from the class a few machines or devices that they are familiar with. Then tell students that they should choose a device that they know well and write a set of instructions for maintaining it, similar to the one in 8. Go through the list of points first. They could do this for homework if you are short of time in class.

3 Rules

Start here

1 Put students in pairs and focus their attention on the photo and table. Ask them to discuss the situation with their partner and then devise a rule to prevent it from happening, stating what action each plane should take. Allow students to come up with their own ideas in this exercise. It is designed to introduce the topic only, so do not correct their answers. The answers are in the reading text in 2.

Reading

2 Tell students that they are going to read a text about the rules of the air. Ask them to identify the rule that the aircrafts in 1 should have followed.

> Only rule 1 solves the problem. Both planes would use odd-numbered flight levels as they are flying E and SE, so rules 2 and 3 would not solve the problem.

3 Students could work in pairs for this activity. Explain that 1–6 are instructions that a trainer gives to a trainee pilot. Ask them to read through the instructions and tick the ones that follow the rules in the text in 2.

> The following instructions are correct according to the text in 2, and should be ticked:
>
> 1, 3, 4 and 6.

Language

unless; present participle

Go through the Language box with the students. Explain that it shows how we can express rules and instructions positively by using *only … if*, or negatively by using *don't … unless*. Point out the use of the gerund that follows the prepositions *after*, *without* and *before*.

Mixed-ability classes

If you feel students need extra practice, write these prompts on the board:

1 enter / the building / you / ask / permission

2 drive / this car / you / check / the brakes

Ask students to write sentences from the prompts, using the forms in the table.

Answers:

1 Only enter the building if/when/after you've asked permission.

Only enter the building after asking permission.

Don't enter the building unless you've asked permission.

Don't enter the building without asking permission.

2 Only drive this car if/when/after you've checked the brakes.

Only drive this car after checking the brakes.

Don't drive the car unless you've checked the brakes.

Don't drive the car before checking the brakes.

4 Ask students to rewrite the instructions to give the same or similar meaning. Explain that they should replace the words in italics with the words in brackets, and that they may need to change the form of the verbs. Allow students to compare answers before checking the answers as a class.

> **1** Your aircraft must only turn if it has enough space to do so.
> **2** You must turn your aircraft without endangering other aircraft.
> **3** The slower helicopter must only change direction after the faster one has passed it.
> **4** A car driver must not overtake another vehicle before checking his mirror.
> **5** Drivers should not start a long car journey unless they have checked brakes, tyres and fluid levels.

Scanning

5 Go through the instructions with the students. Then ask them to turn to pages 116–117 and find the text entitled *Planes just metres apart in near miss*. Remind them that they do not need to read every word in the text, just look for the information which completes the sentences. Ask students to put up their hand when they have finished. Allow the majority of students to finish but check the answers with the first person to put up their hand to see if they were correct and are the winner.

> **1** (just) 180
> **2** Malta
> **3** Italian
> **4** right; 800

Speaking

6 Put students in small groups (of four to six). Focus their attention on the four diagrams and the tables. Explain that each table describes a dangerous mid-air situation and the two diagrams on the right of each table describe the same situation from above and from the side. Tell them that they are going to discuss the two situations in their groups and decide a) which aircraft must take evasive action and b) what action it/they must take.

Ask students to read through the rules of the air (Part 1) on page 40 again. Then divide each group into subgroup A and subgroup B. Ask subgroup A to read Part 2 on page 110 and subgroup B to read Part 3 on page 115. (Note that for situation 1, the rules on pages 110 and 115 are relevant and that for situation 2, the rules on pages 40 and 110 are relevant.)

Give students a few minutes to digest the rules and then ask them to come together in their main groups. Subgroup A explains the rules from Part 2 to the group and Subgroup B explains the rules from Part 3. Go round monitoring and giving help if necessary.

The whole group then discusses both situations together. They work out which of the three sets of rules (including those on page 40) apply to each situation and come to a decision as to which aircraft should take the evasive action and what action the plane/planes must take. Go round monitoring the discussions and giving help.

Although clear-cut answers are given in the key below, there is room for disagreement in some of the situations and discussion should be encouraged. In general, when aircraft are climbing or descending, part 3 of the rules has priority over parts 1 and 2, which relate to situations where both aircraft are cruising, i.e. are at the same altitude. When both aircraft are cruising, then part 1 would have priority. However, if a collision is imminent (i.e. within five minutes, emergency action may have to be taken under part 2 of the rules).

> Situation 1: B has priority as it is descending, so A should take evasive action. Since they are both slightly on the left side of each other, A (and B) should turn right.

> Situation 2: A is at the correct altitude for its heading, so should normally have priority and if there is space, B should change altitude. However, if the distance is very close, A should also turn left or right to avoid collision.

7 Ask students to choose one person to present their group's decisions to the rest of the class and give reasons for them. They can refer back to their notes if necessary.

Writing

8 Tell students that they are free to choose any activity, procedure, sport or game they like and write the most important rules for it. They could do this activity at home, where they can research information on the internet. Tell them to make sure that they use the language they have been studying in this section.

6 Planning

Contents

1 Schedules

Objectives

In this section students will ...

- brainstorm different sources of energy
- listen to a meeting about targets for reducing carbon emissions and consumption, then mark deadlines on a Gantt chart
- study and practise using phrases for agreeing and disagreeing
- study and practise using future modals
- explain the stages of a project using a Gantt chart
- learn vocabulary for setting deadlines

2 Causes

Objectives

In this section students will ...

- study diagrams about processing carbons and answer questions
- match questions and answers to diagrams
- study suffixes that indicate causation
- study ways of expressing causation
- rewrite sentences using verbs and nouns to express causation
- learn verbs for fuel processing

3 Systems

Objectives

In this section students will ...

- use a diagram to describe the system of a geothermal power plant
- prepare and give a short talk on the system
- study and practise using section markers in a talk
- write an email about a talk on geothermal energy
- learn vocabulary for energy and power production

Briefing

This unit looks at plans for solving the problems of over-dependence on non-renewable energy sources and excessive greenhouse gas emissions.

Section 1 deals with setting targets for reducing reliance on non-renewable, carbon-based energy sources, and for reducing carbon emissions. **Fossil fuels** (**hydrocarbons**) are **non-renewable, carbon-based energy sources**, formed from the remains of prehistoric organisms, **oil** and **gas** from marine organisms such as plankton, and **coal** from land vegetation. **Biofuels** in this context refer to **ethanol, diesel** or other liquid fuels made from processing plant material or waste oil. **Bio-ethanol** is usually mixed with petrol, while **biodiesel** is either used on its own or in a mixture with **mineral** diesel. The main **greenhouse gases** contributing to global warming are **nitrous oxide** (N_2O), **carbon dioxide** (CO_2) and **methane** (CH_4). The discussion in audios 18 and 19 is based on the EU Climate Action targets, designed to keep global temperature increases no more than 2°C above pre-industrial levels. At the time of writing, the EU targets include: (A) a 20% reduction of (1) **emissions** of greenhouse gases, and (2) overall energy **consumption**, and (3) 20% of energy consumption to come from renewable energy sources, all by 2020; (B) meeting 10% of transport fuel needs using biofuels by 2020; (C) by 2050, a 50% reduction in emission of greenhouse gases. For more detail, and other targets, see the link below to EU Climate Action.

Section 2 deals with four methods for producing **clean coal** (see Speed search page 117). The first method, **coal washing**, uses a **gravity separator** containing a special fluid in which coal **particles** (small solid pieces) float, and heavier **impurities** sink. The washed coal, separated from the impurities, can then be skimmed off the surface of the fluid. The second method, **desulphurisation** is the process of removing **sulphur** (AmE **sulfur**) from **flue gas** (the gas emitted after coal has been burned). A mixture of calcium carbonate and water is sprayed over the gas. The calcium carbonate reacts with the sulphur in the gas to form gypsum (calcium sulphate), a soft powdery mineral, which can be removed easily (and used in the construction industry for making cements and plasters). The third method, **electrostatic precipitation** (separation of solids from a fluid using static electricity), uses two metal plates, one with a **negative charge**, the other with a **positive charge**. Flue gas is passed between the plates, and the **particulates** (particles of impurities) become negatively charged and are attracted to the positively charged plate, later falling into hoppers and removed. The fourth method, **carbon capture and storage** (**CCS**), pumps the CO_2 emitted from coal burning into spaces deep underground, which prevents the carbon from polluting the atmosphere. In addition to protecting the atmosphere, this method also helps in the extraction of methane (for fuel) and oil (from low-pressure oil fields). When pumped into a **saline aquifer** (underground water channel containing salty water) the CO_2 dissolves and sinks to the bottom, where it remains trapped indefinitely.

Section 3 deals with a **geothermal power station** (AmE **plant**) located above an underground source of **geothermal energy** (energy in the form of heat found below the earth's surface). The heat comes from an underground **layer** of hot rock, whose high temperature is due to radioactive decay. The geothermal energy system consists of **injection wells**, **extraction** (or **production**) **wells**, a **steam separator** and a **generator**. The wells are at least five hundred metres apart to avoid mixing the hot and cold water together in the extraction wells. First, cold water is pumped down to the hot **basement rock** through the injection wells. The pressure of the water creates small **fissures** (cracks) in the hot rock, which allow the water to flow more easily. After some time the fissures join together and create a **reservoir** of hot **geothermal fluid** at 100–200°C. The hot fluid rises to the surface via the extraction wells, driven by the pressure from the pumps and the high temperature of the extra fluid pumped into the reservoir. As the hot fluid rises, the pressure decreases, and the hot water turns into steam before it reaches the surface, where the steam is separated from the water and flows at speed through the turbine generator, creating electricity. Then the steam condenses into water and is returned down to the underground reservoir through the injection wells.

EU Climate Action: Find the European Commission's **Climate Action** website.

Carbon capture and storage: Find the **World Coal Association** website and search for 'Carbon Capture and Storage' and 'Coal and the Environment'.

Clean-coal technology: Find the **BBC Science and Environment** website and search for 'Clean coal technology: how it works'.

Geothermal energy: Find the **International Geothermal Association** website and search for 'Geothermal Energy'.

Teacher's notes

1 Schedules

Start here

1 Ask students to look at the photos. Elicit what they can see in each one (photo 1: hydro-electric dam; photo 2: wind turbines; photo 3: solar panels; photo 4: oil/gas rig). Brainstorm all sources of energy with the class. Elicit more from the lists in the box below if students get stuck and ask students to make a note of them. Ask students what the difference between *energy*, *power* and *fuel* is.

Energy is the general term for any source of useable power such as electricity and coal that makes machines work or provides heat. *Power* is energy (especially electricity) that comes from a source of fuel and is used to operate lights, machinery, etc. Note that you can say there is a *power cut* but not an ~~energy cut~~. *Fuel* is a substance like petrol, oil, coal or gas that is burned to provide heat or power.

> **renewable:** wind power/energy, hydro-electric power/energy, sea power/energy, solar power/energy, wave power/energy, bio fuels; **non-renewable:** coal, oil, nuclear power/energy, fossil fuels; **carbon-based:** coal, oil, fossil fuels, bio fuels; **non-carbon-based:** wind power/energy, hydro-electric power/energy, sea power/energy, solar power/energy, nuclear power/energy

2 ▶ 🎧 18

Tell students that they are going to listen to the first part of a meeting about reducing carbon emissions and cutting energy consumption. Tell them to listen carefully and tick the greenhouse gases that are mentioned.

▶ 🎧 18

[B = Ben; J = Jeff; D = Danielle]

B: Morning, Jeff. Morning, Danielle.

J: Morning.

D: Good morning.

B: Right, let's get started. I know you are both fully aware that there are global targets for reducing carbon emissions, cutting overall energy consumption, and increasing the use of renewable energy.

J: Yes.

B: So first let's just remind ourselves what the targets are. In fact there are two global targets for reducing emissions. And by the way, of course there are other greenhouse gases, such as methane – CH_4 – and nitrous oxide – N_2O – which are bad for the environment, but we're mainly concerned with carbon dioxide – CO_2 – in our company, since that's the only gas we can control. Anyway, the long-term deadline for a fifty percent reduction is the year 2050 …

All are mentioned except ozone (O_3).

3 ▶ 🎧 19

Tell students that they are going to listen to the rest of the meeting. Focus their attention on the Gantt chart. Explain that they should listen out for the deadlines for meeting targets for reducing emissions and cutting energy consumption. As they do so, they should mark the correct date on the chart (they can shade in as shown in the example after listening). Play the recording for students to complete the chart. Allow students to compare answers before checking the answers as a class.

▶ 🎧 19

[B = Ben; J = Jeff; D = Danielle]

B: … but we're mainly concerned with carbon dioxide – CO_2 – in our company, since that's the only gas we can control. Anyway, the *long-term* deadline for a fifty percent reduction is the year 2050. The world is going to have to make a fifty percent reduction in emissions by that date. But the *urgent medium-term* deadline and the one that concerns us most, right now, is the year 2020. By that date the world is going to have to reduce its emissions by twenty percent.

D: Mm.

J: Right.

B: And that means that our company, being the major energy company in the region, will have to do something similar. So let's have your ideas, please. How can we meet the twenty percent target by the year 2020? Jeff, you've done some thinking on this, so would you like to kick off?

J: Certainly, Ben. Well, my view is that we won't be able to meet the target unless we switch from normal coal-burning to CCS. What I mean by that is, we'll have to convert some of our coal-fired energy production to CCS, you know, carbon capture and storage.

D: We'll probably be able to convert about half of our coal-burning power plants.

B: I don't agree, Danielle. CCS technology is still quite a new technology, and untested. I think a lower percentage would be more realistic.

J: Yes, I agree. Our team looked into it and decided on thirty percent.

D: OK, I can go along with that.

B: Good. So we'll agree to convert thirty percent of our coal-fired power plants to CCS. What should the deadline be, Jeff?

J: We're going to have to do it by 2015 at the latest.

B: I'm in complete agreement with you.

D: That's fine by me. But of course that won't be enough to meet the target alone.

B: You're right, Danielle. You have some ideas about our transport fleet, I think. Would you like to bring us up to speed on that?

D: By all means, Ben. At some point we'll have to replace the carbon fuel in our nationwide transport fleet – diesel oil, petrol and so on – with bio fuel.

B: That's right. So what deadline do you think we should fix for that?

D: Well, I think we'll have to convert at least ten percent of the fleet to bio fuel as quickly as possible. I think our deadline for that should be the end of 2014.

J: I'm not sure about that deadline. It's quite tight. I'm sure we won't be able to meet it. I think 2016 would be more realistic.

B: I would disagree with you there, Jeff. Every time we replace an old vehicle, we can buy one that uses bio fuel. We already have a lot of old vehicles in the fleet.

J: You have a good point there, Ben.

B: I think we're going to need to switch to bio fuels as quickly as possible. Ten percent of the fleet by 2014 sounds right. Jeff?

J: Yes, I agree with you.

B: Good. Let's move on. Let's consider our energy consumption, as a company. We need targets for switching part of our energy supply to renewables.

D: You're absolutely right. By renewables, we're talking about wind power, solar power?

B: Yes, and hydro-electric, waves and bio fuels.

D: Well, obviously, we're going to need to get around fifteen percent of our energy from renewables.

J: I can't go along with that. I think we're going to have to increase that to at least twenty percent. I don't think fifteen percent would be enough.

B: Yes, I agree. And we'll probably need to achieve the twenty percent reduction a couple of years before the deadline, in other words by the end of 2018. What do you think?

J: Yes, I think that's correct.

D: I'm happy with that.

B: Good. So finally, and very briefly, let's look at our overall energy consumption. We're going to have to reduce that, too, probably by twenty percent, and, I think, by no later than the end of 2016. Agreed?

D: Agreed. Twenty percent by 2016.

J: That sounds about right.

B: Good. So let's get all this down on paper.

> **1** by 2050   **2** by 2020   **3** by 2016   **4** by 2015
> **5** 2014   **6** 2018

4 Elicit phrases for agreeing and disagreeing from the class. Then tell them to look at the phrases in 4, which are from the listening, and ask them to complete them in pairs. Play the recording again for students to check their answers. Finally, ask them to mark which ones mean *I agree* and which ones mean *I disagree*. Then check answers with the class.

> **1** along with (a)   **4** sure (b)   **7** agreement (a)
> **2** disagree (b)   **5** sounds (a)   **8** go along (b)
> **3** point (a)   **6** right (a)

5 Elicit other phrases students can remember from the recording for agreeing and disagreeing. Tell students to look at the audio script on pages 121–122 and underline them.

> right; certainly; I don't agree; yes, I agree; that's fine by me; you're right; by all means; that's right; I agree with you; yes, I think that's correct; I'm happy with that; agreed

Speaking

6 Put students in groups of three or four to discuss the energy sources they made notes of in 1. They give their opinions on the use of these sources, and use the phrases in 4 and 5 to agree or disagree with each other.

Vocabulary

7 Go through the ways of setting a deadline with the students. Then ask them to rewrite the four statements using the words in brackets. Ask weaker students to do the exercise in pairs and allow students to compare answers before checking the answers as a class.

> *Possible answers:*
> **1** We'll have to finish this job by June 10th.
> **2** The deadline for (completing) the project is the end of the month.
> **3** The last possible date for finalising the report is next Monday.
> **4** We'll have to switch to bio fuels no later than next year.

Language

Future modals

Go through the Language box with the students. Remind them that if we want to emphasise the future, we use *will*, and *be able to* instead of *can*.

Tell them that they will find more information about future modals in the Language summary on page 102.

8 Tell students that they are going to rewrite statements 1–8 by replacing the words in italics with phrases using the words in the box. Explain that they can use the words in the box more than once. Read the first sentence and the rewritten example answer first so that students know what to do. Weaker students could do the exercise in pairs.

> *Possible answers:*
> **1** is going to have to   **5** won't be able to
> **2** won't be able to meet   **6** won't have to cut
> **3** 'll probably be able to   **7** 're going to have to
> **4** won't be able to   **8** won't need to, will have to

Speaking

9 Tell students that they are going to explain the stages of an important project in which they are currently involved to the rest of the class. Tell them to draw a Gantt chart like the one in 3 to show the different stages in the project and the deadlines they have to meet.

10 Ask students to take it in turns to explain their project to the rest of the class, using their Gantt chart in their presentation. In large classes, divide the class into smaller groups. Encourage listening students to make a note of any follow-up questions they can ask at the end of the presentation.

2 Causes

Start here

1 Put students in small groups. Focus students' attention on the diagram and tell them to discuss questions 1 and 2.

See the Briefing section at the beginning of the unit in the Teacher's Book for more information on these four processes. Briefly, Figure 1 shows a process in which impurities are removed from the coal (before it is burnt) by washing and gravity; Figure 2 shows the removal of sulphur dioxide from the flue gas (the gas emitted when coal is burnt) through the chemical reaction of calcium carbonate and water with sulphur; Figure 3 shows the removal of particles from the flue gas by electrostatically charging the particles to make them stick to metal plates and then fall into hoppers; Figure 4 shows CCS (carbon capture and storage), a process of pumping carbon emissions to spaces underground. Note that this is still a new and relatively untested technology. A by-product is that methane and oil from near-depleted oil reservoirs can be pushed up to the surface by the CO_2.

> **1** To make coal cleaner, i.e. to reduce the carbon emissions when it is burned.
>
> **2** In addition to burying and storing the CO_2 away from the atmosphere, the process in Figure 4 also has the benefit of helping to push oil (from low-pressure oilfields) and methane up to the surface where they can be used.

Scanning

2 Go through the instructions with the students. Then ask them to turn to pages 116–117 and find the text on clean coal technology (CCT). Remind them that they do not need to read every word in the text, just look for the information that completes the statements. Ask students to put up their hand when they have finished. Allow the majority of students to finish but check the answers with the first person to put up their hand to see if they were correct and are the winner.

> **1** one trillion   **2** 200   **3** precipitators

After you have checked their answers, go through some of the vocabulary with the students. Check that they understand *ground* (*grind–ground–ground*: crush something into small pieces), *emit* (produce), *react* (when a substance, e.g. a liquid or gas, changes when mixed with another substance), *store* (keep something in a safe place), *pollutant* (a substance that is harmful for the environment) and *impurities* (a substance that is present in another substance which makes it dirty or damages its quality).

Extra activity

Ask students to read the four processes of clean coal technology again. Then put them in pairs and ask them to look back at the diagrams on page 44 and take it in turns to explain each process to their partner.

Reading

3 Ask students to read through the questions and answers about the process of cleaning coal. Put them in pairs to match 1–6 with a–f. Then ask them to match the questions and answers to the diagram in 1.

> **1** e – Figure 3
> **2** d – Figure 2
> **3** f – Figure 1
> **4** a – Figure 4
> **5** c – Figure 4
> **6** b – Figure 4

Vocabulary

4 Ask students to look back at the answers to the questions in 3 and focus their attention on the words in italics. Ask them to change these nouns into verbs. They could look at the questions for the answers, as they will find the corresponding verb in some of them. Point out that some of the nouns will be the same as the verb form.

> **a** store, be present
> **b** force, rise, pressurise
> **c** recover
> **d** desulphurise, react, insert, add
> **e** remove, attract, charge
> **f** purify, rotate

5 Ask students to study the information in the box on suffixes to indicate causation. Ask them to guess the meanings of the words in the task below. They then check the answers in a dictionary or reference book.

Explain that the *-z* spelling (*-ize*, *-ization*) is mainly American English, while the *-s* spelling (*-ise*, *-isation*) is mainly British English. Also point out that the prefix *de-* indicates a negative or opposite action, e.g. *sulphurise* means *add sulphur*; *desulphurise* means *take sulphur away*. You could ask them what *deactivate*, *dehydrate* and *depressurise* mean and ask them if they know of any other words beginning with the prefix *de-*.

> **1** make something more humid or damp (verb)
> **2** the process of converting an atom or molecule into an ion (noun)
> **3** the process of producing ozone, or subjecting (something) to the action of ozone (noun)
> **4** the process of changing (something) into a gaseous state (noun)
> **5** change (something) into a solid state (verb)
> **6** crush something into a fine powder (verb)

Extra activity

Ask students to work in pairs to change the nouns in 1–6 into verbs and the verbs into nouns. Then ask them to underline the stressed syllable in each case. Tell them to say the words out loud as they do so. When checking answers, tell them to note that the stress falls on the syllable before last in nouns ending in *-tion*.

> **1** hu<u>mi</u>dify (verb), humidifi<u>ca</u>tion (noun)
> **2** ioni<u>sa</u>tion (noun), <u>i</u>onise (v)
> **3** ozonifi<u>ca</u>tion (noun), o<u>zo</u>nise (verb)
> **4** gasifi<u>ca</u>tion (noun), <u>ga</u>sify (verb)
> **5** so<u>li</u>dify (verb), solidifi<u>ca</u>tion (noun)
> **6** <u>pul</u>verise (verb), pulveri<u>sa</u>tion (noun)

Language

Causation

Go through the Language box with the students. Tell them that you can use the words in the shaded boxes when you want to explain what makes something happen or how something happens. Ask students to look back at the answers to the questions in 3, find the expressions from the box in the text and underline them.

6 Go through the instructions and the example with the class. Ask students to rewrite each sentence so that the meaning is similar to the original one, using the phrases to express causation in brackets.

> **1** We have to use international time zones owing to the rotation of the earth.
> **2** There's no need to pump the oil due to the pressure of the CO_2.
> **3** The iron filings are moving as a result of the attraction of the magnet.
> **4** The pressure on the methane is caused by the injection of CO_2.
> **5** People must not drink this water owing to the presence of impurities.
> **6** This concrete has flaws caused by the addition of too much water.
> **7** Our astronauts are safe due to the recovery of the capsule from the sea.
> **8** We emit no carbon as a result of the storage of our CO_2 underground.

3 Systems

Start here

1 Put students into small groups. Draw students' attention to the illustration of a geothermal *power plant*. Explain that *power plant* is American English but is also in general use in most English-speaking countries, and that *power station* is mainly British English. Refer students to the American English and British English reference section at the back of the Course Book (page 108) for more information.

Read through the labels on the illustration with the class and check students' pronunciation. Then ask groups to discuss the illustration using all the named labels. Do not check the students' understanding of the diagram at this point as they will be discussing the system in more detail in 2.

See the Briefing section at the beginning of the unit in the Teacher's Book for more information on geothermal technology.

Speaking

2 Put students in groups. Tell them that they are going to prepare a short talk with their group about how the system in the illustration works. Ask them to work through the questions and discuss them in their groups, making notes as they go along. Alternatively, they could appoint one person in the group to make notes.

When the groups have discussed the questions and decided on the answers, have a brief discussion with each group to ensure that their answers are roughly in line with the process shown in the illustration.

1 above a layer of very hot rock, 2–4,000 m below the surface
2 injection wells, extraction wells, a generator and a steam separator
3 five hundred metres (500 m)
4 to avoid mixing the hot and cold water together in the extraction wells
5 It is pumped down to the hot basement rock through the injection wells.
6 the force or pressure of the pumped water
7 The water flows into the fissures and after some time the fissures join together and create a reservoir of very hot geothermal fluid that is continuously heated.
8 The pressure from the pumps above the injection wells, plus the pressure from the high temperature of the fluid in the reservoir.
9 the extraction/production wells
10 in the extraction wells, before it reaches the surface
11 the decrease in pressure as the fluid rises
12 It separates the steam from the water.
13 It flows into/powers the generator.
14 It is returned to the reservoir again via the injection wells.

3 Tell students to look back through their notes and decide how they should divide up the sections of the talk. Go through the example with the class to get them started.

Possible answers:
1 Location (1)
2 Components (2–4)
3 Process (5–14)
3a Injection stage (5–7)
3b Extraction stage (8–11)
3c Surface stage (12–14)

4 Tell students that they are now going to study some section markers to use in their talk. Ask them to read through sentences 1–8 and complete them with the words in the box. After checking answers, tell students to work with their group and add these section markers to the appropriate place in their notes.

1 aim in this talk	5 let's look
2 I'd like	6 like to move on to
3 let's move	7 let's look at
4 I'm going to	8 I'd like to thank

5 Go through the instructions with the class on how to organise their group members to give their talk. You could ask students to make a simple evaluation checklist to use when their colleagues are giving talks. For example:

Evaluation checklist

- communicates meaning clearly ☐
- speaks fluently ☐
- good pace (not too fast or slow) ☐
- clearly marks stages of talk ☐
- clearly marks handover to others ☐
- uses notes/doesn't just read out text ☐
- good eye contact with audience ☐
- good hand gestures ☐
- refers to visual clearly (if using visuals) ☐
- introduces/concludes the talk effectively (if the first or final speaker) ☐

6 Go through the useful phrases first, then ask students to give their talks.

Writing

7 Students write an email giving information about geothermal energy.

Model answer:

Hi Dino

Many thanks for your email earlier today. You asked me some questions about geothermal energy. I'm a bit busy at the moment, so here are some very brief answers to your questions. I can give you some more details when we meet up for lunch at the conference next month.

1 The high temperatures of the rock layers are caused mainly by radiation, not usually by volcanic activity.
2 The fissures are created by the water, owing to the pressure of the pumps.
3 The high flow rate of the fluid up to the surface is due to both pump pressure and also high temperatures.
4 The conversion of hot fluid to steam in the extraction well occurs as a result of the drop in pressure as it rises.

I hope that helps. Let me know if you need any more information.

Best wishes,

Niko

8 Ask students to swap their emails with a partner for them to check grammar, spelling and punctuation.

Review Unit C

Answer key

1 *Possible answers:*

1 The smaller boat has probably turned left immediately in front of the larger boat. Now, the large boat is sailing straight towards the small boat. The large boat will probably strike the small boat in the side.

2 Even if it starts to turn in either direction, it will probably still strike the small boat.

3 The smaller boat would probably turn right and increase its speed.

4 Do not change direction if it will interfere with another boat. (or … unless you have enough space to do so.)

2
1 you have a point there	4 Anyway
2 for instance	5 in other words
3 By the way	6 alternatively

4
1 maintained/kept	4 kept/maintained
2 remains	5 departed
3 regained	

5

1 Bottles of liquid must not be taken through airport security. (E)

2 Seat belts do not have to be worn while the aircraft is cruising. (U)

3 Large quantities of food shouldn't be eaten during the flight. (R)

4 Mobile phones have to be switched off during take-off and landing. (E)

5 Passports do not need to be shown when leaving this airport. (U)

6 Plenty of water should be drunk during a long flight. (R)

7 *Possible answers:*

1 Before long journeys, the brake fluid level must be inspected and topped up if necessary.

2 Every 10,000 km, the old engine oil has to be drained out and replaced with new oil.

3 Every six months, the brakes need to be inspected and adjusted if necessary or replaced if worn.

4 During journeys, the performance of the brakes must be monitored and any necessary action has to be taken.

5 Every 15,000 km, the brake lines need to be checked and mended or replaced if damaged.

6 Before every winter, the radiator must be drained and refilled with a mixture of water and anti-freeze.

8

1 Food must not be taken on site unless the manager has given permission.

2 Those dangerous chemicals should not be handled unless you're wearing protective gloves.

3 You must not walk onto the building site until you have put on a hard hat.

4 These safety boots don't have to be worn if you aren't going to work with live electrical equipment.

5 You should only start a long car journey after topping up all fluid levels.

9 *Model answer:*

The temperature sensor in the room detects a rise or fall in the temperature of the room, and sends this information to the comparator. The comparator then compares the actual room temperature with the desired room temperature. In this example, the actual room temperature is too low. The comparator then sends an error signal to the controller, which sends a correction signal to the boiler. In this example, the boiler switches on to heat up the room.

10 Both systems use a sensor to detect changes (in the environment/in the driver's behaviour) and send this information to a controller, which takes action (by switching on the boiler/by giving the driver a warning).

11
1 should	4 absolutely	7 go
2 agreement	5 sure	8 would
3 agree	6 have	

12 *Possible answers:*

1 The builders will have to construct the foundations by 30th May.

2 The local council workers won't have to remove the waste by the 13th of June.

3 The divers are not going to be able to recover the wrecked ship by the end of tomorrow.

4 The technicians will need to activate the new equipment no later than next week.

5 The radio operator is going to be able to transmit the signal by 12.30 today.

6 The electricians won't need to install the wiring by the end of today.

7 The mining company will have to extract the ores by the end of the year.

8 The drill team won't have to insert the new tubes in the well this week.

13
1 consume	4 desulphurise	7 solidify
2 emit	5 humidify	8 gasify
3 purify	6 liquefy	

14

1 owing to	4 because of	7 due to
2 caused by	5 because	8 because of
3 because	6 as a result of	

15 *Possible answers:*

1 Oxygen is separated from air and introduced into the boiler.

2 The coal is pulverised and combusted in an oxygen-rich environment. As a result, the pollutants are reduced.

3 The ash is removed using electrostatic precipitators.

4 The steam is condensed into water, which is then transferred to the boiler where the combustion is completed.

5 The CO_2 emission from the combustion is recycled and recovered for later capture and storage.

Project

18 At the end of every Review Unit is a project. Students can do their research on the internet.

Ask students to check their work thoroughly when they have finished for any mistakes in grammar, spelling or punctuation. They could also ask a partner to check through their work as well and suggest any improvements.

Part 1: Vocabulary and grammar

1

1 f	2 d	3 e	4 c	5 b	6 a

2

1 keep   2 drifts   3 regains

3

1 inspect   2 monitor   3 mend   4 top up
5 replace   6 adjust

4

1 no later than	3 at the latest
2 deadline	4 date

5

1 purification	4 ionisation
2 liquefaction	5 solidification
3 sulphurisation	6 pulverisation

6

1 must   2 must not   3 have to   4 must not
5 don't need to   6 should

7

1 Warnings from the police or traffic wardens must be obeyed.

2 Horns must not be used in a built-up area between 11:00 p.m. and 7:00 a.m.

3 Seat belts have to be worn in the car.

4 Vehicles must not be left unattended with the engine running.

5 A driving licence doesn't need to be carried with you when driving in the UK, but it is recommended.

6 The lights should be checked regularly to make sure that they are in good working condition.

8

1 when   2 after   3 without   4 unless

9

1 Sorry, I won't be able to finish the report before Friday.

2 Oil companies will need to invest more money in renewable energy.

3 You won't have to finish all the work by the end of the day.

4 The company director will have to give an explanation of the damage to the investigation team.

5 They won't need to inspect the machinery. It's been taken care of.

10

1 The team are unhappy due to the cancellation of the project.

2 The changes occurred owing to the addition of salt.

3 The contamination of the water supply was caused by the presence of pollutants

4 The damage occurred as a result of the incorrect storage of the substances.

Part 2: Reading and writing

Reading

1 This is essential to maintain the mechanical strength of the grate and prevent damage to it owing to the intense heat. (lines 24–26)

2 … waste can be converted into energy. (line 11)

3 There have been concerns from local communities about the health effects caused by emissions from the ash and flue gases (lines 27–29)

4 It is claimed that the benefits of incinerating waste are that it can significantly reduce the volume of waste for disposal; (lines 6–8)

5 … harmful toxins and pollutants in clinical and hazardous waste can be completely destroyed in the combustion process, (lines 8–10)

Writing

Possible answer:

1 Don't give the pilot clearance to land unless it's safe.

2 Check the runways and skies, using binoculars and surface radar.

3 Update the pilot on the local weather conditions.

4 On landing, direct the pilot to an exit taxiway.

5 Give the pilot the radio frequency for ground control.

Review Unit C Quick test

Part 1: Vocabulary and grammar

1 Match the words with their meanings.

1	counter-steer	**a)**	twisting motion
2	detect	**b)**	corrective
3	monitor	**c)**	intentionally
4	on purpose	**d)**	discover
5	remedial	**e)**	check continuously
6	torque	**f)**	steer in the opposite direction

(6 marks)

2 Choose the correct option to complete the sentences.

1 The Lane Keeping Assist system helps drivers to _____ their vehicle in its lane.

   A stay   **B** keep   **C** maintain

2 The system can detect when a vehicle _____ out of its lane.

   A steers   **B** departs   **C** drifts

3 The driver counter-steers and the car _____ its correct position inside the lane.

   A brings   **B** regains   **C** returns

(3 marks)

3 Complete the sentences with the verbs in the box.

adjust   inspect   mend   monitor   replace   top up

1 The mechanic needs to _____ the damage to the car.

2 When you drive your car, you should _____ your brake system for anything unusual.

3 I've had an accident. Can you _____ the car door for me?

4 You need to _____ the brake fluid. The fluid level is low.

5 We need to _____ the brake pads with new ones.

6 This seat belt is uncomfortable. I can't _____ it.

(6 marks)

4 Complete the sentences with the words in the box.

at the latest   date   deadline   no later than

1 They want us to complete the work _____ the end of June.

2 They missed the _____ for completing the work. It was last Friday.

3 We have to meet the target by 2016 _____.

4 The last possible _____ for us to cancel the project is 14 May.

(4 marks)

5 Rewrite the verbs as nouns using the correct suffix: -ification, -efaction, -isation.

1	purify	_____	4	ionise	_____
2	liquify	_____	5	solidify	_____
3	sulphurise	_____	6	pulverise	_____

(6 marks)

6 Choose the correct option to complete these sentences.

1 You **must/shouldn't** obey warnings from the police or traffic wardens.

2 You **have to/must not** use your horn in a built-up area between 11:00 p.m. and 7:00 a.m.

3 You **have to/don't need to** wear seat belts in the car.

4 You **must not/needn't** leave vehicles unattended with the engine running.

5 You **don't need to/shouldn't** carry a driving licence with you when driving, but it is recommended.

6 You **should/have to** check the lights regularly to make sure that they are in good working condition.

(6 marks)

7 Rewrite the sentences in 6 in the passive.

1 _____

2 _____

3 _____

4 _____

5 _____

6 _____

(6 marks)

8 Choose the correct adverb to complete the sentences.

1 Only descend **when/without** air traffic control give permission.

2 Only use this machine **unless/after** reading the instruction manual.

3 Don't drive this car **after/without** replacing the brake discs.

4 Don't leave the building **when/unless** you switch off the electricity.

(4 marks)

9 Rewrite these sentences to emphasis the future. Use *be able to, have to* or *need to.*

1 Sorry, I can't finish the report before Friday.

_____

2 Oil companies need to invest more money in renewable energy.

_____

3 You don't have to finish all the work by the end of the day. You can do it tomorrow.

_____

4 The company director must give an explanation of the damage to the investigation team.

_____

5 They don't need to inspect the machinery. It's been taken care of.

_____

(5 marks)

10 Rewrite these sentences so the meaning is the same, using the verbs in brackets. You will need to make other changes to the sentences.

1 The team are unhappy because the project is cancelled.

_____ (due to)

2 The changes occurred because salt was added.

_____ (owing to)

3 The contamination of the water supply was because pollutants were present.

_____ (caused by)

4 The damage occurred because the substances were stored incorrectly.

_____ (as a result of)

(4 marks)

Part 2: Reading and writing

Reading

Read the text. Find and underline the evidence for the statements below.

> **Burning waste in incinerators**
>
> Unrecyclable waste has traditionally been disposed of at landfill sites. However, more waste is now being incinerated because existing landfills can no longer cope with the quantity of waste produced, and it is becoming increasingly difficult to find space for ⁵ new landfill sites. It is claimed that the benefits of incinerating waste are that it can significantly reduce the volume of waste for disposal; harmful toxins and pollutants in clinical and hazardous waste can be completely destroyed in the combustion process, and ¹⁰ waste can be converted into energy. This occurs due to the intense heat in the incinerator, which produces steam. This in turn drives a turbo-generator which can feed the electricity grid.

> The most common waste-to-energy incinerator in ¹⁵ operation today is the moving grate system. Waste is taken to an EfW (energy from waste) plant and fed down a 'throat' onto a moving grate*. From here it is propelled through a furnace down to an ash pit. Combustion air is pumped up below the grate. The waste must be kept ²⁰ in the furnace at a temperature of at least 850°C for two seconds in order to break down the toxic compounds and completely destroy them. Air is also supplied from below to cool the grate. This is essential to maintain the mechanical strength of the grate and prevent damage ²⁵ to it owing to the intense heat.
>
> There have been concerns from local communities about the health effects caused by emissions from the ash and flue gases. As a result of strict EU regulations, all plants in Europe must have an air pollution ³⁰ control system in place.

grate = frame of metal bars which can hold hot ash

1 Cooling the grate is an important part of the process.

2 Waste can be turned into electricity.

3 People living near the incinerators are worried about their impact.

4 Incinerating waste means that less waste needs to go to landfill sites.

5 The intense heat ensures the complete destruction of harmful substances.

(5 marks)

Writing

Read the information the training officer is giving new local air traffic controllers about landing procedures. Then rewrite the information as five rules, using no more than ten words for each rule.

> **Air traffic control landing procedure for local controllers**
>
> 'First of all, you cannot give the pilot clearance to land before checking that it's safe to land. You must use your binoculars and the surface radar to check the runways and skies above the runways to ensure that it is safe to land. Once you've given the pilot clearance, make sure you give him/her an update on the local weather conditions. When the plane has landed, you must direct the pilot to steer the plane to an exit taxiway, and don't forget to give the pilot the new radio frequency for ground control.'

1 _____

2 _____

3 _____

4 _____

5 _____

(5 marks)

7 | Reports

Contents

1 | Statements

Objectives

In this section students will ...

- identify security systems in photos
- read a newspaper article about an airport security incident and answer questions
- change reported speech into direct speech
- listen to an interview about the incident and compare accounts
- study and practise using reporting verbs
- role-play an interview
- learn vocabulary for security

2 | Incidents

Objectives

In this section students will ...

- read and discuss a case study about a security incident
- read a product review to put illustrations in order, match words in the text with their definitions, then answer questions about the review
- study and practise using the past continuous and present simple with *when/while/as* for interrupted actions
- talk about an international event using the past continuous

3 | Progress

Objectives

In this section students will ...

- compare two types of fingerprint scanners
- listen to a progress report, complete a checklist and discuss recommendations
- label diagrams with words for electrical circuits
- read the transcript of a lecture to match diagrams and answer true/false questions
- prepare and give a talk explaining how capacitive fingerprint scanners work
- learn vocabulary for electrical engineering

Briefing

This unit looks at security technology and procedures.

Section 1 deals with airport security technology, and particularly the **walk-through metal detector (WTMD)**, the large gate-like structure that passengers walk through, and the smaller **hand-held metal detector (HHMD)**, which security staff run over the passenger's body to check for metal objects. The main **concourse** of an airport is the large open area where passengers walk around and wait for their flights after passing through the **security checkpoint** on their way to the **departure gate**. The incident described on page 52 is based on real-life inspections of security procedures, where an inspector, disguised as a passenger, tries to smuggle an imitation weapon or bomb component through the security checkpoint and onto an aircraft, in order to test the effectiveness of the security checks.

Section 2 explains the technology of the WTMD, which uses **pulse induction (PI) technology**, based on the principle of **electromagnetic induction**. An **electromagnet** basically consists of a **coil** of wire which is wound around an **iron core**. When an electric current flows through the coil, the iron core becomes a temporary magnet (for as long as the current continues to flow). **Induction** is the reverse process: if **the magnetic field** from a magnet passes through a metal object (a conductor), an electric current is **induced** (or generated) in the metal object. A **pulse**, or short burst, of electrical current is sent through the coil in the frame of the metal detector. This creates a magnetic field, which passes through the metal object carried by the passenger. The magnetic field **induces** a small current in the metal object, which then acts as a second electromagnet. This new magnet (the metal object) interferes with the magnetic field sent out by a second, **reflected**, pulse of the detector, causing more current to flow in the detector's coil. This increase in current is measured and converted to an **audible tone** or **beep** that becomes louder and higher as the metal object gets closer to the detector. The specific metal detector described on page 54 has eight separate coils which can show eight **detection zones**, or **vertical** locations, from the ground up to the top of the WTMD frame. The **signal strength** shows the **horizontal** location of the object. The **display screen** can therefore show the exact location of the metal object on the passenger's body.

Section 3 deals with **biometric** methods of **identification (ID)** of an individual person, such as **fingerprint scanning**, **iris** (of the eye) **scanning**, **voice recognition** and so on. **Capacitive fingerprint scanners** are more accurate than **optical** ones, because they depend on contact by the actual finger, not just an image of the finger. A **capacitor** consists of two **conductors** (such as **parallel metal plates**) insulated from each other by a **dielectric**, which is often made of an insulating material, but can also contain air or a vacuum. **Capacitance** is the maximum amount of **electrical charge** that can be **stored** by the capacitor. One application of a capacitor is to release a complete charge almost instantly, as with a camera flash. Another application, as in the fingerprint scanner, is to use changes in capacitance as a means of measuring changes in a dielectric. A thicker dielectric (i.e. a greater distance between the conductors) means a lower capacitance, while a thinner dielectric means a higher capacitance. In the scanner, the finger acts as one plate of the capacitor and the **sensor** in the scanner acts as the second plate. When a finger **ridge** (raised part) touches the sensor, the dielectric is thinner (i.e. the finger and the sensor are closer together) so the capacitance is higher. When a finger **valley** (recessed part) touches the sensor, the dielectric is thicker (because of the air in the valley) so the capacitance is lower. The scanner measures the differences in capacitance between all the points where the finger touches the sensors, and builds up a digital image of the shape of the fingerprint.

Walk-Through Metal Detector: Search for the commercial website **Rapiscan Systems** and search for 'Metor 200'.

Capacitive fingerprint scanners: Find the **How Stuff Works** website and search for 'How fingerprint scanners work', 'How capacitors work' and 'How airport security works'.

Electromagnetic induction: Find the website **All About Circuits** and search for 'Electromagnetic induction'.

Teacher's notes

1 Statements

Start here

1 ▶ 🔊20

Tell students that in this unit they will be looking at different security procedures and devices used in airports. Put students in pairs. Ask them to look at the photos and match them with the security systems in the box. Then play the recording for students to check their pronunciation of the devices. Make sure that they are pronouncing *baggage* and *machine* correctly.

▶ 🔊 20

hand-held metal detector

baggage X-ray machine

walk-through metal detector

CCTV camera

A walk-through metal detector (WTMD)
B baggage X-ray machine
C CCTV camera
D hand-held metal detector (HHMD)

Extra activity

You could ask students to discuss with a partner their experiences of going through airport security control: how long it took, if they were searched, how they felt, how security procedures differ at different airports, etc.

Reading

2 Tell students that they are going to read a newspaper article about a security incident at an airport. First, ask students what sort of things security officials look for when passengers are going through the checks at airports. Pre-teach *source* (a person who provides information, in this case, to a newspaper) and *jaw*. Ask students which part of the body the *jaw* is. Then ask them to read the text and answer the questions below.

1 the security official
2 a beep(ing sound)
3 because he was not really a passenger but pretended to be one
4 all the events of the preceding paragraphs after the beeping of the metal detector, i.e. the security official letting the passenger through the security checks

3 Go through the example with the class. Point out that in 1, two possible examples of his exact words are given. The official is giving an *instruction* in both cases but the second one uses a more polite form. You could do the next one with the class. Elicit the answer '*Raise your arms*'. Point out the change in the pronoun form, remind them to use inverted commas, and ask them how they would make this instruction more polite.

You may want to go through the Language box on page 53 with the students at this stage. Or you could simply ask them what tense they think each person would use at the time of speaking. Then ask students to rewrite 2–7, using the exact words spoken by the people in each case. You could ask students to compare their ideas with a partner before asking the class for their answers.

(Other answers are possible than the ones below, and the students should be encouraged to see that form and function do not always match in an obvious way.)
Possible answers:
1 'Stand aside (, please).' or 'Would you mind standing aside, please?'
2 '(Please) raise your arms for a manual search.'
3 'I've recently had surgery on my jaw.'
4 'The surgeon put a metal plate inside my jaw, which made the metal detector beep.'
5 'You can go.'
6 'Stop!'
7 'I'm a security inspector.'

Listening

4 Tell students that following the security incident in the newspaper article, there was an investigation into how it happened. Put students in pairs and ask them to discuss the questions the investigator asked the official who allowed the 'passenger' through the security checkpoint. Get feedback from the class and elicit questions in preparation for 5.

5 ▶ 🔊21

Tell students that they are now going to listen to the interview between the investigator and the security official to compare the investigator's questions with the ones they came up with in 4.

▶ 🔊 21

A: I'm conducting an investigation into the recent security breakdown at the airport. I need to ask you some questions.
B: Fair enough.
A: You were the official on duty at security check-point B between 2 and 4 p.m. on the 18th of this month, is that correct?
B: Yes, that's right.
A: Good. So could you tell me exactly what happened when the passenger walked through the metal detector?
B: He walked through and the detector sounded.
A: What did you do?
B: I told him to step back and then I ordered him to walk through again.

A: Are you sure you instructed him to walk through again?

B: Er, yes, I am. I told him to take his money out of his pockets. I told him to put the money on a tray, and then I ordered him to walk through again.

A: Give me your exact words. What did you say to him? Actual words, please.

B: I said, 'Put your money on the tray. Now walk through again, please.'

A: And then what happened?

B: This time the metal detector didn't sound, so I told him to go on.

A: What were your exact words?

B: No words. I just waved him through.

A: What happened next?

B: My supervisor asked me what had happened and I told him that the passenger wasn't carrying any metal.

A: What were your exact words?

B: I said, 'He isn't carrying any metal.'

A: OK. Now what if I told you that the passenger was, in fact, carrying a knife?

B: What? No, it's not possible!

A: And what if I told you that the 'passenger' was, in fact, a security inspector?

B: Oh.

6 Tell students that they are going to listen to the interview again and compare it with the details from the newspaper article in 2. Tell them that at least four details are different in the article. Point out that as they listen, they should notice what the official says and also what he does not say. You could get them to reread the article first, then play the recording and get them to underline the differences in the text. Then ask them to discuss the differences with a partner and make notes on their conclusions. Do not go through the answers with the class at this stage as students will check them in 9.

The differences are:
- telling the passenger to step back
- telling him to raise his arms
- telling him to walk through again
- telling him to take his money out of his pockets
- telling him to put his money on a tray
- saying that the detector did not sound a second time
- waving him through
- telling the supervisor he was not carrying any metal
- not mentioning the metal plate in the passenger's jaw

7 Ask students to read the sentences from the interview and complete each gap with one word. Then ask them to look at the audio script on page 122 to check their answers.

| **1** to, to | **2** had | **3** wasn't | **4** isn't |

Language

Reported speech

Go through the first Language box with the students on reported words. Point out that after the verbs *tell* and *inform* we use the pronoun *that*, or we can leave it out.

Ask them to underline the verb used in the *Statement* column and say what it changes to in reported speech. Then go through the second box with the students and tell them that with instructions we use *tell/instruct* plus the infinitive.

8 Ask students to change the reported statements into reported instructions. Tell them to use a different reporting verb from the box for each sentence.

Possible answers:

1 The pilot told everyone to leave the plane immediately.

2 The passenger assured the policeman that he was innocent.

3 The security official instructed the man to walk through the gantry.

4 The pilot confirmed that the plane was safe.

5 The policeman ordered the passenger to go with him.

6 The security manager informed his staff that there had been a security incident that morning.

7 The security official promised to be more careful in future.

8 The inspector explained that he had pretended to be a passenger.

Speaking

9 Put students in pairs. Tell them that they are going to role-play the interview between the investigator and the security official. Tell them to use all the information from this section to prepare for the roleplay. They should also look at the audio script on page 122 to check details of the interview. However, they should close their Course Books while doing the roleplay. Tell them to take turns to be the investigator and the security official. While they are doing the roleplay, go round monitoring and giving help.

> **Mixed-ability classes**
>
> You could ask stronger classes to write up a report of the interview for homework. While they are doing the roleplay, the investigator should make notes and use them as the basis for the report. Tell them to use the language they have studied in this section in their reports.

2 Incidents

Start here

1 As a warmer, focus students' attention on the photo and ask them what they can see in the suitcase. Ask them if they can see anything suspicious. Ask them what objects they cannot put in their hand luggage or have on them when they go through a walk-through metal detector.

Tell students that they are going to read a case study about a security incident. Put students in pairs. Ask them to read the text and discuss the question at the end with their partner. Tell them to make a note of their ideas but do not tell them the answer as students will find it themselves in the text in 2.

Extra activity

Put students in two groups, A and B. Tell them that they are going to play a game in which they have to name things that you are not allowed to take in your hand luggage. Students from alternate groups take it in turns to name an object. If they cannot think of one, repeat a word, or name an object which you *can* take in your hand luggage, then they are out. They carry on until one student is left in the game, who is then the winner.

What you can't take in your hand luggage

Apart from the obvious (guns, explosives, knives, etc.), here is a list of items you cannot take in your hand luggage on board a plane (from the UK):

- corkscrews
- large scissors
- non-safety matches
- fireworks
- cigarette lighters
- tweezers
- contact lens solution (more than 100 ml)
- sports equipment: bats and racquets, golf clubs, darts, walking/hiking poles, ice skates, fishing rods, martial arts equipment
- tools: any tool with a blade longer than 6 mm, a drill with drill bit, stanley knives, saws, screwdrivers, hammers, pliers, wrenches or spanners, bolt guns, nail guns, crowbars, blow torches
- chemicals and toxic substances, e.g. oxidisers, peroxides, acids, corrosives and bleaching agents, vehicle batteries, poisons, toxins, infectious substances

You could search the internet to find out about rules for items you cannot take in your hand luggage in your country.

Reading

2 Tell students that they are going to read a product review which will give them the answer to the question about the case study in 1. Revise some of the vocabulary in the text first, e.g. ask what the following words mean: *harmless* (not dangerous), *collapse* (fall down), *interfere* (prevent something from working correctly), *convert* (change).

Then tell students to scan the article quickly to find the solution to the question in 1. Allow students to compare ideas with their partner.

Mixed-ability classes

With stronger students, you could set this as a competition and ask them to raise their hands once they think they have found the solution. Give the other students the chance to find the solution before allowing the first student to raise their hand to give their answer. Check to see if the other students agree.

The metal detector has eight separate electro-magnetic coils, each one at a different height. This shows the height of the metal object. Then the strength of the signal shows the distance of the object from the coil. In the case study, the coil at ground level showed that the metal was in a shoe, and the strength of the signal showed that it was the left shoe.

3 Tell students to look at the illustrations of the walk-through metal detectors and note the differences in each one. Then ask them to read the product review in 2 again and put the illustrations in the correct order. They can then compare their answers with a partner before you check with the class.

The correct order is: A, C, D, B

4 Ask students to scan the text in 2 to find the words to match the definitions 1–5.

1 coil
2 pulse
3 field
4 resistor
5 amplified

5 You could ask students to work in pairs to answer the questions about the product review in 2.

1 The magnetic field from the coil produces a current in the metal object. This current creates the magnetic field.
2 It is caused by the collapse of the magnetic field in the coil.
3 It increases the length of the reflected pulse.
4 It increases the volume.

Language

Past continuous

Go through the Language box with the students. Ask students to identify the two tenses in the first example sentence. Remind students that we often use the past continuous to talk about a situation in progress in the past, and that it is often used with the past simple, which describes a shorter or sudden action. Tell students that when the action in progress is interrupted by a shorter action, we can use *while*, *when* or *as* with the situation in progress but we can only use *when* with the shorter or sudden action.

Then focus students' attention on the second box and explain that when two situations are in progress at the same time, we normally use *while* or *as*. Tell students that they will find more information about the past continuous in the Language summary on pages 101–102.

6 Explain that 1–8 are brief notes which describe either two events in progress at the same time or an event in progress which is interrupted by a shorter or sudden action. Go through the notes for 1 and 2 and the example sentences with the class. Tell students to notice (a) whether the times are happening over a period of time or whether it is a precise time (b), what tenses are used in the examples to describe the actions, and (c) what conjunctions are used. Then ask them to do the same with the notes in 3–8. Tell them to be careful to use the correct conjunctions. Weaker students could do this in pairs.

1 While/As Team A were searching for the man, Team B were looking for the bag.
2 The official was looking at the passenger when (s)he ran away. /
While the official was looking at the passenger, (s)he ran away.
3 While/As the passengers were leaving the plane, the staff were taking the bags off the plane.
4 The police were patrolling Terminal 1 when they suddenly saw the thief. /
While/As the police were patrolling Terminal 1, they suddenly saw the thief.
5 The passenger became ill while/as Flight BA455 was taking off. /
While/As Flight BA455 was taking off, the passenger became ill.
6 While/As KL203 was landing, Flight JL111 was taking off.
7 While/As the passengers were waiting in the terminal, the plane left with no one on board. /
The plane left with no one on board while/as the passengers were waiting in the terminal.
8 The security incident happened while/as thousands of people were using the airport. /
While/As thousands of people were using the airport, the security incident happened.

Speaking

7 Allow students a few minutes to think about an international event that they remember well. Then ask them to tell the class about the situation, where they were and what they were doing at the time. Tell them to give details about when the event happened or when they heard about it, i.e. how long after the event did they hear or read about it? Remind them to use the past continuous and the past simple, and the appropriate conjunctions. Weaker students could practise telling a partner about the event first, then ask a few more confident students to tell the class about their event.

3 Progress

Start here

1 Before you start the lesson, with books closed, you could brainstorm different types of security systems. If necessary, give one example to get students started.

Then ask students to open their Course Books and focus their attention on the photo. Ask them what it shows (a fingerprint scanner) and if it was one of the systems they thought of. Tell them that this section is about fingerprint scanners.

Ask students to read the information about fingerprint scanners and answer the questions. In a feedback session, ask for their opinions about the scanners, but do not confirm the students' answer yet. Encourage them to use the second conditional where appropriate, e.g. *If I was head of security, I would install the capacitive scanner because* ... .

Suggested answer:
The most probable answer is that capacitive fingerprint scanners are more secure because they measure the actual ridges of the finger and need to have an actual finger placed on them. With an optical scanner, someone could, for example, kidnap a bank official, photograph his finger and make an image of it – the scanner would not be able to distinguish between the image and a real finger.

Scanning

2 Go through the instructions with the students. Then ask them to turn to pages 116–117 and find the text on fingerprints. Remind them that they do not need to read every word in the text, just look for the information which completes the statements. Ask students to put up their hand when they have finished. Allow the majority of students to finish but check the answers with the first person to put up their hand to see if they were correct and are the winner.

> **1** Egypt; 4000   **2** 60   **3** do not share   **4** 1905

Listening

3 ▶ 🎧 **22**

Tell students that they are going to listen to a conversation between a manager (Adam) and an employee (Bob). Adam is asking Bob to give him a progress report on his research into finding the most suitable security system for their company. Ask students to look at the list of security methods. Tell them that they should write *D* if the employee has looked into this method, *I* if he is looking into this method at the moment and *P* if he is planning to look into the method. Play the recording for students to complete the checklist, then ask students to check their answers with a partner. If necessary, play the recording again before checking with the class.

> passwords D, pin numbers D, voice recognition D, fingerprint scanning I, optical scanning D, capacitive scanning I, iris scanning P

▶ 🎧 **22**
[A = Adam; B = Bob]

A: Good morning, Bob. I'd like to have a chat about your security project. You've been looking into the different security methods, I believe, is that right?

B: Yes, I'm trying to decide which security system would be best for our offices.

A: Right. So how are you getting on?

B: Fine. I'm making good progress.

A: Good. Have you made any decisions so far?

B: Well, I've looked into passwords, pin numbers, and voice recognition.

A: Aha.

B: And I've decided not to recommend any of those, for various reasons.

A: Right. So what are you looking at now?

B: Well, right now I'm looking into different methods of fingerprint scanning.

A: I didn't know there were different methods.

B: Yes, there's optical scanning, which basically takes a photo of the finger, and there's something called capacitive scanning, which uses electrical current and a capacitor.

A: OK, and what have you come up with?

B: Well, I've decided against optical scanning because it's too easy to forge a fingerprint. I mean, you could place a photograph of a finger onto the scanning plate instead of an actual finger.

A: Oh dear, yes, I see what you mean. So what about the other one, capacitive scanning?

B: I'm looking into that at this very moment. It looks a bit more secure because it measures the actual ridges, not just a picture of ridges.

A: Good. Oh, by the way, what about this new iris scanning technology – a method of scanning the eye? Have you looked into that yet?

B: No, not yet. That's a big research area, so I'm planning to have a look at that next week.

A: OK, I'm glad it's going well. I'll catch up with you next week.

B: Cheers.

4 Ask the class which system they think Bob will not recommend. Stronger students could also give the reason for each answer.

> He will not recommend any of the ones he has researched already: passwords, pin numbers, voice recognition or optical scanning.

5 Ask students to discuss the answer in pairs first, then find out from the class what they think Bob's answer to the question in 1 is.

> The capacitive fingerprint scanner is more secure because it measures the actual ridges of the finger, whereas with optical scanning, it is too easy to forge a fingerprint, e.g. by putting a photo of a fingerprint onto the scanner.

Vocabulary

6 Put students into pairs. Focus students' attention on the first two diagrams and ask them to match 1–7 in diagrams A and B with the words in the box.

1 battery	**4** conductor	**7** earth
2 capacitor	**5** terminal	
3 resistor	**6** switch	

Reading

7 Tell students that they are going to read a transcript of a lecture, in which the lecturer uses the diagrams in 6 to explain how fingerprint scanners work. Ask them first to read the transcript quickly. Then ask them to match figures 1–7 with the diagrams A–G in 6.

A 1 **B** 5 **C** 3 **D** 7 **E** 2 **F** 4 **G** 6

▶ 💿 23

Focus students' attention on the words in the box. Play the recording once through. Then play it again, pausing after each word for students to practise saying them. You could then ask them to listen again and underline the stressed syllable each word.

▶ 💿 23

fingerprint scanner	capacitance
capacitor	ridge
sensor	valley
non-conductive	microchip
dielectric	amplifier

8 Ask students to read the statements and mark them true or false. Then ask them to correct the false statements. Allow students to compare answers before checking the answers as a class.

1 T
2 F – The battery charges it up.
3 F – You decrease it.
4 F – The capacitance is lower because the distance between the finger and the plates is greater.

Writing

9 Tell students that they are going to give a talk on how capacitive fingerprint scanners work. First, they should prepare their talk in small groups. Tell them to refer back to the diagrams in 6, decide on the main points about each one and write these points on cards. Tell students to have a maximum of 30 words on each card, except for Figure 7, which can have up to 60 words. Alternatively, you can advise them to divide Figure 7 into two cards of approximately 30 words each.

If you have computer facilities, the groups can produce the complete PowerPoint slide show, transferring their notes from cards to slides and scanning the visuals (Figures 1–7). Arrange different times for each group to present the completed slide show to the class. This can be practice for a later presentation where the groups choose their own topics and prepare slide shows to present their topics.

Model answer:
Figure 1
Simple capacitor circuit
Capacitor: components
- two metal plates
- dielectric (non-conductive)

How *charge circuit* works:
- switch connects battery to capacitor
- battery charges capacitor
- capacitor holds charge

Figure 2
How discharge circuit works:
- switch disconnects battery from capacitor
- connects capacitor to resistor
- capacitor discharges load to resistor
- example: camera flashgun

Figure 3
Capacitance = amount of charge held by a capacitor
Thickness of dielectric = distance between plates of capacitor
- increased distance → lower capacitance
- decreased distance → higher capacitance

Figure 4
Fingerprint = pattern of ridges and valleys
Each ridge/valley above single sensor cell
Plates in sensor cell = one plate of capacitor
Ridge/valley = other plate of capacitor

Figure 5
Situation 1: cell below *ridge*
Space between two plates: narrow
- Dielectric: thin
- Capacitance below ridge: high

Figure 6
Situation 1: cell below *valley*
Space between two plates: wide
- Dielectric: thick
- Capacitance below ridge: low

Figure 7
Cell measures difference in capacitance
How it works:
- capacitor circuit connected to second circuit
- second circuit passes through inverter amplifier
- capacitance modifies current in amplifier
- high capacitance (below ridge) → voltage 1
- low capacitance (below valley) → voltage 2
- processor reads all voltage outputs
- builds total picture of ridges and valleys

Speaking

10 Students now give their talk to the rest of the class. Ask the listening group to make notes of any questions about the content of the talk, which they could ask the group when they have finished.

8   Projects

Contents

1   Spar

Objectives

In this section students will ...

- find out about the construction of the deepest offshore spar platform in the world
- label a diagram
- listen to news items and complete a specification chart
- complete sentences with the correct verb form
- complete a timeline
- study and practise using the present perfect and past simple passive to talk about past events
- complete and role-play a dialogue
- learn vocabulary for installation, transportation and extraction in the oil industry

2   Platform

Objectives

In this section students will ...

- discuss a photo showing an offshore platform, then read a text to check answers
- complete the text with numbers and units for measurements
- study cohesion in a text
- match words in the text with their synonyms
- study and practise using active and passive adjectives
- study and practise ways of expressing method using *by (means of)* and purpose using *(in order) to*
- learn vocabulary for construction and civil engineering

3   Drilling

Objectives

In this section students will ...

- label a diagram
- discuss the moving of parts of an oil rig, then listen to a description to check answers
- listen to an interview and order stages of a process
- identify active and passive verbs in the description from the recording and say why they were used
- practise using phrases to check understanding
- describe a process using the past simple passive
- make notes and write a report
- learn vocabulary for oil drilling and infrastructure

Briefing

This unit looks at engineering and construction projects linked to the petroleum industry.

Section 1 deals with Shell Oil's **Perdido Spar offshore oil platform** in the Gulf of Mexico. A **spar** is a large-diameter, hollow, single vertical cylinder that floats in the water, with about 90% of the structure under water. The cylinder is fastened to the sea bed and stabilised by means of **mooring lines** (cables). Attached to the top of the cylinder, above the surface of the sea, is the **topside** (platform). Below the cylinder are five risers (vertical oil pipes) that carry oil and gas from the sub-sea oil wells up to the topside. At the time of writing, it is the world's deepest platform, floating in 2,438 metres of water. Shell plan to drill 22 wells in the seafloor below the rig, and another 13 wells nine miles away. On the seabed, Perdido's five risers will branch out into clusters of connected **trees** (**well heads**). Since pressure inside the oil reservoir is low, large **pumping stations** on the seabed will first separate the oil from the gas and then pump both fuels up the pipes. At the time of writing, Perdido Spar is an ongoing project. Some of the news items (audio 24) have not yet taken place at the time of writing but are based on Shell's plans for the completion of the Perdido project by around 2016.

Section 2 deals with the **Troll A fixed oil platform**, which has concrete legs extending down to the seabed. It holds the world record as the tallest structure which has ever been transported from one location to another. The legs of the platform are made of **reinforced concrete** (steel rods inside concrete), and were constructed using the **slip-forming** technique. A **form** is a frame filled with liquid concrete to create the desired shape, and removed when the concrete has **set hard**. In slip-forming, necessary for very tall structures, the form fits around the structure like a ring, and moves (**slips**) slowly upwards over many weeks as more and more liquid concrete is poured into the form in a **continuous pour**. This prevents cracks from appearing in the concrete: if work stops even for a day, the concrete will set hard, and the next layer of concrete will not be bonded with the previous one. Even a hairline crack in the concrete of the Troll A would have weakened the structure and made it unable to support the weight of the oil platform.

Section 3 deals with **drilling** techniques and equipment. The main **lifting** equipment on an oil rig is the **crown block** (at the top of the **derrick**), the **travelling block** (moving up and down, pulled by the **winch** and **cable**), the **hook** attached to the travelling block and the **swivel**. The top half of the swivel does not rotate, but the bottom half does, and is attached to the kelly. The **drilling equipment** consists of the **kelly** (a square shaft that fits exactly in the square hole in the turntable), the **turntable** (which rotates the kelly) and the **drill string** (turned by the kelly). The drill string consists of **drill pipes** screwed together, the **drill bit** attached to the bottom drill pipe, and the **drill collar** which fits over the drill bit to weigh it down. To **lubricate** the drill bit as it cuts into the rock, **drilling mud** is pumped down the inside of the drill pipe, through the drill bit and into the well. Audio 28 gives a step-by-step account of what the drilling crew do to **make up** the drill string (screw the pipes together) and then **trip** the string (lower it) through the kelly and down into the

well. **Horizontal directional drilling** (HDD) is used to install underground pipelines below an obstacle such as a river or road. A **pilot hole** is a narrow **borehole** that is drilled to create a path for the main hole. A **reamer** is a large-diameter tool, wider than the original drill bit, which widens, or **reams**, the borehole that has already been drilled. The **product pipe** is the pipe that will be installed: for example, a pipe to carry water or cables.

Perdido Spar oil platform: Find the **Shell** company website and search for 'Perdido Spar'.

Troll A fixed platform: Find the **Statoil** company website and search for 'Troll A'.

Oil drilling equipment and operation: Find the US Dept of Labour **OSHA (Occupational Safety and Health Commission)** website and find 'eTools' in the A–Z index. Find 'Oil and Gas Well Drilling and Servicing – Drilling'. This explains the drilling process in detail. It also has a very comprehensive glossary of drilling terms.

Horizontal directional drilling: Find the **Northern Directional Drilling** company website and search for 'What is horizontal directional drilling?'.

Teacher's notes

1 | Spar

Start here

1 With books closed, ask students if they can name any parts of an oil rig, e.g. *platform*, *accommodation block*, *spar*. Then put students in pairs. Tell them to open their Course Books and ask them to match the parts of the illustration with the labels in the box. Do not check the students' answers to 1 and 2 yet as they will check their own answers as part of the listening task in 3.

1 topside	**5** pipeline
2 spar	**6** tree
3 riser	**7** pumping station
4 mooring line	

2 Ask students to discuss the questions in pairs. If they do not know the answer, get them to think about where the oceans are the deepest. Then ask the class for their ideas and find out if they all agree.

Perdido Spar in the Gulf of Mexico; the platform is 2,383 metres above the seabed

Listening

3 ▶ 🎧 **24**

Tell students that they are now going to listen to eight radio news items about the deepest spar in the world. Ask them to look at the diagram as you play the recording again for students to check their answers to 1 and 2.

▶ 🎧 **24**

1 This is the News at Ten on Monday, June the 2nd, 2008. Good evening. The Perdido Spar has been towed to its site in the Gulf of Mexico. The spar, which is expected to be the deepest oil spar in the world, weighs about 45,000 tonnes, equivalent to about 10,000 motor vehicles.

2 This is the Nine o'clock News for today, the 14th of August, 2008. Good evening. The Perdido Spar has been secured to the seabed. A total of nine polyester mooring lines were used to moor the world's deepest spar, averaging more than three kilometres in length. It took 13 days to complete the job.

3 June 11th, 2009. This is the Early Evening News with Don Gomez. The topside has been fitted to the top of the Perdido Spar. The topside, which includes the drilling platform and accommodation block, was attached to the spar in calm seas early this morning. The spar itself is 170 metres long and 36 metres in diameter. The depth of the seabed below the spar platform is 2383 metres, which makes it the deepest spar in the world.

4 Good evening, this is the News at Ten for today, November 10th, 2010. The first oil well under the Perdido Spar has been completed. The well, under the world's deepest spar, has a depth of almost 2500 metres below the seabed, making the total depth of the well about 4800 metres below the topside, or spar platform.

5 This is the World Today for March the 12th, 2013. The headlines. A huge pipeline network has been laid under the Perdido Spar, totalling 300 kilometres in length.

6 July 28th, 2014. This is Global News Today. Good morning. Five risers and a pumping station have been built below the world's deepest spar. Far below the Perdido Spar, the pumping station, which is the size of a large truck, will separate the oil from the gas as it flows from the trees, or wellheads. It will then pump both fuels from the trees on the seabed, up the risers to the topside, using 1120 kilowatt pumps.

7 Good evening, this is the Ten o'clock News for April the 15th, 2015. Twenty-two oil wells have been drilled below the Perdido Spar oil platform, and another thirteen wells have been drilled fifteen kilometres away. This brings the total number of wells below the giant spar to thirty-five.

8 This is the World this Weekend on Saturday, October 8th, 2016. More than 46 million barrels of oil have been produced by the Perdido Spar. During the first year of production at the world's deepest spar, an average of 130,000 barrels per day of oil and natural gas were produced by the 35 wells operating from the spar platform.

4 Focus students' attention on the specifications chart. Explain that *b/d* means *barrels (of oil) per day*. Point out to students that the answers in the chart will not necessarily come in order on the recording. Play the recording again for students to complete the chart. Allow students to compare answers before checking the answers as a class. You may need to play the recording one more time for weaker students, pausing after each section if necessary.

Perdido Spar offshore oil platform: Specifications		
Total length of spar	170 m	
Diameter of spar	36 m	
Height of spar platform above seabed	2383 m	
Weight of spar	approx. 45,000 tonnes	
Number of mooring lines	9	
Number of risers	5	
Total number of wells	35	
Average oil and gas production	130,000 b/d	

5 Elicit from the class which form (active or passive) should be used in the sentences (the passive is used in order to focus on the action itself, not who does the action). Ask students which tense should be used and why (the present perfect tense is used because we are talking about events that happened in a period of time that continued from the past up to the present). Ask students why we do not use time expressions with the present perfect (because the time is unspecified). You could do the first sentence with the class as an example. Then ask students to complete the sentences from the news items with the correct form of the verbs in the box. Allow students to compare answers before checking the answers as a class.

1 have been drilled
2 has been completed
3 has been secured
4 have been produced
5 has been fitted
6 have been built
7 has been laid
8 has been towed

6 Go through the instructions with the class, then do an example with them and make sure that they know what to do. Ask them to read through the sentences in 5 and identify which event happened first and write the number down in the correct box. When you have checked with the class, ask students to write the other sentence numbers in the correct box. You could then ask them to look at the audio script on page 123 of the Course Book to check their answers.

Mixed-ability classes

Play the recording again and ask students to write the date next to sentences 1–8 in 5. They can then complete the timeline in 6.

The timeline should be numbered (from left to right): 8, 3, 5, 2, 7, 6, 1, 4

Language

Present perfect and past simple passive

Go through the Language box with the students. Remind them that we use the past simple with completed actions or actions that took place at a specific time, and that we use *be* plus the past participle to make the passive.

Tell students that they will find more information about the present perfect and past simple passive in the Language summary on page 101.

7 Ask students to complete the sentences using the correct passive form of the verbs in brackets. Weaker students can do this activity in pairs.

1 Has the spar been towed
2 It has also been secured
3 was it brought
4 was fixed
5 Has it been fitted
6 has already been installed
7 was the topside attached
8 was taken
9 Have any pipelines been laid
10 have already been lowered
11 was that done
12 were dropped

Speaking

8 Put students in pairs and ask them to practise the completed dialogue with a partner.

Extra activity

If students work in the same company or field of work, you could put students in pairs and ask them to think of a project that they are working on, or invent one, and write a similar dialogue to the one in 7, using the present perfect or past simple passive. They could then perform their dialogue to the class.

Scanning

9 Go through the instructions with the students. Then ask them to turn to pages 116–117 and find the text on the Perdido Spar offshore oil rig. Remind them that they do not need to read every word in the text, just look for the information which completes the sentences. Ask students to put up their hand when they have finished. Allow the majority of students to finish but check the answers with the first person to put up their hand to see if they were correct and are the winner.

1 322
2 45,360
3 2002
4 3,050

2 Platform

Start here

1 Focus students' attention on the photo and ask them to identify the building on the right of the photo (the Eiffel Tower). Ask if anyone knows how high it is and when it was built (total height: 324 m; built: 1887–1889). Then tell students to work in pairs and identify what the other structure is used for and what world records it holds. Do not check students' answers yet, as the answers are in the reading text that follows.

> **1** It is an offshore oil and gas drilling platform.
> **2** It is the tallest construction which has ever been transported from one location to another.

Reading

2 ▶ 🔊 25

Ask students to read the text quickly, ignoring the gaps, and check their answers to 1.

Then go through the figures in the box first and check students' understanding of the abbreviations (t = tonne; mm = millimetres; m = metre; min = minute; m³ = metres cubed; km = kilometres). Remind them that *metre/kilometre* are spelt *meter/kilometer* in American English. Play the recording once for students to hear the statistics. Then play the recording again, pausing after each statistic for students to repeat. Then choose individual students to say one of the statistics out loud and check their pronunciation.

▶ 🔊 25

656,000 tonnes
50 millimetres
1995
303 metres
100,000 tonnes
20 minutes
1.3 trillion metres cubed
472 metres
2,000
200 kilometres
35 metres
245,000 metres cubed

Now ask students to work individually to read the text and complete the gaps with the statistics in the box. They then check their answers with a partner or in small groups.

1	472 m	**7**	303 m
2	2,000	**8**	35 m
3	1995	**9**	20 min
4	656,000 t	**10**	55 mm
5	100,000 t	**11**	200 km
6	245,000 m³	**12**	1.3 trillion m³

▶ 🔊 26

Play the recording once for students to hear the phrases, then play it again, pausing after each phrase for students to repeat.

▶ 🔊 26

reinforced concrete structure
slip-forming
hydraulic cylinders
continuous pour
sub-sea electrical cable
recoverable reserves

3 Ask students to find the words and phrases in the text in 2 and underline them. Then ask students what the words and phrases refer to. Tell them that they will find each answer by looking at the previous sentence. You could get students to add an arrow from the reference word to the word/phrase it refers to.

1 the Troll A platform	
2 the legs	
3 the legs	
4 slip-forming	

4 Ask students to look back at the text in 2 again and find and underline words or phrases which have the same meaning as 1–8.

1 workforce		**4** intense		**7** pour
2 deployed		**5** lengthy		**8** sub-sea
3 reinforced		**6** continuous		

Language

Cohesion; *by (means of)*; *(in order) to*

Go through the Language box with students. The sentences show examples of how to talk about method and purpose. Point out that we can use *by … -ing* and *using/by means of …* to explain how we did something (method), and *in order* + infinitive to explain why we did something (purpose).

5 Ask students to read through phrases 1–6 from the text in 2. Tell them to identify the function in each by writing *M* for method or *P* for purpose.

1 P	**2** P	**3** M	**4** M	**5** P	**6** M

6 Go through the example with the class to show students how the two sentences can be joined into one. Remind them to use the language from the Language box in their answers but also to take care to include words such as the articles *the* and *a*, which might be left out of the notes. Ask students to rewrite the notes as single sentences retaining the same meaning given in the notes.

> **1** The highest structure in the world was built using 330,000 m³ of concrete.
> **2** The concrete was made in a single pour (in order) to prevent cracks from forming.
> **3** The topside was fitted to the top of the Perdido Spar by deploying hydraulic winches.
> **4** The pumping station was installed below the spar (in order) to separate the oil from the gas.
> **5** The spar was secured to the seabed by means of/ using nine mooring lines.
> **6** Five risers were built below the spar (in order) to carry oil and gas up to the platform.

Vocabulary

7 Go through the examples with the class. Point out the passive ending *-ed* in *reinforced* and the active ending *-ing* in *reinforcing*. Ask students to do the exercise individually. They can then compare their answers with a partner before you check with the class.

> **1** reinforcing
> **2** reinforced
> **3** pressurised
> **4** pressurising

3 Drilling

Start here

1 Ask students to look at the photo and ask them to say what is happening. Then ask them to look at diagram A and label the parts of the oil rig with the words in the box. Do not check students' answers yet as they will check their own answers in the listening task in 3.

> **1** drill bit   **4** hook   **6** cable
> **2** turntable   **5** travelling   **7** winch
> **3** swivel   block   **8** drill pipe

2 Focus students' attention on diagram B, which is an enlarged section of diagram A. Put students in pairs to discuss the movements of this part of the rig and to label the diagram *R*, *U* or *RU*. Do not check students' answers yet as they will check their own answers in the listening task in 3.

> **1** RU   **2** R   **3** R (lower part only)
> **4** U   **5** U   **6** U   **7** U   **8** RU

3 ▶ 🔊 27

Tell the students that they are going to listen to a description of the diagrams in 1. Play the recording for students to check their answers in 1 and 2.

▶ 🔊 27

If you look at Diagram A – that's the diagram of the oil rig on the left – you can see all the main moving and non-moving parts. The derrick is the actual tower of the oil rig and stands solidly on the drilling platform. So the derrick and the platform obviously don't move because they support all the other equipment.

Right, so, as Diagram A shows, right at the top of the derrick is the crown block. This is fixed to the top of the derrick and doesn't move up or down although of course it rotates when the winch pulls or releases the cable. Below the crown block is the travelling block, attached to the cable, which moves up and down and raises or lowers the hook with the drilling equipment attached to it.

The hook at the bottom of the travelling block is attached to a swivel. The top part of the swivel can't rotate but the lower part can.

The lower part of the swivel is attached to a kelly, as you can see in Diagram B, and the kelly fits into and goes through a turntable. Below the turntable, the kelly is attached to the drill pipe. When the diesel engines are switched on, the turntable rotates and this makes the kelly rotate. The kelly then makes the drill pipe rotate.

At the bottom of the oil well, a drill collar fits over the drill pipe just above the drill bit. The drill collar helps to weigh down the drill bit. When the drill pipe rotates, this makes the drill bit turn and cut into the rock.

4 ▶ 🎧 28

Tell students that they are going to listen to a TV interview with an oil worker. First, ask them to read through the stages (A–J) for preparing to drill an oil well. Then tell them to listen to the recording and put the stages in the correct order. You could ask them to check their answers in pairs first. If necessary, play the recording again, then check answers with the class.

1 G	2 D	3 I	4 B	5 C	6 A	7 E
8 J	9 F	10 H				

▶ 🎧 28

[I = Interviewer; AK = Asif Khan]

I: Here I am on the Western Desert oil rig, one of the biggest land rigs in the world, and I'm talking to one of the drilling crew, Asif Khan. Asif, I understand that you were the driller on the day that the first well was drilled from this rig.

AK: Yes, that's right. With my team. We drilled the first well here.

I: So could you talk us through what you and the others did in that first drill?

AK: Well, first of all we made up the drill pipe and the drill bit.

I: Sorry, could you just explain what you mean by 'made up'?

AK: Yeah, what I mean is, we attached the drill pipe to the drill bit, we screwed them together.

I: I see, thanks.

AK: And then we slid the drill collar over the drill pipe so that it sat on top of the drill bit.

I: Right.

AK: And then we made up the pipe with the kelly.

I: Made up? Oh, yes, I remember. You joined the kelly to the drill pipe?

AK: Yes, that's right. So then we lowered the string …

I: Excuse me, what do you mean by 'string'?

AK: The string – you join different parts together to make a long section. So the string is the drill bit, the collar, the drill pipe and the kelly all joined together. The whole string rotates inside the well hole.

I: Oh right, I see, thanks.

AK: So then we lowered the string – the kelly, the drill pipe, the drill collar and the drill bit – we lowered it through the rotary table until the kelly fitted tightly in the hole in the rotary table.

I: I see.

AK: And then the mud pump was switched on, to make the drilling fluid flow down to the drill bit.

I: Was that to lubricate the drill bit?

AK: That's right. And then the drilling mud hose was checked for leaks.

I: Sorry, I didn't catch that. It's the noise. Could you repeat that, please?

AK: Sure, the mud hose was checked for leaks.

I: Who did that? Did you do it?

AK: No, someone else. The derrick hand did that.

I: Right, and then after the hose was checked …?

AK: Then the rotary table was switched on.

I: You didn't do that?

AK: No, that's the job of the motor hand. He did that.

I: Then you started drilling?

AK: That's right. I slowly tripped in …

I: Sorry to interrupt you, but what does 'tripped in' mean?

AK: Tripped in? That means lowered the drill string into the well. So I tripped in, or lowered the drill bit to the rock below the platform.

I: And that's how the drilling on the first well was begun?

AK: That's right.

I: And how many metres have been drilled so far?

AK: About fifty metres up to now.

I: That's great. Well, Asif, thanks for talking to us.

AK: My pleasure.

5 Go through the instructions with the class. Tell them to mark the stages in 4 with either *A* for active or *P* for passive. Tell them not to refer to the audio script as they do this. They can check their answers in pairs when they have finished but do not check as a class.

As an alternative, ask students to listen to the interview again and mark the sentences *A* for active or *P* for passive according to what they hear.

6 Play the recording again for students to check their answers. Ask students whether the driller used active or passive verbs and why he used them in each case.

> They were all active in the audio except for A, C and E, which were passive. This is because the speaker himself did not do the actions in A, C and E. They were done by someone else.

7 Read through the sentences with the class. Elicit any other expressions that students know for asking someone to explain something more clearly or repeat something. Then ask them to complete the phrases. Then you could get students to answer questions 1, 2 and 4 in pairs.

> 1 what you mean by
> 2 what do you mean by
> 3 I didn't catch that; you repeat that, please
> 4 interrupt; what does

8 Put students in pairs. Tell them to use the past simple passive to describe to each other how the well was drilled. They can refer back to the Language box on page 61 if they need help. They should take turns with A describing the first half and B the second half of the process. Remind them to use the language in 7 and practise interrupting each other to ask for explanations and repetitions, as in the audio.

Speaking

9 Put students in groups of four, assigning roles A to D in each group. Go through the instructions with the class and ask students to look at their relevant pages. Tell students to make notes about the processes, using the factsheets at the back of the Course Book and the diagrams on page 63. Note that both Student A and Student B need to study Figure 1 on page 63.

As they explain their process to their group, tell the listening students to ask for clarification by asking the speaker to repeat anything they did not understand and to give clearer explanations.

Writing

10 Students work individually to complete the report of how a tunnel was drilled and a pipe installed below the River Avon. Remind them that they should use the past simple passive where appropriate and that they should refer to the notes from their meeting in 9. They could also try to include expressions for method and purpose that they studied in the previous section.

Possible answer:

Report

Drilling a borehole and installing a water pipe below the River Avon

The aim of the project was to drill a borehole below the River Avon using horizontal directional drilling, in order to install a water supply pipe below the river.

Stage 1A: Drilling the pilot hole

The purpose of this stage was to drill a pilot hole with a small diameter. First a drill bit with a narrow diameter was attached to a drill string. A narrow pilot hole was drilled through the rock, and enlarged using a wash pipe. Drilling fluid was then pumped through the drill string to lubricate the drill bit. The rock was broken into small pieces by the action of the drill bit and the pressure of the drilling fluid. The rock pieces were carried back to the entrance hole at the rig. When the drill bit reached the exit point, it came out of the ground. Then the drill bit was detached from the string and attached to the reamer.

Stage 1B: Electronic guidance system

The purpose of the guidance system was to control the direction of the drilling along the planned path. First an electronic transmitter was fitted immediately behind the drill bit. This sent a signal to a locator at the surface, directly above the drill bit. The exact location of the drill string was indicated by the locator, which took a reading every 2 to 5 metres to check the position of the drill bit. If the location was incorrect, the direction of the drill bit was adjusted. When the drill bit reached the exit point, it came out of the ground and the transmitter was detached from the string.

Stage 2: Reaming

The purpose of this stage was to ream the pilot hole until it was wide enough for the product pipe. After leaving the ground, the drill bit and the transmitter were removed from the drill pipe and a reamer was attached to the string. The reamer was then pulled backwards from the exit point towards the drill rig and rotated to cut and enlarge the hole. While it was rotating and moving backwards, drilling fluid was pumped through the drill string to remove the rock pieces, and to enlarge the hole more. A layer of bentonite was deposited behind the reamer, to make the hole clean, hard and stable.

Stage 3: Pulling back the product pipe

The purpose of this stage was to fit the product pipe inside the reamed hole. First the reamer was removed from the drill string, and the string was attached to a swivel, which was attached to the product pipe. This was done in order to prevent the rotating drill string from twisting the product pipe. As the reamer was pulling the product pipe along the drill hole, drilling fluid was pumped along the hole to lubricate the product pipe and to allow it to pass along the hole smoothly. Finally, the product pipe filled the hole completely.

Review Unit D

Answer key

1
1 'Don't fire but stand ready.'
2 'I'm not a police officer but I am trained in security procedures.'
3 'I've introduced a new pay system for all the staff but don't worry; your pay will rise by 5%.'
4 'I checked your computers yesterday and found no viruses but be careful in future.'

2
The official told the passenger to stop and take off his shoes. The passenger agreed. Then he asked the passenger to put his bag on the rollers but the passenger refused. The officer asked him again. The passenger then said that he didn't want to put the bag through the X-ray. He explained that the bag contained undeveloped film. He told the officer that he didn't want to damage it. The officer advised the passenger not to worry. He informed him that the X-ray wouldn't damage his film. He then instructed the passenger to put his bag on the rollers, and the passenger complied.

4 *Model answer:*
The red and the blue cars were driving at the same speed in two lanes next to each other. The white van was driving in front of the red car, and the green car was driving in front of the van. While this was happening, the green car suddenly indicated to turn right, and started to turn. While it was turning, the van moved into the next lane to overtake it, as it was now moving slowly. As the van was doing this, the red car hit the green car, pushing it across the side road onto the pavement. While this was happening, the blue car struck the van and made it cross over the central line.

The yellow car and the white car were coming in the opposite direction on the other side of the road when the van suddenly crossed over the central line. The yellow car tried to avoid it by moving in front of the white car, but while this was happening, the van struck the white car and the rear of the yellow car.

5
1 transmitter; transmission
2 detector; detection
3 amplifier; amplification
4 producer; production
5 generation; generator
6 reflector; reflection

7 *Model answer:*
The purpose of an electric motor is to convert electrical current into rotational movement. It operates on the scientific principle that when electric current is passed through a wire coil, it generates a magnetic field in a nearby conductor.

The motor has a permanent magnet and an electromagnet which consists of a coil (made of copper wire), an armature (a solid bar made of iron or steel), steel brushes and a steel commutator. The coil, which goes around the armature, is connected to a power source via the commutator and the brushes. When the current is switched on, it flows through the coil and magnetises the armature. The armature now becomes an electromagnet.

The north pole of the armature is pushed away by the north pole of the permanent magnet and rotates 180 degrees around the axle. Then the south pole of the armature changes to the north pole, and it rotates another 180 degrees.

The brushes are connected to the power source. One has a positive charge and the other has a negative charge.

As the armature rotates, the commutator touches a negative brush and then a positive brush. When the commutator touches a different brush, it changes the magnetic pole of the armature.

8
Both devices use induction, in which a current sent through a coil magnetises a nearby conductor.

9
1 by installing
2 to link
3 by pouring
4 to search
5 to allow
6 by generating

10
1 The spar has been transported to its site in the Atlantic Ocean.
2 The spar has been moored to the sea floor using cables.
3 The topside has been attached to the top of the spar.
4 The pipeline network has been set up below the spar.
5 The foundations for the pumping stations have been dug below the sea bed.
6 The risers have been constructed and the pumping stations have been installed.

11
1 been plastered
2 has already been installed
3 was the wiring put in
4 was finished
5 have the paints been bought
6 have been chosen
7 have already been ordered
8 was the order made
9 was sent

13 (The estimated date of completion of this bridge is 2012.)

Possible questions:

What's the name of the bridge?/What's it called?
Where is it (located)?
What's the purpose of the bridge?
How much did the bridge cost?
How many arches does the bridge have?
How high is the highest arch?
What record has this bridge made/broken?
What makes this bridge a great achievement?
How long is it?
What is the height of the deck?
How much steel was using to construct the bridge?
What do the foundations consist of?
How deep are the foundation piles?
How were the piles constructed?

15 *Model answer:*

The world's tallest arch bridge has been completed in Dubai in the UAE. The Sheikh Rashid bin Saeed Crossing (also called the Sixth Crossing) has been built to connect the localities of Al Jaddaf and Bur Dubai. It is an example of extreme engineering, because it has been built not on a bed of hard rock but on a bed of sand. And it has broken the world record for the tallest arch: it is twice the height of the Lupu Bridge in Shanghai, China, which was the tallest arch bridge until yesterday. The larger of the bridge's two arches is 205 metres high, and the total length of the bridge is 1.6 km. The height of the road deck above the water is 15 metres and a total of 140,000 tonnes of steel was used in the construction.

The foundations of the bridge consist of 200 steel-reinforced-concrete piles, 40 metres long and 2 metres wide. The piles were constructed by drilling holes 40 metres deep into the sand, and then filling the holes with reinforced concrete.

Project

16 At the end of every Review Unit is a project. Students can do their research on the internet.

Quick test answer key

Part 1: Vocabulary and grammar

1 | 1 c | 2 d | 3 b | 4 a |

2 | 4 conductor | 5 resistor | 6 capacitor |

3
1 ~~Capacitor~~ Dielectric	4 ~~dielectric~~ capacitor
2 ~~fingerprint scanner~~ amplifier	5 ~~amplifier~~ fingerprint scanner
3 ~~plates~~ valleys	

4 | 1 hook | 2 drill bit | 3 risers | 4 swivel |
| 5 mooring line | 6 spar |

5
| 1 reinforced | 3 Reinforcing |
| 2 pressurising | 4 pressurised |

6 | 1 said | 2 told | 3 promised | 4 me |

7 | 1 in order to | 2 by means of | 3 using | 4 to |

8
1 explained that he couldn't find his passport
2 informed her that her bags were over the weight limit
3 told me not to touch the bag
4 said that he'd packed his bags himself
5 reported that (s)he hadn't seen anything suspicious
6 instructed the passengers that they could go to Gate 12

9
1 While I was getting on the plane, I dropped my passport.
2 When they were building the spar, there was an accident.
3 While one mechanic was checking the brake pads, another mechanic was removing the wheel.
4 As the man was leaving the shop, the alarm sounded.
5 As the woman was walking through the security checkpoint, an officer was waiting for her on the other side.

10
| 1 has been towed | 3 was brought |
| 2 has been secured | 4 was lowered |

Part 2: Reading and writing

Reading

| 1 9,156,400 m³ | 2 6,809 MW | 3 168 m high |
| 4 600,000 acres | 5 79.7% | |

Writing

Model answer:

Thursday, 25 June

There has been an explosion at an offshore oil rig in the North Sea. Twenty-two people have been injured and they were immediately taken to hospital by helicopter. The other workers on the rig were evacuated early this morning by ship. An investigation into the incident has begun. The cause of the explosion is not certain. However, while doing a routine maintenance check the day before, an engineer discovered a possible gas leak on the rig. He said that he filled in a report sheet. Chief Engineer John Cox explained that the firefighting system on the rig wasn't working. Due to damage caused by the fire, the platform has been completely destroyed.

Review Unit D Quick test

Total _____/55

Part 1: Vocabulary and grammar

1 Match the security systems and procedures 1–4 with their definitions a–d.

1 walk-through metal detector

2 baggage X-ray machine

3 CCTV

4 hand-held metal detector

a) a small device used by a security officer to detect metal objects

b) a video system that transmits signals to a specific place for surveillance purposes

c) a device that passengers pass through and a reflected pulse detects any metal on their person

d) a device that obtains images of the contents of suitcases, rucksacks, etc.

(4 marks)

2 Correct the incorrect labels in this diagram.

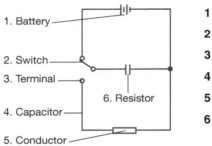

1. Battery
2. Switch
3. Terminal
6. Resistor
4. Capacitor
5. Conductor

1 _____
2 _____
3 _____
4 _____
5 _____
6 _____

(3 marks)

3 One word in each sentence is incorrect. Correct the word.

1 Capacitor is used to describe a material such as rubber that doesn't conduct electricity.

2 The fingerprint scanner is used to increase the voltage of the signal.

3 A fingerprint is formed by a series of ridges and plates.

4 A dielectric is an electronic component that holds electricity.

5 This amplifier uses sensors to detect ridges of the finger.

(5 marks)

4 Complete the sentences with the nouns in the box.

| drill bit   hook   mooring line   risers   spar   swivel |

1 Attach the drilling equipment to a _____ and lower it to the rock layer.

2 The _____ cuts the rock in the seabed.

3 The oil is pumped from the seabed up _____ to the topside.

4 Only the bottom part of the _____ can rotate.

5 They mended the _____ securing the platform, which was broken in the storm.

6 The seabed is 2,382 metres below the _____ platform.

(6 marks)

5 Complete these sentences using *reinforced/reinforcing* or *pressurised/pressurising*.

1 Over 110,000 tonnes of _____ concrete was used in the foundations of the Burj Khalifa.

2 The _____ pump was detached from the water tank.

3 _____ steel bars, or *rebars*, are commonly used in the building industry to strengthen concrete structures.

4 So that passengers and crew can breathe normally, air in the cabin is _____.

(4 marks)

6 Complete the sentences with the words in the box.

| told   me   said   promised |

1 The announcer _____ that there was a delay.

2 The officer _____ us that there had been an accident.

3 The assistant _____ me the airline would pay compensation for the loss of my bags.

4 The alarm sounded and the security official told _____ to open my bags.

(4 marks)

7 Choose the correct option to complete these sentences.

1 Plastic was used **in order to/by means of** make the wing lighter.

2 The structure was transported **by means of/to** towing to its location.

3 The bridge was strengthened **using/by** steel girders.

4 Drilling fluid was used **by/to** lubricate the drill bit.

(4 marks)

8 **Rewrite these sentences using reported speech.**

1 'I can't find my passport,' explained the man.

The man _____.

2 'Your bags are over the weight limit, madam,' the check-in assistant informed her.

The check-in assistant _____.

3 'Don't touch the bag,' the officer said to me.

The officer _____.

4 'Yes, I've packed my bags myself,' said the man.

The man _____.

5 'I didn't see anything suspicious,' reported the passenger.

The passenger _____.

6 'Passengers for flight BA 287 can go to Gate 12.' instructed the announcer.

The announcer _____.

(6 marks)

9 **Write sentences using these prompts. Use the past continuous and past simple.**

1 while / I / get on / the plane / I / drop / my passport

2 when / they / build / the spar / there / be / an accident

3 while / one mechanic / check / the brake pads / another mechanic / remove / the wheel

4 as / the man / leave / the shop / the alarm / sound

5 as / the woman / walk through / the security checkpoint / an officer / wait for / her / on the other side

(5 marks)

10 **Complete these sentences with the correct passive form of the verbs in the box.**

bring	lower	tow	secure

1 The boat _____ to the shore.

2 The platform _____ to the seabed by nine mooring lines.

3 The chief engineer _____ to the platform yesterday by helicopter.

4 The drill bit _____ to the seabed yesterday.

(4 marks)

Part 2: Reading and writing

Reading

Read the text. Then complete it with the statistics in the box.

79.7%	168 m high	600,000 acres
6,809 MW	9,156,400 m³	

The Grand Coulee Dam

The Grand Coulee Dam stands on the Columbia River in Washington State, USA. It is one of the largest concrete structures ever built, containing approximately [1]_____ of it. The dam is the fifth largest producer of hydroelectric power in the world and the largest one in the USA. It has four power plants, containing 33 turbines which have the overall capacity to generate [2]_____ of electricity. The top producing dam in the world is the Three Gorges Dam which when fully operational will produce 22,500 MW of electricity. The Grand Coulee Dam stands [3]_____ and is roughly 1,592 m long. At its base it is about 150 metres wide. It was built between 1937 and 1942, originally for the purpose of irrigation (it provides water for [4]_____ of Columbia river basin farm land), but as the need for electricity grew, power generation became its primary function and for many years it was the largest producer of hydroelectricity in the world. About [5]_____ of Grand Coulee's use is for hydropower, but it serves other purposes too, such as flood control, water storage and delivery, as well as providing recreation, fish and wildlife areas.

(5 marks)

Writing

Write a short news report about this incident using the notes below.

Today's date – Thursday 25 June

Incident – explosion – offshore oil rig – North Sea

Casualties – 22 injured – immediate transportation hospital by helicopter

Rescue operation – evacuation other workers 6 a.m. 25 June by ship

Investigation – in progress

Cause – not certain

Maintenance – routine maintenance inspection 24 June – engineer discovers possible gas leak – 'I filled in a report sheet', he said.

Safety – 'Firefighting system on rig not working during fire' says Chief Engineer John Cox.

Damage – fire – complete destruction of platform

Thursday, 25 June

_____

_____

_____

_____

_____

(5 marks)

9 Design

Contents

1 Inventions

Objectives

In this section students will …

- discuss the design of an unusual motorbike
- listen to a test report and choose the correct statements
- study and practise using modifying comparatives
- compare two types of light bulb in a table
- discuss a product design, plan and write a proposal
- discuss how to improve a familiar product and present a proposal to the class
- learn vocabulary for automotive and electrical engineering

2 Buildings

Objectives

In this section students will …

- discuss three buildings and their structural design
- learn vocabulary for shapes and use it to describe buildings
- read and match fact sheets to buildings
- identify and correct false information in statements
- study and practise using modifying superlatives
- choose the winner of an award for best architectural design and explain reasons for the choice
- learn vocabulary for architecture and design

3 Sites

Objectives

In this section students will …

- identify two buildings on a site plan from photos
- match buildings on a site plan with descriptions of their shapes
- listen to a talk and complete a matching task
- match sketches with photos of buildings
- describe buildings for a partner to locate on a map
- learn vocabulary for technical and architectural drawing

Briefing

This unit looks at **innovative design**, with automotive, electrical and architectural examples.

Section 1 begins with a review of a motorcycle with an unusual design, the Can-Am Spyder Roadster, which has two wheels in front and one behind, half way between a car and a motorcycle. Like a car (and unlike a motorcycle), it has a single **brake pedal** (and no **levers**) for all the brakes. The Spyder is assessed in terms of braking **power, braking efficiency** (a measure of how much effort is required to stop a vehicle), **maximum speed, acceleration** (how quickly a vehicle reaches a specific speed), **effort** (or work) required to turn the **handlebars, suspension** (system that insulates the **chassis** from shocks transmitted through the wheels), **stability** (ability for all wheels to remain in contact with the road) while turning, and **storage space**. To improve turning stability, the Spyder uses a **Vehicle Stability System** which ensures that if the inside wheel lifts off the road, light braking is automatically applied. The energy-saving properties of **incandescent lamps (light bulbs)** and **compact fluorescent lamps (CFLs)** are compared. Incandescent lamps emit light as a result of being heated, and therefore waste a lot of energy. An electric current heats a **filament** (very thin wire) until it glows. The light of a CFL is not caused by heat and so wastes much less energy (CFLs are often called **energy-saving lamps**). An electric current causes **electrons** to **collide** with mercury atoms in a gas-filled tube. This produces **UV light** which is converted into **visible light**. The **LED (light-emitting diode) lamp** on page 69 is the award-winning Frogware prototype, which uses a high-output LED as the light source. This prototype uses half the power of a CFL while lasting ten times longer.

Section 2 deals with architectural concepts and shapes, focusing on three iconic modern award-winning buildings: Capital Gate in Abu Dhabi, Hearst Tower in New York and Swiss Re in London. All three have a **diagrid** (diagonal grid) structure, which uses diagonal **support beams**, made of steel, forming **triangular** structures around the *outside* of the building. Diagrid structures require much less **structural steel** than a normal steel frame, and no **columns** are needed. The **plan** of a building is the two-dimensional shape you would see looking down on the building from above. The **floor area** of a building is total space covered by all the floors or **storeys** (AmE **stories**) in a building; its **footprint** is the area of the land which the building covers (roughly equivalent to the area of a *single* storey). Linear shapes used in describing features of buildings include **straight, curved, zigzag** (changing direction sharply several times). Two-dimensional shapes include **circular** (round), **oval (elliptical), rectangular (oblong)**. Three-dimensional shapes include **cylindrical, conical, cuboid** (in the shape of a **rectangular prism**). A **tapered (tapering)** object becomes gradually narrower or thinner towards one end, for example a cone. A line or shape can be **inclined (at an angle)** to another line or shape, or to the **vertical** or **horizontal**. When a shape **bulges**, it swells outwards (as does the Swiss Re building just above the base). The Tornado Tower, Doha, Qatar, and the Bahrain World Trade Centre, Manama, Bahrain have won 'Best Global Design' awards in different years.

Section 3 deals with **architectural plans** and **drawings**. A **site plan** is the drawing of the plan of a completed building site, showing the arrangement and footprints of buildings, **landscaping** (gardens, trees, lakes and so on), roads and paths and other features. The informal terms **doughnut-shaped** (AmE **donut-shaped**) and **ring-shaped** are commonly used to refer to a **torus**. On an architectural or **technical drawing**, the **plan** of a building or component is the two-dimensional shape as viewed from above, and the **(front / rear / side) elevation** is the 2-D shape as viewed from one side. A **solid line** (in a plan or elevation drawing) indicates a line which can actually be seen be seen, while a **broken line** is used to indicate a line which is hidden from view. A **hatched (shaded) area** or **hatching** can be used to highlight a surface or feature on a drawing.

Can-Am Spyder: Find the **Motorcycle USA** magazine website and search for 'Can-am spyder'.

Architectural awards: Find the website of the **(CTBUH)** and search the 'Awards' section for 'Past winners', including the Tornado Tower, the Bahrain World Trade Centre and the Hearst Tower.

Capital Gate and Swiss Re buildings: Find the **E-Architect** website and search for 'Capital Gate' and 'Swiss Re'.

LED lamp and other innovative designs: Find the **Business Week Innovation** website and search for 'The Best Global Design of 2008'.

Teacher's notes

1 Inventions

Start here

Warmer

As a warmer, ask students to discuss in small groups the design of their ideal car or motorbike. What particular features would they include?

1 Put students in pairs. Ask them to look at the photo, answer the questions on the design of the vehicle and make comparisons with a normal motorbike and a sports car. Tell them that they should consider the features in the box when discussing the design, as well as any others that they think are important. Tell them to make notes on their ideas but do not check answers at this point. See the Briefing section at the beginning of the unit in the Teacher's Book for information about these vehicles, though most of the key information is in the audio script.

Listening

2 ▶ 💿29

Tell students that they are going to listen to a test report which compares the performance of the Spyder roadster with that of the Zoomster XL motorcycle. Tell them to read the statements in the checklist first so that they will know what to listen out for. Play the recording for students to tick the correct statements according to what they hear. Do not check students' answers yet as they will check their own answers in the listening task in 3.

The correct statements are: 1, 2, 4

▶ 💿 29

A: I've just finished testing the new Can-Am Spyder roadster and comparing it against the Zoomster XL motorcycle.
B: So what were the main differences?
A: Well, of course, the first thing to mention is the wheels. While the Zoomster has two wheels, the Spyder has three – that's two in front and one behind.
Having three wheels means having three sets of brakes. And here's another obvious and very striking difference between the Spyder and any motorbike, not just the Zoomster. Most motorbikes have a brake pedal for the back wheel and a lever on the handlebar for the front brake. But the Spyder has a single brake pedal, located on the right side, for all the brakes, and it has no lever. So it was a bit confusing at first but I soon became accustomed to the new layout.
B: How did the brakes perform in your test?
A: Well, I found that the Spyder's brakes were much more efficient and a great deal more powerful than the Zoomster's.
B: How about speed?

A: Well, I found that the Spyder went just as fast as the Zoomster. The maximum speed of both vehicles was almost the same, at 260 kilometres per hour. So that's the good news.
B: What's the bad news?
A: Well, although the Spyder's speed was as good as the Zoomster's, its acceleration wasn't as good. I would say the Spyder's acceleration was about ten percent slower. Another problem is that the two front wheels meant that it was quite a lot harder to turn the handlebars to steer the Spyder.
A further issue was that whenever the Spyder's two front tyres went over a hole or bump in the road, I felt a lot of up-and-down movement in the handlebars. The Zoomster had much better suspension and went over the bumps without too much movement in the bars.
B: So what about safety?
A: The Spyder is equipped with safety systems which keep all three wheels in contact with the road at all times. So turning round a bend at speed is much more stable and safer than on the Zoomster. On the whole, I felt that the Spyder was much less dangerous than most normal motorbikes. Perhaps that makes it less exciting? I'll leave that for you to decide.
Oh, before I forget, the storage space at the front of the Spyder is very roomy. It's about twice as large as the container on the back of the Zoomster.
B: And what's your overall assessment?
A: All in all, the Spyder proved to be a useful and ultra-safe innovation in the motorcycle market – much safer than the Zoomster. It will perhaps be more attractive to slightly older riders. That's just as well because the Spyder is about fifty percent more expensive than the Zoomster.

3 Play the recording again for students to check their answers in 2 and correct the false statements.

> **3** the Spyder accelerates (ten percent) less quickly/ more slowly
> **5** the Spyder has much worse suspension/the Zoomster has much better suspension
> **6** the Spyder is much more stable on bends
> **7** the Spyder is much safer
> **8** the Spyder is fifty percent more expensive

Language

Modifying comparatives

Go through the examples in the Language box with the students, which show how to modify comparisons in order to make general and specific comparisons. Point out that this can be done by using the words and phrases in the shaded box before comparative adjectives.

Refer students to the Language summary on page 103.

4 ▶ ⏱30

Focus students' attention on the headings in the chart and the photos of the two types of light bulb. Explain that they are going to compare these light bulbs using the information in the chart. Explain that *CFL bulb* is an abbreviation for *compact fluorescent light bulb*. Go through the phrases in the box. Ask them what *kWh means* (*kilowatt hour*) and if they can explain what *lumen* means (a measurement of the amount of brightness that comes from a source of light). Play the recording for students to hear the phrases. Play the recording again, pausing after each phrase for students to repeat. Then choose individual students to say one of the phrases out loud and check their pronunciation. Ask them to underline the stressed syllables in *fluo<u>res</u>cent* and *incan<u>des</u>cent*.

▶ ⏱30

compact fluorescent light bulb

CFL

incandescent light bulb

thirteen watts

eight hundred and ten lumens

one hundred and thirty kilowatt hours

at fifty-five euro cents per kilowatt hour

Without looking at the information in the chart, ask students to say what they think the main differences are between the two light bulbs. Then go through the example with the class and ask students to use the information in the chart to make more comparisons.

Possible answers (It is possible to say 'normal' instead of 'incandescent'):

An incandescent bulb consumes much more energy/ many more watts than a CFL bulb.

A CFL bulb lasts more than six times as long as/six times longer than an incandescent bulb.

A CFL bulb has slightly less output in lumens than an incandescent bulb.

For 10,000 hours, you need more than six times as many incandescent bulbs as CFL bulbs.

A CFL bulb costs almost twice as much as an incandescent bulb.

An incandescent bulb uses more than four times as much electricity as a CFL bulb.

The total cost of using an incandescent bulb is almost five times greater than using a CFL bulb.

Speaking

5 Put students in pairs and explain that they are going to design a new type of light bulb for a design competition. Go through the instructions with the class and ask them to turn to their respective pages at the back of the Course Book and read the information. Tell them to use this information and the table in 4 to discuss and plan their proposal for designing a new type of light bulb.

Writing

6 Go through the instructions with the class. Make sure that students start the proposal with a separate introductory paragraph explaining how their design meets the needs of society today. Go round as they are writing, giving help where needed. When they have finished, ask them to read through their proposal carefully and to check for grammar, spelling and punctuation mistakes.

Ask pairs to read out their proposals, or you could put their proposals on the classroom walls and ask the class to read each proposal. Then take a vote on which proposal they think is best.

Task

7 Put students in pairs. Allow them a few minutes to think about a product that they use regularly in their daily lives or at work. You could brainstorm ideas with the class first. They then discuss with their partner how they could improve the design so that it works better for them.

8 Ask students to write their proposal, comparing it with other products in the market. Again, ask students to check carefully for grammar, spelling and punctuation mistakes when they have finished.

Model answer:
[Give a brief description of the design as shown in the photograph.]
Our new design of light bulb is neither fluorescent (CFL) nor incandescent. It consists of an LED light source inside a plastic bulb. It has the same shape and form as a normal light bulb and it is screwed into the socket in the same way.
[Write a short explanation of how your design meets a need in society today.]
Our design meets an important need. Because of the dangers of global warming and climate change, many societies want a bulb that gives better light but consumes much less energy. They also want a safer product.
[Compare your design with similar products, explaining how it improves on them.]
Our LED light bulb is safer than other types of light bulb because it has solid-state components, is made of unbreakable plastics and contains no mercury. It uses fifty percent less power than a CFL and about one-tenth less power than an incandescent light bulb. It has the same light quality as an incandescent bulb and slightly better quality than a CFL bulb. It can also be dimmed, something which is impossible with a CFL bulb. It lasts ten times longer than a CFL bulb and more than 60 times longer than an incandescent light bulb. We believe that this new design will be very popular with the public.

9 Ask students to take turns to present their product to the class. Ask the rest of the class to make notes and at the end of the presentation, ask any questions on points they would like clarified.

2 Buildings

Start here

1 Put students in pairs. Ask them to look at the photos of the buildings and discuss the questions. Note that as the students are unlikely to know all this factual information, the answers are given on page 111. Students should be encouraged to say what they know about the buildings before they check the answers.

> **1 & 2** Photo 1: Capital Gate, Abu Dhabi
> Photo 2: Hearst Tower, New York
> Photo 3: 30 St Mary Axe (also called Swiss Re or the Gherkin), London
> **3** All three buildings use a diagrid (diagonal grid) structure as the outer shell of the building.

Listening

2 Check that students know the shapes *circular*, *oval* and *rectangular* by asking a volunteer to draw the shapes on the board or give examples of things from real life that are these shapes. Then ask students to imagine the base of each of the buildings in the photos in 1 and to decide which is circular, which is oval and which is rectangular in shape.

> **1** the Gherkin
> **2** Capital Gate
> **3** Hearst Tower

3 ▶ 🔊 31

Play the recording for students to listen to the pronunciation of the words in the box. Then play it again, pausing for students to repeat. Then ask individual students to repeat the words to check their pronunciation.

▶ 🔊 31

straight

curved

zigzag

cylindrical

conical

diagonal

inclined

at an angle

vertical

horizontal

rectangular

oval

elliptical

tapered

Extra activity

To check students' understanding of the words in the box, put students in pairs and divide the words equally among the pairs. Ask pairs to think of a few objects from real life to illustrate each of their shape words. If students are unsure of the meaning of any word, allow them to use a dictionary, or draw the shape on the board for them. Students then say their real-life objects for the rest of the class to guess the shape word. Check students' understanding of all the shape words before you move on to the next activity.

Brainstorm any further shape words students might know, e.g. *square, triangular, oblong, cubed, pentagonal, octagonal, egg-shaped, star-shaped, heart-shaped*. Then put students in pairs. Without naming or identifying the buildings, ask students to take turns to describe them, using words and phrases for shapes in the box, or any other ones that they came up with in the brainstorming session. Ask the listening student to guess the building that their partner is describing.

Possible answers:

1 (about Capital Gate) This building is tall and curved. It is not vertical but inclined at an angle to the horizontal. It has an oval base.
2 (about Hearst Tower) This building is vertical and it has a rectangular base. It has flat surfaces with zigzag edges.
3 (about the Gherkin) This building has a circular base and it is partly cylindrical and partly conical. It has curved sides.

Extra activity

Ask students to identify the odd word out according to the stress.

1 inclined   oval   tapered
(in<u>clined</u>: The stress falls on the first syllable in the other two words.)
2 cylindrical   elliptical   horizontal
(hori<u>zon</u>tal: The stress falls on the second syllable in the other two words.)
3 conical   diagonal   vertical
(di<u>ag</u>onal: The stress falls on the first syllable in the other two words, and they have three syllables, not four.)

---

9 | Design

Reading

4 Tell the students that they are going to read three fact sheets about the buildings in 1. They should write the name of the building at the top of each fact sheet. Ask students to find another word to mean *approximately* in the texts (*roughly*). Then ask them what the difference between *approximately/roughly* and *virtually* is (*roughly* and *approximately* mean *about*; *virtually* means *almost* or *nearly*).

> 1 Hearst Tower
> 2 'the Gherkin'
> 3 Capital Gate

5 Tell students that they are going to read some information about the three buildings in the photos in 1. Explain that some of the information is incorrect. Ask them to read the statements and compare them with the information in the fact sheets in 4. Students should underline the incorrect information and correct it.

Tell them that *floor* and *storey* mean *level in a building* but *floor* also has another meaning as used in the text; ask them what it is (*ground or flat area you walk on*). Tell them that in British English the spelling is *storey* (plural: *storeys*), whereas in American English it is spelt *story* (plural: *stories*).

> 1 The top of the tower is the least tapered ...
> 2 delete: *with the least extensive floor area.*
> 3 the widest part is *at the sixteenth floor*/delete *the fewest storeys and*

Language

Modifying superlatives

Go through the examples in the Language box with the students. We can use *easily* or *by far* to modify superlative adjectives in order to exaggerate them more.

Remind students they will find more information about modifying superlatives in the language summary on page 103.

6 Go through the instructions and example with the class. Ask students to describe each building briefly, using superlative adjectives. Remind them that they should not name the buildings.

Speaking

7 Put students in small groups. Tell them that they are going to decide on the winner of an architectural award for the best tall building. Refer them back to the photos of the Hearst Tower, the Gherkin and Capital Gate in 1, which have been short-listed for the award, as well as two more buildings: the Tornado Tower, Doha and Bahrain World Trade Centre, Manama, Bahrain, which they can find at the bottom of page 71.

Go through the example criteria for choosing the building for the award. Tell them that they should decide the criteria for their award and decide which building best meets their criteria and should win. Tell them that they should make a note of their group's reasons for the decision.

8 Tell students that they are now going to report back to the class on their group's decision for the best building award. Say that they should first explain their group's criteria for their award, then tell the class what building they chose and why they decided on that particular building.

After all the groups have presented their buildings, ask the class to vote on which building should win the award.

3 Sites

Start here

1 Ask students to look the site plan of the new Samundra Institute of Maritime Studies, near Pune in India, and the photos of two of the buildings on the site. Ask students to identify these two buildings in the site plan. Tell them to pay particular attention to the shapes of the buildings and to imagine the shapes of their bases. You could ask them to try and draw what they think the bases would look like before looking for them on the site plan.

1 G   **2** H

2 Ask students to read through all the descriptions first before matching them with the buildings in the site plan in 1. Check that they understand *doughnut* and explain that in American English this is spelt *donut*. Point out that here it means *ring-shaped* but it is also a small cake, which can have a similar shape. Then ask students to match the buildings. Weaker students can do this in pairs.

1 A   **2** D   **3** F   **4** B   **5** E   **6** G   **7** H   **8** C

Listening

3 ▶ 💿 32

Tell students that they are going to listen to the award ceremony at an architectural festival. Point out that the buildings are not mentioned on the recording in the same order as they appear in the questions. Also point out the compass on the site plan and draw students' attention to the direction of north. Students should listen and write the letters of the buildings from the site plan (A–H) next to their names (1–8). Students can then compare their answers in pairs. Play the recording a second time, pausing after each building is mentioned for students to check their answers.

With weaker groups, pause for students to identify each building at the first listening. Then get them to check their answers in pairs before checking with the class.

Ask students for the names of the buildings shown in the photo (the Administration Building and the Student Hostels).

1 G   **2** C   **3** D   **4** F   **5** H   **6** E   **7** A   **8** B

▶ 💿 32

… and our design for the new Institute of Maritime Studies has recently been shortlisted as best site in the Learning category at the World Architecture Festival. So could you all please look at the plan of the site of the new campus? You can see that the complete site is enclosed by water on three sides and the main highway on the fourth side. Two canals on the east and west sides flow into the large lake on the south side of the site. In other words, there is plenty of water around, which is appropriate for maritime studies.

Right, so I'm now going to point out some of the main buildings of the site. Let's begin with the building in the furthest north-east corner of the site. It's the long, curved building adjacent to a curved and tapering stretch of water. Do you see it? It's right next to the small curved area of water. That's the new administration building.

OK, so I'd like to move on to another building, the hostels where the students will have their accommodation. The student hostels are in the long narrow rectangular building on the opposite side of the curved lake from the admin building.

Right, so the next building that I would like to mention is the Academic Block, which contains the main lecture theatres and classrooms. This is the curved building which looks like a set of teeth. This building is on the opposite side of the road from the student hostels.

Just south west of the Academic Block you can see a rectangular blue pool of water, enclosed in an oval or elliptical building. This is the swimming pool.

Just south of that there are two buildings. One is a doughnut-shaped, or ring-shaped building. This is the Research Centre. Immediately adjacent to the Research Centre, to the east of it, is a rectangular building. This is the Workshop.

On the opposite side of the sports field, the oval building, pointed at both ends, is the Services Building.

And right next to the lake is a structure which is semi-circular at one end and straight on the other end. This is the campus ship. It's a ship where the maritime students can practise their seafaring skills.

Vocabulary

4 Make sure students understand the difference between *plan* and *elevation* first. Then ask them to match sketches (a) and (b) with the photos in 1.

> **1** b   **2** a

5 Focus students' attention on the words and phrases in the box and ask them to use them to describe the sketches in 4.

Tell students that they are now going to read a text about the administration building and the students' hostel in the photos in 1. Tell them to read the text once through, ignoring the gaps and referring to the photos as they do so. Then ask them to complete the text, using the words from the box.

1 tapered	**4** perpendicular	**7** elevation
2 arch	**5** hatched	**8** solid
3 horizontal	**6** plan	**9** broken

Speaking

6 Put students in pairs. Tell them that they are going to take turns to describe the buildings in the site plan to their partner. Ask Student A to turn to page 114 and Student B to 115 and read the instructions. They then take turns to describe the buildings in the site plan in random order for their partner to identify. Remind them to use the language to describe shapes from 2 and 5. Point out that if their partner fails to identify a building, they should explain it again in a more detailed way, so as to distinguish it from all the other buildings on the site plan.

Scanning

7 Go through the instructions with the students. Then ask them to turn to pages 116–117 to find the information for this unit. For weaker classes, you could tell students there are four texts. Remind them that they do not need to read every word in the text, just look for the information which answers the questions. Ask students to put up their hand when they have finished. Allow the majority of students to finish but check the answers with the first person to put up their hand to see if they were correct and are the winner.

> **1** 15,140.4 metric tonnes
> **2** the Cinema dei Piccoli, at the Villa Borghese, Rome
> **3** beneath the waters of Susami Bay, Japan; for passing divers to post letters
> **4** 285 m (935 ft)

Extra activity

Ask students to work in pairs and describe a famous building, or if they come from the same town or city, a well-known building from there, for their partner to guess the building. Remind them to use the language they have studied in this section. If their partner is having problems, help them by drawing the base of the building.

Speaking

8 In their pairs, students try to remember what world records have been mentioned in the Course Book and other world records. They should also say what world records have been broken recently.

10 | Disasters

Contents

1 Speculation

Objectives

In this section students will ...

- speculate about what can cause a bridge to collapse
- listen to technical experts speculate about a bridge collapse
- match phrases that have a similar meaning
- study and practise using present perfect modals for speculation
- categorise statements as possible, certain or impossible
- rewrite statements as speculations
- talk and speculate about events from personal experience
- learn vocabulary for structural engineering and describing damage

2 Investigation

Objectives

In this section students will ...

- label a diagram with civil engineering words
- listen to an interview and complete an action report
- complete statements from the interview
- study and practise using *should/shouldn't* and the perfect infinitive to criticise actions in the past
- study and practise using the third conditional to speculate about the past
- discuss and explain the collapse of a hotel walkway; speculate what caused it and what should have been done
- learn vocabulary for civil engineering

3 Reports

Objectives

In this section students will ...

- match section headings for reports with their explanations
- read an investigative report and match headings to sections of the report
- answer questions about the report
- discuss sections of the report and say where they should go in the report
- write a report on an investigation

Briefing

This unit looks at **investigations** into major accidents or disasters, culminating in **investigative reports**.

Section 1 deals with the types of **structural failure** of metal parts that can lead to bridge collapse. Such failure is usually due to **stress** (a force that causes **deformation**, or change of shape), such as excessive **compression** (squeezing, pushing), or **tension** (stretching, pulling). If a structural part such as a **girder** (steel beam) or **strut** (a smaller supporting rod) is unable to support a **compressive load** applied at each end towards the centre, it may **buckle**, that is, bend out of shape so that the middle part bulges outwards. A **fracture** is the separation of an object into two or more pieces due to long-term stress or sudden **impact** (powerful force or shock applied over a short time period). **Fatigue** (weakening) occurs when a metal is exposed to **cyclic**, or repeated, loads over a long period of time: the stress level may be well below the **yield strength** (stress limit) of the material, but the damage is caused by the repetitive and similar nature of the stress. **Thermal shock** is a cracking of the metal caused by rapid temperature change (from extreme heat to extreme cold, or vice versa), and therefore rapid **expansion** and **contraction**. **Wear** is the **erosion** (or removal) of material from a solid surface by the movement of another surface against it. **Corrosion** (commonly called **rusting**) is the **disintegration** (break-up) of a metal due to the reaction of electrons in the metal with water and oxygen. A **bearing** (in a bridge or building) is a part that supports weight. (In other contexts, as in **ball bearing**, it is placed between two moving parts to allow them to move easily.)

Section 2 deals with the collapse of the I-35W bridge in the USA in 2007. The basic facts of this disaster and the investigation that followed it can be found on pages 78 and 79 (see also references below). The **deck** of a bridge is the horizontal section that carries the traffic. A **truss** is a framework of girders or beams arranged in triangles to form a strong, rigid supportive structure. A **node** is the point where two or more girders connect in the truss. In the left-hand diagram on page 76, the truss is the metal framework below the road deck of the bridge. In the right-hand diagram, the truss rests on the bearing (support), which in turn rests on the concrete **pier**. The nodes of the truss are connected by means of **gusset plates**. The weakness of some of the gusset plates was found to be one of the main causes of the bridge collapse. Cracks were also found in some girders, which engineers attempted to repair by drilling holes to stop the cracks from spreading, and by adding extra struts to reinforce the damaged girders. The main details of the collapse of the **walkways** above the **atrium** of the Hyatt Regency hotel in Kansas City, USA, can be found in the Extra Material section on pages 110, 112, 114 and 115. The investigation into this disaster is often used on training courses as a case study on ethics and good practice in communication between engineers, architects and **building contractors** (builders). The builders did not follow the original design (which used a single rod to connect the walkways) but, during the construction stage, changed the design from one single rod to two separate rods without (it was claimed in court) receiving written approval from the engineers.

Section 3 provides the main details of the investigation into the I-35W bridge collapse, adapted from the official government report into the causes of the collapse (which were later confirmed by an independent academic study by the University of Minnesota). A lot of evidence was uncovered (stated in the 'Findings' section): some gusset plates and bearings were corroded, and others (at one of the nodes, known as 'U10') were cracked; some gusset plates were too thin to support the loads on the bridge; earlier inspections had not discovered the problems with the gusset plates; the load on the bridge had been increased (extra concrete added to the road and construction machinery on the day of the collapse). However, the report concluded that the main reason for the collapse was most probably the over-thin gusset plates.

Official investigation into the I-35W bridge collapse: Find the US government **National. Transportation Safety Board (NTSB)** website and search for 'Collapse of I-35W Highway Bridge Minneapolis, Minnesota August 1, 2007'.

Independent study of I-35W bridge collapse: Find the **Science Daily** website and search for 'Independent Study Of The I-35W Bridge Collapse Results Parallel NTSB Report'.

Hyatt Regency walkway collapse: Find the website of the **University of Utah Dept of Mechanical Engineering** and search for 'Kansas City Walkway Collapse'.

Teacher's notes

1 Speculation

Start here

Warmer

As a warmer, focus students' attention on the title of the section and elicit the meaning of *speculation*. You could begin the lesson by putting students in small groups and asking them to discuss some examples of events where the cause is not immediately known, such as police detectives speculating about suspects of a crime or firemen speculating about the cause of a fire or oil rig disasters. Then ask the class for their ideas.

1 Put students in small groups. Focus their attention on the photo and tell them that in this unit they are going to speculate about the causes of disasters. Pre-teach some basic bridge vocabulary, such as *pier, deck* and *girder*. Ask students to point to these items in the photos.

Then ask them to answer the question and make a list of possible causes for a bridge to collapse (e.g. due to factors such as weather conditions, intense traffic, destruction because of vehicles, trains, etc. colliding into pillars, terrorism, structural failure, etc.) After eliciting ideas from the class, you could ask students if they can name any famous bridge collapses (Tacomo Narrows Bridge, Washington State, USA, 1940; Hyatt Regency walkway, Kansas City, USA, 1981; Minneapolis I-35W bridge, Minneapolis, US, 2007; Tuo River Bridge, China, 2007). Do not spend a lot of time on this and do not go into any detail about the collapse of the road bridge over the Hyatt Regency walkway or the Minneapolis I-35W bridge if students mention them.

See the Briefing section at the beginning of the unit in the Teacher's Book for more information about the causes of bridge collapse, though most of the key information is given in the audio script. Essentially, the list of causes in 3 along with their synonyms in 4, is a checklist of the causes of bridge failure.

2 Focus students' attention on the bridge collapse and the damage in the photo. Ask them to read the information about the incident. Then, in their groups, ask them to discuss the possible causes of this bridge collapse. Note that students are just speculating at this stage; the cause of the collapse (gusset plates which were too thin) will be given later in the unit. If students mention structural failure, ask them to give more details if they can.

Possible answer:
From the main picture, it looks as though there has been some structural failure to the bridge – corrosion or weakness of the bearings (where the girders rest on the piers) could have caused the collapse.

Listening

3 ▶ 🎧 33

Tell students that they are going to listen to a radio phone-in show in which listeners speculate over the possible causes of the bridge collapse in 2. Ask them to read through the list of possible causes first, then tick the ones that are mentioned.

The following speculations are mentioned: 3, 4, 5, 7, 9

▶ 🎧 33

[P = Pete; J = Jerry; T = Tom; S = Susan; R = Richard; Ja= Jason]

P: Welcome back to Mississippi Calling. I'm Pete Hanson, your host, and we're talking about the terrible event that's dominating all the news channels and all the phone-ins tonight, and that's the tragic collapse of the I-35W bridge over our Mississippi river earlier this evening.
We'd like anyone out there who's a civil engineer, or any kind of technical expert on bridge design or bridge construction, to call in and tell us about your theories, speculations and ideas about why this bridge might have collapsed.
So what might have caused the collapse? We'd like to hear from you. OK, now we have Jerry from Minnesota. What's your idea, Jerry?

J: Well, I think that one or more of the girders might have buckled, Pete …

P: You're an engineer, Jerry?

J: I'm a technician working in a civil engineering company. I think the collapse might have been caused by a girder buckling.

P: And now we have Tom on the line, from Chicago. What's your take on this, Tom?

T: Well, I reckon the collapse could have been due to metal fatigue.

P: You sound like a bridge engineer, too – is that right, Tom?

T: Yeah, I've worked on quite a lot of bridge projects. I think that years and years of the same loads over and over again might have caused some metal fatigue in the truss.

P: And now we have Susan, a civil engineer from Texas. Susan, can you shed some light on this?

S: I'll try, Pete. My own view is that one of the bearings must have corroded and rusted away.

P: You say it must have corroded? You sound pretty certain of that.

S: Yeah, well, I've seen it happen before, on two other bridges that collapsed. When they did the investigation, they concluded that the collapse was caused by corroded bearings.

P: And now we have Richard on the line. Well, Richard, what do you think went on here?

R: Well, I think the collapse could have been caused by thermal shock. It was an extremely hot day and if the bearings and plates were also corroded, the heat could have caused too much contraction.

Vocabulary

4 Ask students to read through the phrases and then match them with the words and phrases in 3, which have the same or similar meaning.

> **a** 9   **b** 7   **c** 6   **d** 3   **e** 4   **f** 8   **g** 5   **h** 10

> **Extra activity**
>
> Elicit the verb form of some of the nouns in 3: *compress, shock, corrode, wear, impact, buckle, fracture*. Ask students which words have the same noun and verb form (*shock, wear, impact, fracture*).

Language

Modals + perfect infinitive: *could/must/may/can't have*

Go through the Language box with students. Go through the example sentences and explain that we can use *could, may* or *might* + perfect infinitive to talk about the possibility that something happened in the past, and *could/may/might not* + perfect infinitive to talk about the possibility that something did not happen in the past. Point out that to express certainty that something happened in the past, we use *must*. To express certainty that something did not happen in the past, we use *can't/couldn't*. Then go through the examples of the passive form in the second box with the class.

Tell students that they will find more information about speculating about the past in the Language summary on page 105.

5 Ask students to read through the statements and think about how certain the speakers were about their speculations. Tell them to mark the statements P for possible, C for certain and I for impossible. They could underline the modal verbs in the sentences as they go along and refer back to the Language box for help.

> **1** I   **2** P   **3** P   **4** C   **5** P   **6** C

6 Tell students that they are going to read statements about investigations into other disasters. Ask them to read through the statements. Check understanding of the phrase *the plane itself* in item 4. Then ask them to rewrite the sentences as speculations using the words in brackets. Then they should write *P, I* or *C* after each statement to show the degree of certainty.

Weaker students could do this exercise in pairs. Go round helping the students as they write their sentences.

> **1** The Challenger disaster could have been caused by a faulty O-ring seal. (P)
> The seal might have broken away from a fuel tank and damaged it. (P)
> **2** The wing of the Columbia shuttle must have been damaged by an insulating tile. (C)
> The tile may have fallen off the nose cone at launch. (P)
> **3** The Warsaw radio mast may have collapsed because of human error. (P)
> The cables securing the mast might not have been fastened correctly. (P)
> The mast must have bent and then snapped into two. (C)
> **4** The crash of the Air France Concorde can't have been caused by a fault in the plane itself. (I)
> One of its tyres must have been cut by a metal strip lying on the runway. (C)
> Another aircraft could have dropped the strip on the runway some minutes before. (P)

Speaking

7 Put students in pairs. Allow them a few minutes to think of some dangerous or unusual events that have happened to them personally. Then ask them to discuss these with their partner and speculate on the causes of the events. You could give them an example of something that has happened to you to get them started. While they are doing the activity, go round the class monitoring the students and checking they are using the language correctly. Go through any errors with the class at the end of the activity. You could ask one or two pairs with good stories to share them with the rest of the class.

2 Investigation

Start here

1 Focus students' attention on the diagrams and ask them what they show. Then ask them to match the words in the box with labels 1–6. Students may have difficulty with *truss*, which is a structure which has one or more triangular units.

> 1 deck
> 2 truss
> 3 girder
> 4 gusset plate
> 5 bearing
> 6 pier

Scanning

2 Go through the instructions with the students. Then ask them to turn to pages 78–79 and scan them to find the answers to the questions. Remind them that they do not need to read every word in the text, just look for the information which answers the questions. Ask students to put up their hand when they have finished. Allow the majority of students to finish but check the answers with the first person to put up their hand to see if they were correct and are the winner.

> 1 140
> 2 four
> 3 17
> 4 261,000 kg

Listening

3 ▶ 🔊 34

Tell students that they are going to listen to an interview between an investigator and the company that managed the collapsed bridge. First ask them to read through the actions in the table. Then play the recording for students to tick the things the company did or did not do.

> YES: 2, 4, 5, 6, 7
> NO: 1, 3, 8, 9, 10, 11

▶ 🔊 34

[I = Inspector; CR = Company Representative]

I: Your company should have inspected the bridge annually. Did a competent employee of your company carry out an annual inspection?

CR: The bridge was inspected every year, although it wasn't in 2007.

I: Why not?

CR: The main reason was that there was a lot of construction work going on the bridge.

I: Well, the bridge should have been inspected in 2007. What did previous inspection reports say?

CR: In 1990 a report stated that there was significant corrosion in its bearings.

I: Were the bearings repaired or replaced immediately afterwards?

CR: No, I'm afraid nothing happened as a result of the report.

I: Well, the bearings shouldn't have been left on that bridge. If your company had replaced the bearings, maybe the bridge wouldn't have collapsed. What did other reports on the bridge say?

CR: A 2001 inspection stated that there was cracking in some of the girders.

I: Was any action taken after that report? The cracks should have been drilled to stop them from spreading.

CR: Yes, this remedial action was carried out.

I: But that's not enough. Support struts should also have been added to the cracked girders to prevent any more cracking.

CR: Yes, this was done after the report.

I: All right. What about 2006? There was an inspection then. What did that find?

CR: Signs of metal fatigue were observed in the bridge. The report mentioned the metal fatigue.

I: In my opinion, the bridge should have been closed then, in 2006, immediately after the signs of metal fatigue were discovered. But of course that never happened.

CR: No, that's correct.

I: The bridge should have been replaced immediately.

CR: Yes, you're right.

I: Did anything happen after that inspection in 2006?

CR: Yes, we planned to carry out some steel reinforcement on the bridge. But the project was cancelled.

I: Why?

CR: We found that the reinforcement work might have weakened the bridge.

I: You shouldn't have cancelled the steel reinforcement. You should have found a way to do it without weakening the bridge.

CR: Yes.

I: Look, in our investigation, we've found a design error in the gusset plates which connect the girders together in the truss structure. The plates were too thin to support the girders. You should have discovered this error in one of your annual inspections. Did you?

CR: No, we didn't.

I: And the undersized gusset plates should have been replaced with larger ones. Were they?

CR: No, they weren't.

I: Well, if you had replaced the gusset plates, the bridge would probably not have collapsed.

4 Ask students to read the sentences from the second part of the recording of the investigation and complete the sentences with the words in the box. They can then check their answers in the audio script on page 125 of the Course Book.

> 1 have
> 2 have been
> 3 have been
> 4 had; wouldn't have

Language

should/shouldn't have

Go through the Language box with the students. Explain that we use *should/shouldn't have* + past participle when we want to criticise an action that happened in the past which we think was wrongly done or not done. Go through the examples showing the active and passive forms.

5 Tell students to look back at the actions that were *not* carried out in 3, i.e. the ones they marked *NO*. Ask them to write sentences criticising why these actions were not carried out. They can then compare their sentences with a partner. Weaker students can discuss the sentences in pairs first, then write their sentences together.

1 The bridge should have been inspected every year.
3 The corroded bearings should have been repaired or replaced.
8 The bridge should have been closed after the metal fatigue was discovered.
9 The steel reinforcement should have been carried out on the bridge.
10 The design error in the gusset plates should have been discovered before the collapse.
11 The undersized gusset plates should have been replaced with larger ones.

Language

Third conditional

Go through the Language box with the students. Focus their attention on the first clause in each sentence. Explain that we are speculating about unreal events in the past. In the second clause, we are talking about the result of doing these things differently. Point out that in the third conditional, we use *if* + past perfect in the first clause. In the second clause we use *would/wouldn't* + perfect infinitive to talk about results in the past and *would/wouldn't* + present infinitive to talk about result happening in the present.

Tell students that they will find more information about the third conditional for speculating about the past in the Language summary on pages 102–103.

6 Go through the example sentence, then do the first question as an example with the class. Students could then work in pairs to read through the sentences and speculate about the unreal situations in the past. Then get feedback from the class.

1 If the main column had not buckled, the building would not have collapsed.
2 If the plane's fuel tank had not fractured, the fuel would not have exploded.
3 If the ship hadn't crashed into the bridge pier, the pier wouldn't be cracked now.
4 If friction hadn't worn down the brake pads, the brakes would work now.
5 If tensile forces hadn't stretched the cables, they wouldn't have snapped.
6 If compressive forces hadn't pressed down on the columns, they wouldn't be fractured in three places now.

Task

7 Focus students' attention on the photo and ask if anyone can identify this disaster. Put students in groups of four (A–D) and go through the instructions with them. Each student in the group should then turn to the relevant page at the back of the Course Book and study the information. Then they discuss the questions in their groups.

8 Ask students to take turns to explain their group's conclusions to the class.

Model answer:

(What happened?)

Without warning, two walkways crashed to the floor of the Hyatt Regency hotel in the USA in 1981.

(What caused it to happen?)

In the original design, the two walkways were connected to the same long vertical rods. You can see this in Figure 1. Here the two walkways were supported by the roof.

But the builders changed the design without getting the approval of the engineering firm. They replaced the long vertical rods with shorter ones. You can see this in Figure 2. Now the lower walkway was supported by the upper one.

This doubled the weight on the upper walkway. When people stood on the lower walkway, it pulled the upper walkway down and both walkways collapsed.

(What should have happened?)

The builders should not have changed the design. They should not have replaced the longer rods with the shorter ones.

The lower walkway should have been suspended from the roof, not from the upper walkway.

If the builders had followed the original design, perhaps the walkways would not have collapsed. Or perhaps they would have collapsed anyway because there were also some problems with the original design.

The engineering firm and the builders should have communicated effectively with one another.

3 Reports

Start here

Warmer

Discuss with students what types of reports they have to write in their jobs. Then ask them what problems they have writing reports and what they think makes a good report.

1 Explain to students that it is vital when you write a report to organise it into clear sections. Put students in pairs and ask them to match the report section headings with their explanations. Then discuss the questions with their partner.

Point out that in report writing, *Abstract* is the same as *Summary* and *Method* is the same as *Procedure*.

> **1** c **2** f **3** a **4** h **5** b **6** d **7** e **8** g
> *These are the standard headings for a report of an investigation, and the sections are usually in this order (1–8).*

Reading

2 Tell students that they are going to read an investigation report on the I-35W bridge collapse. Tell them that the report has been divided up into sections on pages 78 and 79. Explain that these sections are not in the correct order. Ask them to read quickly through the sections and write the headings from 1 in the correct places.

> *These are the headings, in the order presented in the text:*
> **8** Attachments
> **6** Conclusions
> **4** Method
> **7** Recommendations
> **2** Introduction
> **5** Findings
> **1** Abstract
> **3** Background

3 Ask students to answer the questions about the report.

> **1** the gusset plates joining a group of girders (at the U10 nodes)
> **2** At 13 mm, some of the gusset plates were too thin for the loads on the bridge.
> **3** There was construction equipment on the bridge (adding an extra 261,000 kg) and four lanes were closed (concentrating traffic load into the remaining four lanes).
> **4** CCTV camera footage; wreckage from the collapsed bridge; photos and documents of previous inspections

Task

4 Put students in pairs to discuss which sections of an investigative report would contain the sentences. After getting feedback from the class, elicit which verb form is used in each case and why.

> **1** Conclusions (*must* + perfect infinitive to indicate certainty)
> **2** Recommendations (modal *should* to indicate a recommendation)
> **3** Conclusions (*should* + perfect infinitive to indicate criticism)
> **4** Findings (or Background) (past simple passive to focus on the action rather than the agent)
> **5** Introduction (present simple used here as a fixed formal expression)

Extra activity

You could ask students to read through the report sections and underline any other language they think would be useful in writing a report, e.g. *The purpose of this document* in the introduction. Then put students in pairs to compare.

Writing

5 Ask students to form the same groups as they were in for the task they worked on about the Hyatt Regency disaster on page 77. Tell them that they should now produce their report on their investigation into the disaster. Ask them to use the same format as the one used in 1 and 2 above. Tell them to choose a group leader and divide the group up, so that each member writes one or more sections. The group leader should make sure that the work is shared out equally. Tell them to use the verb forms they studied in this section and some of the phrases they underlined in the report. When they have finished, remind them to check their work carefully for any grammar, spelling or punctuation mistakes.

See the Briefing section at the beginning of the unit in the Teacher's Book for more information about the Hyatt Regency collapse and investigation.

Model answer:

1 Abstract

This report presents the results of the investigation into the collapse of two walkways in the Hyatt Regency hotel. It describes the method of investigation, including wreckage, video footage, documents and interviews with witnesses. The main findings are (1) the failure of the ceiling rod connections, (2) the change of design during construction and (3) the absence of prior approval by the engineers. The investigation concludes that the main cause of the collapse must have been (1) the change of design during the construction phase and (2) poor communication between builders and engineers. The report recommends (1) no change of design during construction without written approval and (2) better communication between builders and engineers.

2 Introduction

This is the report of our investigation into the causes of the Hyatt Regency walkway collapse. It presents our findings, conclusions and recommendations.

3 Background

On 17 July 1981, two walkways crashed to the floor of the Hyatt Regency hotel in Kansas City during a crowded party. 114 people were killed and over 200 injured. Millions of dollars in costs resulted from the collapse.

4 Method

Wreckage from the collapsed walkways was collected. In addition, video footage of the collapse was examined and witnesses were interviewed. Diagrams of the original design of the walkways were studied.

5 Findings

The second and fourth-floor walkways were supported by ceiling rods. The evidence showed that these connections failed and then the walkways collapsed.

As can be seen in Figure 1 (see Attachment), in the original design, the two walkways were connected to the same long vertical rods. In the original design, the two walkways were supported by the roof.

During construction, the builders replaced the long vertical rods with shorter ones, as can be seen in Figure 2 (see Attachment). In the changed design, the lower walkway was supported by the upper one.

The builders changed the design without getting the approval of the engineering firm before construction.

6 Conclusions

This investigation concludes that the collapse must have been caused by the change of design. The new design must have doubled the weight on the upper walkway. When people stood on the lower walkway, the weight must have pulled the upper walkway down.

The lower walkway should have been suspended from the roof, not from the upper walkway.

The builders should not have changed the design during construction. They should not have replaced the longer rods with the shorter ones. They should have shown their plans to the engineering firm and received approval before construction.

The engineering firm should have checked the changed design carefully.

If there had been better communication between the builders and the engineers, the collapse would probably not have happened.

7   Recommendations

7.1 Builders should not change designs during construction without written approval from engineers.

7.2 An improved system of communication between building contractors and engineers should be set up.

8 Attachments

Figure 1 and Figure 2.

Review Unit E

Answer key

1 *Possible answers:*
1 The Nokia is slightly longer than the iPhone.
2 The iPhone is a great deal wider than the Nokia.
3 The iPhone is much thinner than the Palm Pre.
4 The Nokia is a little heavier than the Apple.
5 The Nokia has a lot better/sharper resolution (or has a lot more megapixels) than the Apple.
6 The display (screen) on the iPhone is slightly larger than the one on the Palm Pre.
7 The Palm Pre has a far shorter (maximum) talk time than the iPhone.
8 The Nokia has a much greater capacity than the Palm Pre.
9 The Nokia is a lot less expensive than the 32 GB iPhone.

2
1 The capacity of the 32 GB iPhone is exactly four times as great as/greater than the capacity of the Palm Pre.
2 The display (screen) of the Palm Pre is roughly ten millimetres smaller than the screen of the Nokia.
3 The Apple is approximately 25% thinner than the Palm Pre.
4 The Nokia has virtually twice as many pixels as the Palm Pre.
5 The talk time of the Nokia is exactly four times longer than/as long as the talk time of the Palm Pre.
6 The iPhone 32GB model is almost £40 more expensive than the Nokia.

4
1 Capital Gate is much shorter/less tall than Hearst Tower.
2 The Gherkin has a slightly smaller floor area than Capital Gate.
3 Hearst Tower is a little taller than the Gherkin.
4 The Gherkin consumes half as much energy as a normal tower.
5 Capital Gate is about five times lighter/five times less heavy than/one fifth as heavy as the Bird's Nest in Beijing.
6 Hearst Tower uses about 25% less steel than a normal building.

5
1 C	2 B	3 D	4 A

7
1 E	2 C	3 D	4 A	5 B	6 G	7 J
8 F	9 H	10 I				

9
1 The automatic locks on the fire doors should not have been disabled.
2 The fire sprinklers should have been inspected every month.
3 The fire extinguishers should not have been taken away for servicing all at the same time.
4 Fire drills should have been carried out on a regular basis.
5 Two of the fire escapes should not have been demolished.
6 The fire alarm system should have been tested every two months.

10 *Possible answers:*
1 In future, the steel used in ship hulls should not be made of metal which becomes brittle in cold temperatures.
2 All rivets used in hulls should be made of the best quality and should not contain any slag.
3 Binoculars should be used at all times by lookouts. Alarms should be given in plenty of time to allow ships to turn out of danger.
4 Enough lifeboats should be provided to hold all the crew and passengers of a ship.

11
1 metal fatigue	4 wear
2 thermal shock	5 tension
3 impact; fracture	6 corrosion

12
1 had been mixed; would not have collapsed; would still be standing
2 had used/had been using; had been invented; would not have collided
3 had not fallen; would not have struck; would not have come; would be
4 had been equipped; would have been stopped; would have been ejected

13
1 If the engineer had not tripped the wrong switch, the electrical system would not have broken down last night.
2 If the buildings had been built with earthquake-proof foundations, the earthquake would not have destroyed over 20% of the town.
3 If the police had not taken down all the speed cameras from this section of the road, the 27 accidents would not have taken place.
4 It the cloud had not prevented the pilot from seeing the other plane, he would have taken evasive action.

Project

14 At the end of every Review Unit is a project. Students can research their projects on the internet. Ask them to prepare their talk by writing notes and dividing the notes into sections as in lesson 10.3. They then take turns to give their presentation to the class.

Quick test answer key

Part 1: Vocabulary and grammar

1
1 curved	**3** cylindrical	**5** elliptical
2 zigzag	**4** conical	

2
1 arch	**5** tapered end
2 broken line	**6** line which is
3 solid line	perpendicular to the
4 hatched area	horizontal

3 **1** b   **2** c   **3** d   **4** a   **5** e

4 **1** truss   **2** pier   **3** girder   **4** gusset plate

5
1 slightly longer than	**4** far more slowly than
2 a third shorter than	**5** twice as expensive as
3 easily the deepest	

6
1 must	**4** must have	**6** couldn't
2 must	been	
3 couldn't	**5** must have	

7 **1** If they had built the tower with enough structural support, the tower wouldn't have collapsed.
2 If the airport staff had checked that the runway was clear of debris, it's possible that Concorde would be operating now.
3 If we had seen the corrosion, we would be driving the car now.
4 If they had made the columns from strong, flexible materials, the columns wouldn't have fractured.
5 If the mechanic had replaced the brake pads, we wouldn't have had the accident.

8 **1** You should have checked the strength of the material.
2 The engineers should have seen the signs of metal fatigue.
3 The mechanic should have replaced the (badly worn) wheels.
4 Diesel fuel shouldn't have been put in the car.

Part 2: Reading and writing

Reading

1 It was in a bad condition. Large cracks and blocks of concrete falling onto the road below had been reported.
2 Designing a bridge on which it was impossible for detailed inspections to be made, placing the steel reinforcements in one area and poor communication.
3 Not putting the rebars in the correct place, using low-quality concrete and poor communication.
4 Not closing the bridge when concrete blocks were falling on the road, not maintaining the bridge well enough and poor communication.
5 Better inspections to detect wear in old bridges and more spending on maintenance and rebuilding.

Writing

Model answer:
The table compares high-speed rail transport in France, Japan and China. It shows that the rail network in China is far more extensive than in the other two countries. There are about twice as many kilometres of tracks that operate high-speed trains in China as there are in France. China has by far the most kilometres of tracks under construction, whereas France has the least. High-speed trains that operate in Japan travel slightly more slowly than the trains in France, but China has easily the fastest high-speed trains, which can run at a speed of 350 km/h.

Review Unit E Quick test

Total _____/50

Part 1: Vocabulary and grammar

1 Label the illustrations with the words in the box.

| conical   curved   cylindrical   elliptical   zigzag |

1 ....

2 ....

3 ....

4 ....

5 ....

(5 marks)

2 The names of the shapes are in the wrong places. Put them in the correct places.

1 a hatched area

2 a solid line ------

3 a tapered end ———

4 a line perpendicular to the horizontal

5 a broken line

6 an arch

(6 marks)

3 Match the types of damage with their causes.

1 buckling   **a)** a crack in the material
2 wear   **b)** being bent due to a great force
3 corrosion   **c)** use over a period of time
4 fracture   **d)** a chemical or rust
5 tension   **e)** being pulled apart or stretched

(5 marks)

4 Complete these definitions with words to describe parts of the structure of a bridge.

1 A _____ is a triangular shaped structure or frame which is used to give shape to a bridge.

2 A _____ is the main support for a bridge, on which the bridge superstructure rests.

3 A _____ is a beam which can be made of steel or wood, etc., to give support to a structure.

4 A _____ is a rectangular or triangular steel plate which is used to strengthen an angle of a structure.

(4 marks)

5 Fill the gaps with modifying comparatives and superlatives using the words in the box and the adjectives in brackets.

| a third   easily   twice   far   slightly |

1 (Overall length: Seikan Tunnel, Japan = 53.85 km, Channel Tunnel, UK to France = 50 km)

The Seikan Tunnel is _____ (long) the Channel Tunnel.

2 (Length under seabed: Seikan Tunnel = 23.3 km, Channel Tunnel = 37.9 km)

The length of the Seikan Tunnel under the seabed is about _____ (short) the Channel Tunnel.

3 (Depth below seabed: Seikan Tunnel = 140 m, Channel Tunnel = 45 m, the Eiksund Tunnel = 287 m)

The Eiksund Tunnel is _____ (deep).

4 (Construction: Seikan Tunnel = 1971–1988, Channel Tunnel = 1987–1993)

The Seikan Tunnel was built _____ (slow) the Channel Tunnel.

5 (Cost of Channel Tunnel: original estimated cost = £4.8 billion, final cost = £10 billion)

The final cost of constructing the Channel Tunnel was _____ its original estimated cost.

(5 marks)

6 Choose the correct option to complete these sentences.

1 I think the bearings **could/must** have broken.

2 I'm certain the damage **might/must** have been caused by metal fatigue.

3 No, lightning **mightn't/couldn't** have caused the damage.

4 The fire **could have/must have been** caused by a faulty wire.

5 A virus **must have/must have been** infected your computer.

6 I'm sorry, the exhaust pipe **can/couldn't** have been fitted properly.

(6 marks)

7 Rewrite the sentences to speculate about unreal situations.

1 They didn't build the tower with enough structural support so the tower collapsed.

If they _____, the tower _____.

PHOTOCOPIABLE

2 The airport staff didn't check that the runway was clear of debris so Concorde isn't operating now.

If the airport staff _____,
it's possible that Concorde

_____ now.

3 We didn't see the corrosion and as a result we can't drive the car.

If we _____,
we _____ now.

4 They didn't make the columns from strong, flexible materials so the columns fractured.

If they _____, the columns

_____.

5 The mechanic didn't replace the brake pads so we had the accident.

If the mechanic _____,
we _____.

(5 marks)

8 Rewrite the sentences with *should* or *should have* and the correct form of the verbs in italics.

1 You didn't *check* the strength of the material.

You _____.

2 The engineers didn't *see* the signs of metal fatigue.

The engineers _____.

3 The wheels weren't replaced by the mechanic. They were badly worn.

The mechanic _____.

4 The car isn't starting because diesel fuel was put in it by mistake.

Diesel fuel _____.

(4 marks)

Part 2: Reading and writing

Reading

Read the extracts from a report and answer the questions.

De la Concorde Overpass in Laval, Quebec, Canada

Background

De la Concorde Overpass was built in 1970 and was estimated to last for 70 years. … On 30 September 2006, a 20-metre section collapsed, killing five people in their cars as they were driving under the bridge and injuring six others.

Findings

… large cracks had been reported … Shortly before the collapse blocks of concrete were seen falling onto the highway from the overpass. A sight and sound test was done to check the damage by a maintenance inspector who decided that there was no immediate danger and the road stayed open. He asked for an inspection of the bridge, but this could not be done until two days later.

Conclusion

The investigating team concluded that the bridge collapsed due to a horizontal plane fracture, which caused a part of the abutment below it to break away. They identified three main reasons for the fracture: firstly, the design of the bridge, in which steel reinforcements were concentrated in one area, causing a weak plane. Secondly, during construction, the rebars were placed in the wrong locations, which severely weakened the bridge. Thirdly low-quality concrete was used in the abutments … Other factors were that the bridge design made it impossible to conduct a detailed inspection, and poor communication during the design, construction and in the maintenance of the bridge.

Recommendation

The report recommended that increased efforts should be made to detect wear in old structures, and that there should be more spending on infrastructure maintenance and rebuilding.

---

1 What was the condition of the overpass shortly before it collapsed?

2 What mistakes did the designers of the De la Concorde overpass make?

3 What mistakes did the construction workers make?

4 What mistakes did the people in charge of maintaining the bridge make?

5 What did the investigating team recommend for constructing overpass bridges in the future?

(5 marks)

Writing

Read the information in the table. Complete the description below. Use expressions for making comparisons.

High speed trains: July 2010

	France	Japan	China
High-speed rail network	1,872 km of track	2,452 km of track	3,529 km of track
Tracks under construction	234 km	590 km	6,696 km
Average speed	272 km/h	Over 260 km/h	350 km/h

The table compares _____

_____

_____

_____

_____

_____

_____

(5 marks)

11 Materials

Contents

1 Equipment

Objectives

In this section students will ...

- complete and explain a chart about the properties of materials in sports equipment
- listen to a phone call and answer questions
- identify text type and answer questions about a letter
- listen to a website audio and complete a table
- study and practise using a range of verbs for expressing properties
- learn vocabulary for materials and their properties

2 Properties (1)

Objectives

In this section students will ...

- identify the properties different materials contain
- match adjectives and adjectival phrases with their meaning
- change nouns to adjectives
- study related verb, noun and adjectival phrases and write a chart using different language patterns
- read and complete a text about a material and its properties
- write a chart about materials and their properties; write a short description based on the chart

3 Properties (2)

Objectives

In this section students will ...

- discuss ideas for improving the performance of an Olympic team through training, clothing and equipment
- listen to a meeting and answer questions, then complete the minutes of the meeting and suggestions
- study and practise using ways of making suggestions
- study *able to/capable of -ing*, then rewrite sentences using these forms
- prepare a meeting about reducing the budget for equipment and training for the Olympic team, and write a memo reporting on the outcome
- learn vocabulary with *-proof* and *-resistant*

Briefing

This unit looks at materials and their properties, particularly in the field of sports technology.

Section 1 deals with materials commonly used in sports equipment, and their properties. **Fibres** (AmE **fibers**) are thin, elongated strands (or **filaments**) of material that can be **natural** like cotton, or **synthetic** (manufactured) like nylon. **Graphite fibre** (or **carbon fibre**) consists mainly of carbon atoms and can be combined with a **polymer resin** to form a **composite** (combined) material. A 'graphite' ski pole is actually made of a composite of graphite and polymer. The football boot described on page 84 has good **torsional stability**, which means that it resists a twisting force (**torsion**). It is partly made of **aramid fibre**, a synthetic fibre which has great strength and heat resistance. **Polyurethane** is a polymer that can be made into a soft foam for padding inside the boot and also a tough, elastic material for the sole of the boot. **Thermoplastics** can be re-melted into a new shape; **thermosets** are heat-resistant and cannot be melted after they have set hard the first time. **Impact resistant** materials **resist** the shock of impact (like the *outside* of a safety helmet), whereas **impact absorbent** materials **absorb** (take in) the shock (like the lining *inside* a safety helmet).

Section 2 deals with more ways of describing the properties of materials. **Compressive strength** is the power to **resist** a compressive (squeezing) force; **tensile strength** is the power to resist a tensile (stretching) force; **shear strength** is the ability to **withstand** (resist) two sideways forces in opposite directions, like the **shearing** (cutting) caused by the two blades of shears or scissors; and **torsional strength** is the strength to **tolerate** (withstand, resist) a twisting force. A **malleable** material can be hammered into a new shape, and a **ductile** material can be pulled without breaking until it forms a thinner shape, such as a wire. **Kevlar®** is the proprietary name of an aramid fibre patented by Dupont which has a number of properties that make it suitable as a **bullet-proof** or **stab-proof** vest (used by police and the military) as well as in many sports. A further property of Kevlar® is its resistance to **abrasion** (excessive **erosion** or wearing down caused by friction). Its other main properties include: high tensile strength at low weight; structural rigidity; low electrical conductivity; high chemical resistance; low thermal shrinkage; high toughness; excellent dimensional stability; high cut resistance; flame resistance and self-extinguishing ability.

Section 3 deals with the technology which is increasingly being introduced to help teams win in the Olympic Games. The products mentioned in the meeting in audio 39 on page 88 are based on the following technologies and products: (1) Speedo LZR Racer swimwear uses a woven elastane-nylon and polyurethane material designed to hold the body in a more hydrodynamic position, while expelling water and allowing for improved oxygen flow to the muscles. It also has ultrasonically welded seams to avoid drag. (2) In the Beijing Olympics, sailing teams used a Doppler LIDAR system, which scans the surface of the sea with laser beams and measures beam scatter to provide a real-time readout of wind speed and direction over a large area. This works even when there is little or no wind. (3) Technology borrowed from Formula One racing, aircraft design and the defence industry has been modified to help in training rowing and sailing teams. Miniature sensors are fitted to paddles and rowing blades to measure the force of each stroke. This is combined with data on the boat's speed from a GPS sensor. The combined data gives the coach an accurate picture of how each athlete is performing. (4) Nike Flywire sprinting shoes (used at Beijing) weigh 67 grams each, 40 per cent less than the previous year's model. Nike reduced the weight by stitching the shoe together with thin filaments like a spider's web, then covering it with see-through, super-lightweight fabric. (5) The Japanese shoe engineer for Asics became famous after the rain-soaked marathon of the 2004 Athens Games for his lightweight shoes with soles that grip the pavement in wet weather. His shoes for the Beijing marathon were angled forward slightly to improve motion and reduce fatigue.

Article about technology and the Olympic Games: Find the **Guardian** (London) newspaper website and search for 'Sporting technologies vie for Olympic gold in Beijing'.

Article about sailing technologies, e.g. use of Doppler LIDAR: Find the **e! Science News** website and search for 'New technology may help Olympic sailing'.

Information about the properties of plastics: Find the **American Chemistry** website and search for 'Plastics' and 'Learning Centre – Athletic excellence'.

Article: 'Top 10 new technologies that will change the Olympics forever': Find the **DVICE** website and search for the article.

Teacher's notes

1 Equipment

Start here

Warmer

Brainstorm sports with the class. Then ask students what equipment they need for each sport.

1 Focus students' attention on the photo and ask them to cover the table. Ask them to identify the sport (climbing). Elicit the equipment climbers use to help them get up and down a mountain (rope, helmet, climbing boots, gloves, crampons, ice axe, harness, devices for helping you control the descent on a rope, e.g. belay devices, rappel devices). Explain that a particular type of material is used in rope for mountain climbing. Elicit what material the rope is made of and why. Then focus students' attention on the table to check their answers and to read through the other example.

Put students into small groups and ask them to choose another sport. Tell them to make a list of the main equipment used for the sport they have chosen, with one person taking notes. Finally, ask them to write the notes into a chart, as in the example.

See the Briefing section at the beginning of the unit in the Teacher's Book for more examples of the materials (and their properties) that are used in some popular sports equipment.

2 Ask each group to write their chart on the board. Then they explain their chart to the class, telling them what materials were used and why they are used in the sport they have chosen. Go through the list of properties the students listed in the chart on the board with the class, and make sure that they understand what they mean.

Listening

3 ▶ 🎧 35

Tell students that they are going to listen to a phone call. Ask them to read the questions first. Play the recording for students to answer the questions. Then ask them to compare their answers with a partner before you check with the class.

> 1 Albert wants to follow up his presentation of football boots to Ramón's team the previous day.
> 2 Albert gave a presentation about his new boot design to Ramón's team.
> 3 Albert will get a formal proposal to Ramón by special delivery the next morning.

▶ 🎧 35

[RO = Ramón Ortega; AW = Albert Weston]
RO: Ramón Ortega.
AW: Hello, good morning, Ramón. This is Albert Weston. How are you?
RO: Ah yes, Albert. How are you doing? Thanks very much for coming along yesterday. The team were very impressed with your presentation.

AW: Oh good, I'm glad to hear it. It was good to meet the team.
RO: Yes, and they really liked the look of the new football boot that you've designed. We all think that maybe we'll buy your boots for the next season. But we'll have to look into it a little bit more, discuss the price and so on.
AW: Great. That's why I'm phoning, in fact. I was wondering what the next move is. Would you like me to send you a formal proposal?
RO: Yes, that would be excellent. In the proposal, just summarise the main points you made in your presentation yesterday. Give a bit of technical background about the properties of the materials used in the boot. And of course confirm your unit price, delivery dates and so on.
AW: OK, will do. I'll get the proposal to you by special delivery tomorrow morning.
RO: Very good. Thanks, Albert. We'll see you soon, I hope.
AW: Of course. I look forward to it. Bye now.
RO: Bye.

Reading

4 Ask students to read through the words and phrases in the box and tell you when and why they would write or use them (e.g. a letter of thanks, to thank someone for a present they have just received; an invitation, to invite someone to a wedding; an invoice, to ask someone for payment for work done; a presentation, to demonstrate how a new product works; a proposal, to make a suggestion about future work; an attachment, to send a document with an email; a covering letter, a letter with a CV explaining who you are and why you want a job, etc.; a personal letter – to give news about yourself, family and friends; an application, to apply for a job.)

Then ask students to read the letter. When they have finished, ask them to look at the words and phrases in the box and choose one which best describes the letter. Then ask students to explain briefly why the new design would help the team win the Cup final (it gives the players protection and stability because of the way the studs are moulded onto the bottom of the boot, allowing the players greater speed and also lightness and comfort because of the materials used).

proposal

5 Ask students to read through the questions first. Then tell them to answer the questions about the letter. Allow weaker students to compare answers in pairs before checking the answers as a class.

> 1 He gave a presentation and then phoned Ramón to follow it up.
> 2 He wants Ramón to make a firm order for football boots.
> 3 by referring to Beckham's and Rooney's foot injuries
> 4 'The boot gives the player torsional stability.'
> 5 No, because they are injection moulded as part of the bottom (sole).
> 6 The proposal will lapse and he will have to ask for a new price.

Listening

6 ▶ 🎧 **36**

Tell students that they are going to listen to an audio from a website about the DesignerSport football boot. Go through the descriptive words in the box first and make sure students understand them all. For example, ask them what the difference is between a material that is *impact resistant* (not damaged by being hit with force) and a material that is *impact absorbent* (it can absorb or reduce the effect of the shock or energy of hitting something).

Focus students' attention on the table and ask them to read the information. Tell them that they need to complete 1–8 in the third column with words from the box that describe the materials in the second column. Then play the recording for students to complete the table.

1 lightweight	5 soft	
2 flexible	6 impact absorbent	
3 strong in tension	7 tough	
4 impact resistant	8 elastic	

▶ 🎧 **36**

Thank you for clicking on the link to find out more about the materials we use in the revolutionary new DesignerSport football boot.

The upper or top part of the boot is made of a combination of two materials, carbon fibre and aramid fibre. Carbon fibre of course is a very light and flexible material, able to bend easily in all directions. And that's great for comfort and ease of movement. But the player also needs some protection against impact. I'm sure you'll remember the metatarsal injuries that David Beckham and Wayne Rooney suffered in their feet. So that's why we have added aramid fibre to the upper part of the shoe. Aramid fibre is strong in tension, which means that it doesn't stretch when another foot smashes into it. This makes the upper impact resistant. The player's foot is completely protected from injury from outside the boot.

Inside the boot we've put a generous amount of padding, made of polyurethane foam. This material is very soft but also highly impact absorbent, which means that if the boot strikes (or is struck by) something hard, the padding absorbs the blow and reduces its impact on the foot.

Finally, we have the sole plate on the bottom of the boot. This is made of thermoplastic polyurethane, or TPU, which is a tough plastic, which means that it can't be broken or split by pressure or impact of any kind. But it's also very elastic, which means that it can bend or twist out of shape and then return to its original shape immediately.

▶ 🎧 **37**

Play the recording for students to listen to the words in the box. Then play the recording again for students to repeat. Check their pronunciation of *fibre* and *polyurethane*.

▶ 🎧 **37**

carbon fibre

aramid fibre

polyurethane foam

thermoplastic polyurethane

TPU

impact absorbent

impact resistant

Extra activity

You could play the recording once more for students to underline the stressed syllables.

<u>car</u>bon fibre

<u>a</u>ramid <u>fi</u>bre

poly<u>u</u>rethane foam

thermo<u>plas</u>tic poly<u>u</u>rethane

impact ab<u>sor</u>bent

impact re<u>sis</u>tant

Language

Verb forms for expressing properties

Go through the Language box with the students. Tell them that they will find more information about describing properties in the Language summary on page 105.

7 Ask students to read through the sentences and then complete them with the correct form of the verbs in the box. Point out that they can use some of the verbs more than once. Allow students to compare answers before checking the answers as a class.

> 1 weigh, bent
> 2 stretched, breaking
> 3 reduces, transferring
> 4 break, stretched/bent, return

2 Properties (1)

Start here

Warmer

Play hangman to revise materials and properties from Section 1. Demonstrate the activity first. Think of a word to revise, e.g. *lightweight* and write gaps up on the board to represent each of the letters in the word (_ _ _ _ _ _ _ _ _ _ _). Ask students to guess a letter. If the letter is in the word, write that letter on the line in the appropriate place (e.g. _ _ _ _ _ _ E _ _ _ _). If the letter is not in the word, draw one line of the hangman picture, starting with the base of the frame. Then, for each subsequent incorrect letter, draw lines to represent the parts of the man's body until the students guess the word or the hangman picture is completed and they lose the game.

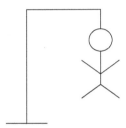

1 Tell students that in this section they will continue looking at materials and their properties for use in other technical fields. Focus students' attention on each of the photos. Tell students to focus on the diving board/springboard in photo 1, the rope in photo 2, the road in photo 3 and the red hot metal in photo 4. Then ask them to look at the words to describe properties in the box. Ask them to match each word with the correct photo.

> 1 flexibility
> 2 tensile strength
> 3 compressive strength
> 4 malleability
> Note: a bungee-jumping rope has to have some elasticity so that it can stretch a certain amount but its most important property is tensile strength so that it does not break or stretch too much.

▶ 💿 38

Play the recording for students to listen to the words in the box. Then play the recording again for students to repeat. Make sure that they are stressing the correct syllable. Ask the class to underline the stressed syllable in *re<u>sis</u>tance*, *ri<u>gid</u>ity* and *non-flamma<u>bil</u>ity*.

▶ 💿 38

malleability

tensile strength

flexibility

compressive strength

2 Ask students to work in pairs and discuss the properties that the items 1–4 must have.

> 1 non-flammability
> 2 rigidity
> 3 water resistance
> 4 heat resistance

Scanning

3 Go through the instructions with the students. Then ask them to turn to pages 116–117 and find the information for this unit. Remind them that they do not need to read every word in the text, just look for the information which answers the questions. Ask students to put up their hand when they have finished. Allow the majority of students to finish but check the answers with the first person to put up their hand to see if they were correct and are the winner.

> 1 three (carbon fibre, fibreglass, polycarbonate)
> 2 carbon fibre; fibreglass
> 3 five (carbon fibre, fibreglass, nylon, polycarbonate, polyester)
> 4 spandex; nylon

Vocabulary

4 Ask students to match the adjectives and adjectival phrases (1–6) with their meanings (a–f).

When checking answers, choose one student to call out a word from 1–6 for another student to give the answer.

> 1 e   2 f   3 b   4 a   5 c   6 d

5 Ask students to change the nouns into adjectives. Weaker students can do this in pairs.

> 1 malleable
> 2 non-flammable
> 3 tolerant
> 4 ductile
> 5 durable
> 6 absorbent

6 Ask stronger students to rewrite the sentences so that the meaning stays the same, then compare their answers in pairs. Weaker students can do the exercise in pairs.

> *Possible answers:*
> 1 Steel cable is very strong in tension.
> 2 Concrete is extremely strong in compression.
> 3 Nylon has excellent tensile strength.
> 4 This metal is very strong in torsion.
> 5 This steel has high compressive strength.
> 6 Kevlar is very strong in shear.

Language

Related verb, noun and adjectival phrases

Go through the examples in the Language box with the students on ways to describe properties of *resistance* and *tolerance*.

Tell students that they will find more information about describing properties in the Language summary on page 105.

7 Ask students to make a chart like the one in the Language box for sentences 1 and 2. Then ask them to check their answers in pairs before checking with the class.

This plastic tolerates heat extremely well.	verb
This plastic is highly heat tolerant.	adjectival phrase
This is an extremely heat-tolerant plastic.	hyphenated adjective
This plastic has very good tolerance to heat.	noun phrase
This plastic has excellent heat tolerance.	noun phrase

This plastic resists chemicals very well.	verb
This plastic is highly chemical resistant.	adjectival phrase
This is an extremely chemical-resistant plastic.	hyphenated adjective
This plastic has very good resistance to chemicals.	noun phrase
This plastic has excellent chemical resistance.	noun phrase

8 Ask students to complete the text with the correct option in brackets.

1	rigidity	**7**	resist
2	tolerance	**8**	lightweight
3	resistance	**9**	rigidity
4	durable	**10**	rigid
5	resistant	**11**	absorbs
6	stretch resistant	**12**	stability

Writing

9 Focus students' attention on the chart and read through the examples. Ask students what main materials are used in their technical field. Elicit reasons why these particular materials are used. Then explain that students should draw a chart similar to the one in the Course Book, with information on the main materials that they use in their technical field and their properties.

> **Extra activity**
>
> Ask students to underline the stressed syllable in the word pairs below to show how stress can shift in related words.
>
> 1 flexible   flexibility
> 2 ductile   ductility
> 3 rigid   rigidity
> 4 elastic   elasticity
> 5 plastic   plasticity
> 6 durable   durability
> 7 stable   stability
>
> Then ask them to say the words out loud. Make sure they pronounce *rigid* and *durable* correctly.

10 Ask students to write a short description based on their chart in 9.

> **Extra activity**
>
> As an additional speaking exercise, if there are computing facilities, you could ask the students to prepare a PowerPoint presentation based on their table, and then talk through the information on the screen to the rest of the class.

3 Properties (2)

Start here

1 Ask students to look at the photo of the Olympic cyclists. Put students in groups (if appropriate, in the countries that they come from). Tell students to imagine that they are managers and trainers of their country's Olympic team and ask them to discuss the two questions.

Listening

2 ▶ 🎧 39

Tell students that they are going to listen to the manager of an Olympic team discussing plans for a future Olympics. Ask students to read the two questions so that they know what to listen for. Then play the recording for students to answer the questions.

> **1** equipment and team training
> **2** (a) running (for 100/200/400 m and long-distance/ marathon) (b) swimming, rowing and sailing

▶ 🎧 39

A: OK guys, I've called this meeting to discuss our plans for our national team for the next-but-one Olympics. We need to make some decisions soon on two important issues – and I'm sure you know what I'm talking about. So let's start with the first issue: equipment. What about running shoes for the 100, 200 and 400 metres?

B: Well, I think we need a more lightweight model. Last year's model gives good impact resistance in the sole but it's not light enough compared with what other teams have.

C: Why don't we try the new Flite shoes? I've tried them out and they withstand impact extremely well. But they're also incredibly lightweight. They weigh 67 grams each, 40 percent less than last year's model.

A: OK, that sounds good, Jane. We'll look into that. Right, another equipment issue is the long-distance shoes for the marathon. Any ideas?

B: Yes, we need to find a shoe than can tolerate very wet roads and resist slipping. Last year's model doesn't have enough grip on wet surfaces.

D: Let's try using the newest Marathonites. They're made by the same Japanese company that designed shoes for the rain-soaked marathon of the Athens Games. They have good impact absorbency but the most important property is that they're totally slip resistant on wet surfaces.

A: Thanks for that suggestion, Anil. Can you look into these shoes a bit more and do me a report? Thanks. All right, I've just one more equipment issue before we move on. What about swimsuits for our swimmers? Are they aerodynamic enough?

E: You mean hydrodynamic, don't you?

A: Yes, that's right, they're racing through water, not air. So can we improve the hydrodynamic properties of our swimsuits?

B: We need to find a material that reduces drag in the water. Perhaps a material like a shark's skin?

C: Hmm, shark's skin. Can I make a suggestion? We could look at the new SpeedShark swimsuit. The manufacturers claim that it is 10 percent more hydrodynamic than other models.

A: Good, why don't we look into that? But we'll have to be careful here. The Olympic Committee may put a ban on new materials for swimsuits, so we'll keep an eye on that, OK?
Right, so let's move on to our second important issue of the meeting, namely training. Are there any suggestions for using new technology to improve team training?

B: I would suggest that we need to invest more in sensors that are able to tell us how well each athlete is performing.

D: How about starting with the rowing team? There are very good sensors now that you attach to the rowing blades. They're capable of sending accurate information in real time to the coach.

A: Can they measure the force that the rowers use in each stroke?

D: Yes, they have the capability of providing data on both force and speed.

A: Excellent. Any other suggestions? What about for our sailing team?

B: We need a device that's capable of reading wind speed and wind direction, and presenting the information clearly to the sailor.

E: In the Beijing Games they used a Doppler lidar system. It scans the sea with laser beams. It has the ability to provide a real-time readout of wind speed and direction.

A: Very good. Let's look into all these suggestions and make a full report.

3 Focus students' attention on the minutes of the meeting from the listening. Ask them to read the information, then listen again to complete the minutes with the properties of the equipment or material that is being considered. After you play the recording, students could compare their answers in pairs.

> **1** withstand impact
> **2** lightweight
> **3** impact absorbent
> **4** slip resistant
> **5** hydrodynamic
> **6** data about force and speed
> **7** a real-time readout of wind speed and direction

4 Ask students to try to complete the sentences used in the meeting from memory. Ask weaker students to check their answers in pairs. Then play the recording again for students to check their answers.

> **1** don't we
> **2** Let's
> **3** make; could
> **4** would; that
> **5** about
> **6** Let's

Language

Suggestion phrases

Go through the examples in the Language box with the students on the different ways of making suggestions. Tell students that they will find more information about ways of making suggestions in the Language summary on page 105.

Speaking

5 Put students in pairs or small groups. Ask them to brainstorm ways to improve their college, work place, a sporting team or an everyday device.

When the students have finished their brainstorming session, they could share their best suggestions with the rest of the class.

Language

able to/capable of -ing

Go through the examples in the Language box with the students. Explain that we can use all these ways to express the ability or inability to do something. Point out that we use -ing after the preposition of.

6 Ask students to read the sentences and then rewrite them to give the same meaning, using the language from the Language box. Tell them that they should use the words in brackets instead of the words in italics, but point out that they may have to change other parts of the sentence as well. Weaker students could do this exercise in pairs.

> **1** Kevlar is used in bulletproof vests because it is capable of resisting severe impact.
> **2** Polypropylene is used inside crash helmets because it has the capability of absorbing impact and softening a blow to the head.
> **3** Nylon is commonly used in waterproof jackets because it has the capacity to withstand water and to prevent it from passing through.
> **4** Wood is rarely used nowadays for making a boat hull because it is incapable of stopping rocks from cutting into the hull.

Vocabulary

7 Ask students to read through the definition of *fireproof/ fire-resistant* door. Then go through the words with *proof* and *resistant* in the table and explain the difference between the two words. Point out the use of the hyphen in the adjective for *fire-resistant* door. You could ask students to work in pairs or small groups to build up a list of similar words that are useful in their technical field. Then ask students to share some of the words in their word bank with the rest of the class in a feedback session.

Task

8 Put students in groups of four. Go through the instructions with the class. Ask the groups to decide who will be their chairperson (Student D). Then ask each student in each group to turn to a different page at the back of the Course Book and read their notes for the task. They then have the meeting and reach a decision on how to reduce the budget.

Writing

9 Explain to the students that they must write a memo as chairman of their Olympic team to the head of the national Olympic team, explaining the decisions their team has made. When they have finished, remind them to check their memo for grammar, spelling and punctuation mistakes. Groups could read out their memos to the class and have a vote on the best one.

12 | Opportunities

Contents

1 | Threats

Objectives

In this section students will …

- study graphs and discuss predictions
- listen to a message from the future to check present-day predictions about the environment
- make comparison between the situation in 2060 and now
- study and practise using the future perfect
- complete a SWOT analysis chart about a present-day company or industry; make notes of actions to be taken and tell the class about their predictions for the industry
- learn vocabulary for the environment

2 | Innovation

Objectives

In this section students will …

- study, discuss and make notes on a wind-powered land racer
- read a technical description about the wind-powered land racer, compare notes and answer questions about the text
- study and practise using a range of forms for expressing similarity and difference
- write a short explanation about how a vehicle works
- learn vocabulary for aerodynamics, marine and automotive engineering

3 | Priorities

Objectives

In this section students will …

- discuss electric car systems based on information in illustrations
- study information about different electric car systems and practise decision-making by choosing the best one for future large-scale use
- write a report of a meeting
- have a debate on the best technology for the future environment
- learn vocabulary for energy sources and electrical and automotive engineering

Briefing

This unit looks at threats to the environment and opportunities for innovative solutions.

Section 1 deals with predictions for the future of the environment up to the end of the twenty-first century. They are based on predictions of the Intergovernmental Panel on Climate Change (IPCC), a UN body, for (1) amount of CO_2 emitted, measured in **Gigatonnes** of carbon per year (**Gt C/Yr**), (2) **concentration** of CO_2 in the atmosphere, measured in parts of carbon per million parts of atmosphere (**ppm**), (3) sea level rise (metres), and (4) average global temperature change (°C). Each prediction is presented by the IPCC as four **scenarios** (possible chains of events), simplified here as the **best-case** (most optimistic) scenario and the **worst-case** (most pessimistic) one. The solid line on each graph gives the *actual* situation (as measured up to approximately the present day), and the broken line gives the *extrapolated* (expected, predicted) future trend. A **SWOT analysis** is a strategic planning method used to evaluate the **S**trengths, **W**eaknesses, **O**pportunities, and **T**hreats involved in a future project. The first two are *internal* factors, and the second two are *external* factors. To use the method, write S, W, O and T in four quarters of a square, and then brainstorm ideas for each one in turn.

Section 2 deals with the Ecotricity 'Greenbird' project, which aims to produce fast land vehicles powered only by the wind. Greenbird broke the land speed record for a wind-powered vehicle in 2009 at 202.9 km/h. The Greenbird uses the principle of **aerodynamic lift** (often called **the Bernoulli effect**) in two ways: to push the large, solid vertical 'sail' forward at high speed and to force the smaller horizontal 'wings' downwards to create stability. In this way, it combines racing car, sailing boat and aircraft in one high-performance vehicle. It also uses the phenomenon of apparent wind (a combination of true wind and man-made wind caused by the movement of the vehicle) to maximise acceleration and speed. The **apparent wind** speed is much faster than the true wind speed, allowing the Greenbird to travel at 3–5 times the true wind speed. Aerodynamic lift is (partly) the result of the wing's shape: the larger surface area of the upper wing makes the air move faster, which lowers the air pressure; the smaller surface area of the lower wing makes the air move more slowly, which increases the air pressure. The difference in pressure causes the wing to rise.

Section 3 deals with four methods for **recharging** (renewing the electrical charge of) an **electric vehicle (EV)**. **Non-contact recharging** allows a driver to re-charge an EV without a connecting cable, simply by parking it in a designated spot, much like charging an electric toothbrush or shaver. Electric power is supplied via **magnetic induction** from a **primary (power-supply) coil** in the surface of the parking space to a **secondary coil** on the vehicle. When the primary coil is electrically charged, it generates a magnetic field that **induces** current in the secondary coil, and so charges the batteries with no wired connection. **Battery exchange** uses a network of **charging points** around a city, where EV owners can exchange their flat batteries for fully-charged ones. The process is fully automated, and the driver does not even get out of the car. It takes between 3–5 minutes, less time than it takes to fill a petrol tank. The system is similar to changing a gas cylinder for an oven. A deposit is paid at the beginning for the first battery. This deposit can be returned if the car is sold and the battery returned. Then, every time the battery is changed, the driver only pays for the electricity. In the **hydrogen fuel cell**, hydrogen is pumped into the system at a **negative terminal**, and oxygen is pumped in at a **positive terminal**. A **catalyst** (substance that accelerates a chemical reaction) helps electrons to break free from the hydrogen atoms. There is a **membrane** (thin layer of material) that allows hydrogen ions through, but blocks the electrons. The electrons are channelled through a circuit to provide power for the vehicle. The electrons and hydrogen ions then combine with oxygen to form water, which is the waste product. The **solar panel** contains **photovoltaic (PV)** cells which produce electrical current when sunlight hits them. The current can travel to the batteries for storage and later use, go directly to the motor controller, or a combination of both. The current sent to the controller powers the vehicle.

Climate change predictions: Find the website of the **Intergovernmental Panel on Climate Change (IPCC)**.

The IPCC graphs on climate change can be found on the **GHG Online** website. Search for 'Predictions'.

Ecotricity Greenbird: Find the **Ecotricity** website and search for 'About Ecotricity – Greenbird project'.

Hydrogen fuel cells: Find the **BBC News** website and search for 'Honda makes first hydrogen cars'.

Solar cars: Find the **Solar Car TAFE SA** (South Australia) website and search for 'Solar cars'.

Non-contact charging: Find the **Nissan Global** commercial website and search for 'Non-contact charging'.

Battery exchange: Find the **Guardian** (London) newspaper website and search for 'UK charges up for electric car future' (15 April 2009) in 'Environment' section.

Teacher's notes

1 Threats

Warmer

Put students in small groups. Ask them to imagine that they have been transported to the year 2100. Ask them to think for a couple of minutes about the changes that have happened to the environment on Earth. Then ask them to discuss the changes in their groups. Finally, ask the groups to share their ideas with the class.

Start here

1 Focus students' attention on the photo and ask students what they think it represents (the environment). Then look at the four graphs with the class and elicit what they show (predicted changes to the environment from the year 2000 to 2100). Check that they understand *Gt* (*Gigatonnes*) and *ppm* (*parts per million*). Then ask them to discuss the questions about the graphs.

> **2** The green dotted lines show the best-case scenarios and the red dotted lines represent the worst-case scenarios.
>
> Fig 1: best-case: 6 Gt per year; worst case 29 Gt
>
> Fig 2: best-case: just over 500 ppm; worst-case c 900 ppm
>
> Fig 3: best-case: c 0.1 m; worst-case c 0.8 m
>
> Fig 4: best-case: just over 1°C; worst-case almost 6 °C
>
> **3** Students' own answers.

Listening

2 Tell students to imagine that they have received a radio message from people in the year 2060. Ask them if they think the message brings good or bad news and what they think the news might be about.

3 ▶ 🔊 40

Tell students that they are going to listen to the first part of the message from the future, in which the speaker talks about what has actually happened to the environment by the year 2060. As they listen, students should look at the information in the graphs in 1 and make a note of what the figures are for 2060 according to the speaker. Alternatively, you could ask them to correct the graphs themselves.

After you have checked their answers, ask students for their opinions about the new figures in the graphs: how likely do they think these scenarios are? And how would people in 2060 feel about people from the early 21st century?

> Figure 1: CO^2 emissions: 80 Gt per year
>
> Figure 2: CO^2 concentrations: 2,000 ppm
>
> Figure 3: sea level rise: 1.2 m
>
> Figure 4: world temperature rise: 8°C

▶ 🔊 40

[S1 = Scientist 1; S2 = Scientist 2; V = Voice Message]

S1: Hey, something's coming through. Someone's speaking. It's a V from the future. Someone's speaking to us from the year 2060. Can you believe that? Shhh. Let's listen.

V: … the world's temperature has risen by eight degrees Celsius since your time … fires have burnt down huge areas of forest … most of the world's forests have now been destroyed … the Arctic ice cap has completely disappeared … the glaciers on the world's mountains have melted and turned into rivers …

S2: What was that? Did you catch it? What did it say?

S1: Something about mountain glaciers. He says that they've all melted.

V: … sea levels around the world have risen by one point two metres since your time … many low-lying countries have been flooded … tropical cyclones have destroyed large parts of many of the world's major cities … water in many villages has dried up and their populations have died because of the drought … every year the emissions of carbon dioxide into the atmosphere have increased …

S2: Did you hear what he said just then?

S1: Yeah, he's talking about carbon dioxide now. Emissions have increased year by year.

V: … now emissions of carbon dioxide have risen to eighty gigatonnes per year … and the concentration of carbon dioxide in the atmosphere has also gone up every year since your time … now the concentration of carbon dioxide has risen to two thousand parts per million …

4 Go through the list of locations and the example about forests with the students. You could ask them to predict what else has happened to the other locations by the year 2060 before you play the recording. Then tell students to listen again and make a note of what has happened to these locations.

> Fires have burnt down huge areas of forest.
>
> The Arctic ice cap has completely disappeared.
>
> The glaciers on the world's mountains have melted and turned into rivers.
>
> Many low-lying countries have been flooded.
>
> Tropical cyclones have destroyed large parts of many of the world's major cities.
>
> Water in many villages has dried up and their populations have died because of the drought.

5 Go through the information and instructions with the students. Then put students in pairs. Ask them to read through the text about present-day society's mistakes first and think about what they have done wrong. Then ask them to fill in as many gaps as they can with their partner. Point out that they should not worry if they cannot fill in every gap. Do not check answers at this stage as students will be checking their answers with the recording in 6.

6 ▶ 🔊 41

Tell students that they are going to listen to the next part of the message to check their answers in 5. Explain that if they have any gaps that they could not fill in the text, they should listen out for the words and fill them in. Point out that there is radio interference on the recording and they will not be able to hear all the words, so they should not worry if they cannot hear them. After they have listened to the recording, they should try and guess them.

▶ 🎧 41

V: Your society should have reduced your … of oil and other fossil fuels. You should have invested more in renewable energy. Your governments shouldn't have encouraged cheap air flights; instead, they should have put higher taxes on air fuel to … the cost of air travel. Everyone should have … their own energy in their homes. They should have … wind turbines and solar panels on their houses. Why didn't your society and governments do these things? If you had …out these actions, the world's temperature probably would not have … by eight degrees Celsius. If your government had … better decisions, the sea level would probably not have … by one point two metres, and low-lying areas would have been … .

5 & 6
Other words are acceptable in exercise 6 (where the words cannot be heard) if they have a similar meaning.

1 reduced	11 didn't
2 use/consumption	12 carried
3 have	13 have
4 shouldn't	14 risen/gone up
5 should	15 had
6 have	16 taken/made
7 raise/increase	17 would
8 have	18 have
9 produced	19 risen/gone up
10 installed	20 flooded

7 Ask students to join another pair and discuss the answers to the text in 5 that they had to guess. Tell them that they should explain why they think their choice of words is correct. Alternatively, with weaker students, you could do this exercise as a class.

Speaking

8 Go through the instructions and example with the class and make sure that they understand what to do. Then have a class discussion.

Possible answers:
The actual increase in CO_2 emissions by 2060 will be more than 160% higher than the worst-case predictions today.
The increase in CO_2 concentrations will be more than twice (as high as) the worst-case predictions today.
The temperature rise will be eight times higher than the best-case predictions.
The sea level rise will be 50% higher than the worst-case predictions.

Listening

9 ▶ 🎧 42

Tell students that they are going to listen to a scientist from the present day talking about the message from the future. Ask them to read through the extract of the scientist's summary. Then play the recording for students to complete the summary.

▶ 🎧 42

[B = Boss S = Scientist]
B: You heard the message from the future, didn't you?
S: Yes, that's right.
B: So could you please summarise very briefly what will have happened by the year 2060, according to the message?
S: Certainly. By 2060, CO_2 emissions will have risen to 80 gigatonnes per year. CO_2 concentrations in the atmosphere will have increased to 2,000 ppm. The world's temperature will have gone up by 8 degrees from today's levels. As for the sea level …

1 will have risen
2 will have increased
3 will have gone

Language

Future perfect
Go through the explanation and examples in the Language box for the active and passive forms of the future perfect with the students. Tell students that they will find more information about the future perfect in the Language summary on page 102.

10 Ask students to complete the sentences about what will have happened by the year 2060. Tell them to use the future perfect and explain that they will need to use the passive form in one instance.

1 Fires will have burnt down huge areas of forest.
2 Most of the world's forests will have been destroyed.
3 The Arctic ice cap will have completely disappeared.
4 Mountain glaciers will have melted and turned into rivers.
5 Tropical cyclones will have destroyed large parts of many of the world's major cities.
6 Water in many villages will have dried up (and their populations will have died because of the drought).

Speaking

11 Put students in pairs. Go through the instructions with the class and make sure that students know what to do. See the Briefing section at the beginning of the unit in the Teacher's Book for more information on SWOT charts.

12 Ask students to refer to their SWOT charts in 11 and, in the same pairs, discuss the actions they think should be taken soon to avoid threats and to increase opportunities. Ask them to make notes of the decisions they make.

13 Go through the instructions and the example with the class. Then ask students to take it in turns to tell the class about their predictions for their chosen industry by 2025. Point out that they should state what will happen if the actions they noted in 12 have or have not been taken.

2 | Innovation

Start here

Warmer

Focus students' attention on the photo and ask them to cover the text. Ask them what type of vehicle this is, how it moves, how fast they think it can travel and if they would like to be in control of it.

1 Ask students to uncover the text and read the information about the vehicle in the photo. Then put students in groups. Ask them to discuss the question in their groups and make notes. Do not check the students' answers yet as the information is given in the reading text and students will check their answers in 3. You could pre-teach some vocabulary in the text by asking students to explain what *lift* (forces that push the plane upwards) and *drag* (forces that pull the plane backwards) mean.

You might like to know, for your own information, that the shape of the vertical wing (or sail) allows the apparent wind to propel it at high speed. The efficiency of the design and lightness of the materials reduce the drag or friction and the shape of the horizontal wings gives it stability.

See the Briefing section at the beginning of the unit in the Teacher's Book for more information about apparent wind and aerodynamic lift (the Bernoulli effect).

Reading

2 Focus students' attention on the illustration. Explain that it is a diagram of the Greenbird land racer in the photo in 1, as seen from above. Allow students to study the diagram for a couple of minutes. Ask them to explain what the difference between apparent wind and true wind is. (Apparent wind is the flow of air acting on the sail – it's the wind as it appears to sailors on a boat as they are in motion, whereas true wind is the wind as it appears to someone who is stationary.) Then ask them to read the article about the Greenbird and compare the information with the notes they made in 1. Again, do not check answers until 3.

3 Ask students to look back at the text in 2 and work individually to answer the questions. Allow students to compare answers before checking the answers as a class. Weaker students could discuss the questions in pairs.

> **1** a) similar to aircraft: shape of rigid sail; different: on land
> b) similar to racing car: on land, has horizontal wings for stability; different: no engine, has vertical sail
> c) similar to sailing boat: has a sail, different: sail is rigid and has skates
> **2** five times the speed of the wind
> **3** one tonne
> **4** drag, or friction
> **5** the horizontal ones
> **6** it would go much more slowly

Vocabulary

4 Write _very good_ sailboat on the board (underlining _very good_). Then elicit stronger adjectives which you can use to replace _very good_. Accept any answers (e.g. _amazing, incredible, fantastic,_ etc.). Then ask students to look back at the information about the Greenbird in 1 and find a strong adjective for _very good_ (_spectacular_) and underline it. Ask the students to find four other strong adjectives in the text in 2. Then ask them why they think the writer chose to use these adjectives in the text.

> staggering (= very good)
> exceptional (= very good)
> massive (= very great)
> tremendous (= very great)
> The writer uses them for impact and variety, and in order to impress and persuade the reader about how great the vehicle is.

Language

Forms for expressing similarity and difference

Go through the examples of ways of expressing similarity and difference in the Language box with the students. Tell students that they will find more information about expressing similarity and difference in the Language summary on page 106.

5 Go through the example with the students and ask them to describe objects 1–6 in a way which expresses their similarity to and difference from other objects. While they are doing the activity, go round the class checking students are using the language correctly. Go through any common errors with the class at the end of the activity.

Possible answers:
> **1** A surfboard is like a small boat but uses a flat board instead of a hull.
> **2** A hovercraft goes over the sea like a boat but it doesn't actually sit on the water. Instead, it floats (hovers) a short distance above it.
> **3** A seaplane is like an aeroplane but instead of wheels, it lands on a pair of floats.
> **4** A helicopter flies through the air like an aeroplane but it uses blades instead of wings.
> **5** A submarine can float on water like a ship but unlike a ship, it can also submerge below the surface.
> **6** A space shuttle is like an aeroplane but instead of flying only in the atmosphere, it can fly outside the atmosphere like a space rocket.

> **Extra activity**
> Ask students to think of something their company produced, which has been replaced by a new version of it, or a gadget that they have replaced, e.g. a new mobile phone, mp3 player, etc. Put students in pairs. Ask them to tell their partner how the new product or gadget is similar to/different from the old one.

Scanning

6 Go through the instructions with the students. Then ask them to turn to pages 116–117 and find the information for this unit. Remind them that they do not need to read every word in the text, just look for the information which completes points 1–3. Ask students to put up their hand when they have finished. Allow the majority of students to finish but check the answers with the first person to put up their hand to see if they were correct and are the winner.

> **1** 160
> **2** a V12 Ferrari
> **3** 240

Writing

7 Ask students to write a short explanation of how the Greenbird works, using the ideas from their group discussion in 1. Point out that they should not look at the text in 2.

When they have finished, remind them to check through their work, looking out for grammar, spelling and punctuation mistakes. They could then swap their work with a partner for them to read and check for mistakes. You could also tell them to give positive feedback on their partner's work and, if appropriate, make suggestions for improvement.

3 Priorities

Start here

1 Focus students' attention on the illustrations (Figures 1–4) in this section. Allow them to study the illustrations for a couple of minutes and answer any questions on vocabulary that they may have. Then ask them to discuss the two questions in pairs.

> Similarities: they are all methods for charging the batteries of an electric car.
>
> Differences: they all use different charging methods. The hydrogen fuel cell method charges the battery internally, whereas the other three use an external source of energy. Two of the three use an external electric current (non-contact and switch station), whereas the solar car uses sunlight. In the switch station method a newly-charged battery replaces the old one, whereas in the non-contact method the battery is charged in the car itself (using induction).

Task

2 Ask pairs of students to join two other pairs to form groups of six. Tell them that they are going to have a meeting to decide on the best electric car system for future large-scale use in their countries. Ask them to turn to page 113 and read the information about the four systems. Allow students time to take in the information and ask you any questions on vocabulary.

Then explain that each student in a group (Student A–Student F) should choose a different argument. When they have done this, explain that they have to prepare their arguments for their meeting according to their role and using the information on page 113. Tell them that they should decide on four options for their argument, and when they have done that, to rank their options in order of priority from 1 (best) to 4 (least good). Go round the class as they prepare for the meeting, giving help if needed.

> *Suggested rank order for the six factors for Students A to F (where '1' is the best option):*
>
> Student A: the cheapest system to buy: 1 battery exchange; 2 non-contact; 3 solar; 4 hydrogen fuel cell
>
> Student B: the cheapest system to run: 1 solar; 2 non-contact; 3 battery exchange; 4 hydrogen fuel cell
>
> Student C: the safest system: 1 non-contact; 2 battery exchange; 3 solar; 4 hydrogen fuel cell
>
> Student D: the simplest and most convenient system: 1 battery exchange; 2 non-contact; 3 hydrogen fuel cell; 4 solar
>
> Student E: the system that is quickest to refuel/recharge: 1 battery exchange; 2 hydrogen fuel cell; 3 non-contact; 4 solar
>
> Student F: the system that is least harmful to the environment: 1 solar; 2 non-contact; 3 battery exchange; 4 hydrogen fuel cell
>
> *Note that some would argue that the hydrogen fuel cell is harmless to the environment because of its zero emissions but others would argue that the means of production of hydrogen can be very polluting and energy-intensive.*

3 In their groups, students hold the meeting. Ask them to make notes of the meeting's agreed order of options and reasons for their decisions.

Writing

4 Tell students to work individually and write a report of the meeting using their notes. Before they start, go through the points they need to include in their report and make sure that they know what to do. Ask them to make a plan of their report first, writing the points they want to mention in each paragraph. Then they should write a draft of their report. While students are writing their draft, go round giving them help with vocabulary if required. Make sure that they are following the instructions, writing their report in the paragraphs stated.

When they have finished, remind them to check through their report, looking out for grammar, spelling and punctuation mistakes. They could then swap their work with a partner for them to read and check for mistakes. Students could also give positive feedback on their partner's work and, if appropriate, make suggestions for improvement.

Model answer:
Report of meeting
Introduction
Our group held a meeting on [actual date] to decide on the best electric car system for future large-scale use in [country]. The four systems were the solar-powered car, battery exchange, the hydrogen fuel cell and non-contact charging. This is the report of the meeting and the decisions that we made.

Technical description
First of all, here is a brief technical description of the four systems:

1 Solar-powered car
The sunlight hits the cells of the solar array, which produces an electrical current. The energy (current) can travel to the batteries for storage, go directly to the motor controller, or a combination of both. The energy sent to the controller is used to power the motor that turns the wheel and makes the car move. Generally, if the car is in motion, the converted sunlight is delivered directly to the motor controller but extra energy is stored in the batteries for later use. When the solar array can't produce enough energy to drive the motor at the desired speed, energy from the batteries powers the motor.

2 Battery exchange
1 The car enters the switch station (similar to a car wash) and the car and battery are identified. 2 A robotic arm removes the depleted battery. 3 The car moves forward. The depleted battery is put into the bay to be recharged. The robotic arm then inserts a fully charged battery. 4 A systems check makes sure that all systems are working correctly, and the driver drives away.

3 Hydrogen fuel cell
1 Hydrogen is constantly pumped in at the negative terminal. 2 Oxygen is pumped in at the opposite positive terminal. 3 The catalyst helps the electrons to break free from the hydrogen atoms. 4 The membrane allows the hydrogen ions through but blocks the electrons.
5 The electrons flow through the circuit to the positive terminal and drive the motor or charge the battery.
6 The electrons and hydrogen ions combine with oxygen, forming water. Water vapour is emitted as exhaust.

4 Non-contact charging
Electric power is supplied via magnetic induction from a primary power-supply coil in the parking surface to a secondary coil on the vehicle. When the primary coil is electrically charged, it generates a magnetic field that induces current in the secondary coil, and so charges the batteries with no wired connection.

Decisions of the meeting
After some discussion, our group decided that the order of priority of the four systems was as follows:
1 (best option) battery exchange; 2 non-contact; 3 solar; 4 (worst option) hydrogen fuel cell.

Reasons for decisions
The main reasons for this decision were as follows: battery exchange is the simplest system, the cheapest for the driver to buy and the quickest to use (since the battery is simply replaced), so drivers will like it. It is also a very safe system (although non-contact is slightly safer) and good for the environment (although solar and non-contact are slightly better). Non-contact is the second-best option, mainly because it is the safest system and is also very cheap and simple. Solar cars have many advantages and are the least harmful to the environment but they are expensive to buy and very complicated to use. Finally, the hydrogen fuel cell is the most expensive and least safe system. Driving a car with a hydrogen cell is good for the environment because it emits no carbon gases but our group thought that hydrogen production caused harmful emissions.

Speaking

5 Tell students that they are going to have a debate on *The best technology for the future environment*. Ask them to note down a list of technologies which may help us to avoid an ecological disaster in the future. Tell students that the list can include technologies which they have come across in the Course Book. Allow them plenty of time to make the list and then ask them to put the technologies in order of most helpful to least helpful, making notes of their reasons.

6 Students now take part in the debate, giving reasons for their opinions, using the notes they made in 5. Depending on the size of your class, you could conduct this either as a class discussion or put students in groups.

Give each speaker/group a time limit of three to four minutes to argue their case. You should act as chairperson of the debate, or choose a volunteer student. The chairperson should introduce the speakers, make sure that they stay within their time limit and control the question session. When each speaker has made their point and given reasons for their opinion, the chairperson opens the debate up for the other students to ask the speaker questions. When they have finished, the chairperson can then ask for a vote on the best technology for the future environment.

Answer key

2
1 This plastic does not melt when you heat it.
2 The frame of this mountain bike has great strength but does not weigh very much.
3 You can pull aramid fibre with great force, but it does not break or stretch.
4 This highly elastic polymer can be stretched a little when it is pulled, and then it is capable of returning to its original shape.
5 The soft plastic foam inside this helmet absorbs impact, and the polycarbonate external shell is able to resist impact.
6 The fibre used in this cloth can be heated to a high temperature, without burning or transferring the heat to the body.

3
1 The cables in a suspension bridge need to be very strong in tension.
2 The diving suit used by a scuba diver has to have total water resistance.
3 The concrete used in the bridge piers must have very good compressive strength.
4 The steel used in the axle of a racing car must be very strong in torsion and in shear.
5 We need to design a new running shoe that has much more flexibility and toughness than the old one.
6 Some of the materials used in earthquake-proof building need to have slight elasticity.
7 Gold has great malleability and ductility, and has high corrosion resistance.
8 The fire doors are made of a new material that is non-flammable and very heat resistant/thermally resistant.

4
1 inability	3 capacity	5 capable
2 incapable	4 unable	6 ability

6
Model answer:
Dear [Mr/Mrs/Ms] [name],
Thank you very much for inviting me to make a proposal to supply your firefighting unit with FireProtect's range of protective clothing for your firefighters.
At the presentation I gave at your fire station a few days ago, I demonstrated the clothing and explained how I think we can help to protect your firefighters against fire and other dangers when they are on duty. In our phone conversation soon after, you kindly invited me to send you a proposal.
As I explained at the presentation, our clothing is designed to give protection against flame, heat, water and chemicals, as well as giving lightness and comfort to the wearer.
Our protective clothing combines the thermal and moisture resistance of Nomex with the breathability of Gore-Tex and the comfort of viscose. The outer shell of the jacket and trousers is made of Nomex, a meta-aramid fibre, which is extremely resistant to heat, flames and chemicals. It can resist heat of temperatures above 350°, and it does not melt when it is exposed to flame. The material is strong, durable and resists abrasion very well. The middle layer of the clothing is made of Gore-Tex, which provides a moisture and thermal barrier. This material is a high-performance weatherproof fabric which is waterproof and windproof, and allows the body to breathe. Finally, the inner lining is made of a mixture of Nomex and viscose, which is smooth, soft and comfortable next to the body.
My company proposes to supply this protective equipment at the unit price (per set of jacket and trousers) of €359.00. Package and delivery is free of charge, and free delivery is within three weeks of placing the order. The offer is open for 28 days from the date of this letter.
I look forward to hearing from you with a firm order in due course.
Best wishes,
[signature]
[name]
Technical Sales Manager

8 *Possible answers:*
1 By 2060, I think all prisons will have closed down because biometric tracking and monitoring of all offenders will have been introduced, to replace the prisons.
2 I would imagine that, by 2060, the disease of malaria will have completely died out, because a deadly virus will have wiped out all the mosquitoes in the world.
3 Probably, by the year 2060, a United Nations task force of radio specialists will have succeeded in communicating with an extra-terrestrial broadcaster on a planet in another galaxy.
4 My prediction is that a system of giant floating mirrors will have been constructed in space, probably using the International Space Station as a construction site. The cities of the Arctic Circle will have been given extra hours of daylight by the mirrors.
5 I predict that, by 2060, the computer chip industry will have died out and that a new optical-based computer technology, based on laser beams, will have been invented and put into operation.

9 Please refer to the information in the Briefing section at the beginning of this unit for more information about the items described in this exercise.

Possible answers:

1 The new DMG lathe turns curved shapes just as the old one does, but instead of being operated by hand, it's operated by computer. Unlike the old design, this one has a complete safety shield around the whole machine, with large safety windows which give high visibility to the operation. Instead of hand controls, the operator uses control panels with password access, and 19-inch monitors, which can be rotated and swivelled. Another difference is that the new lathe has an optional seat for the operator.

2 This forklift truck does exactly the same as a traditional lift truck, but unlike the old design this one is actually comfortable for the driver. It has a huge operator compartment which is much larger than the cab in the old truck, and has much better visibility. It is more user-friendly than the old design, as the top of the compartment acts as a desktop, with a document clip and storage area for tools.

3 This outdoor lamp post has exactly the same function as a traditional street light, but the source of the light is at the base of the post, instead of at the top. The light is transmitted to the top of the post by means of fibre optics. Instead of a fixed beam of light, as in the old design, in the ZIPlux the angle and spread of light can be controlled. And instead of one single beam, one light source can illuminate different spots on the ground. Maintenance of the ZIPlux is carried out at ground level instead of at the top of the lamp using ladders. Finally, the ZIPlux can use solar energy, unlike many standard street lights.

Project

11 At the end of every Review Unit is a project. Students can do their research on the internet.

Quick test answer key

Part 1: Vocabulary and grammar

1   1 rigid   2 tension; resistant   3 elastic; absorbent

2
1 water resistant   3 tensile strength
2 compressive strength   4 childproof

3
1 absorbency   4 flexible   7 rigidity
2 ductile   5 malleability   8 tolerant
3 durability   6 non-flammable

4   1 flood   2 forest fire   3 drought   4 cyclone

5   1 staggering   2 exceptional   3 massive

6   1 d   2 a   3 b   4 c

7   1 break   2 be broken   3 break   4 breaking   5 breaks

8
1 incapable; resisting   3 the capability;
2 the ability; resist   withstanding

9
1 Let's try using these new ski boots.
2 How about testing the compressive strength of the material?
3 Why don't we encourage staff to cycle to work?

10
1 won't have melted
2 will have been burnt down/will have burnt down
3 will have met

11
1 This material is similar ~~as~~ to Kevlar, except that it costs more.
2 This car is unlike my old one. It uses hydrogen instead ~~from~~ of petrol.
3 The building is different from all the others. It resembles ~~like a~~ the sail of a boat.

Part 2: Reading and writing

Reading

1 True.
2 False. The speedometer is in the same place, but the rev counter has been replaced by a charge indicator and the fuel gauge has been replaced by a power gauge.
3 False. The suspension is tight because of the weight of the battery. This makes the Mini E less responsive than normal cars.
4 True.
5 False. The car is not for sale to the general public at the moment (it is not in production), as they are still doing research on the Mini E in the USA.

Writing

Model answer:
Spandex is a synthetic fibre with a polymer base. It is an excellent material to use in cycle shorts because it is very comfortable. This is because of its elasticity and flexibility, and also because it is incredibly lightweight, highly absorbent and abrasion resistant. Cycling shorts made of spandex are very durable because the material is stretch resistant, so it never loses its shape. The material also increases the performance of the cyclist because it is lightweight and wind resistant, which makes it extremely aerodynamic.

Review Unit F Quick test

Total _____/55

Part 1: Vocabulary and grammar

1 Complete the sentences with the words in the box.

> absorbent elastic resistant rigid tension

1 Carbon fibre is a _____, lightweight material. It is very strong when stretched or bent. It is ideal for racing boats.

2 Aramid fibre, also known as Kevlar, is used to make protective clothing as it's strong in _____ and impact _____.

3 Polyurethane foam is used in the car industry. It can be made into a soft, _____ material, which is also impact _____. It is therefore ideal for seats and headrests.

(5 marks)

2 Write synonyms for these words.

1 _____ = resistant to water

2 (good) _____ = strong in compression

3 (good) _____ = strong in tension

4 _____ = guaranteed that children cannot hurt themselves using it

(4 marks)

3 Complete the table.

Verb	Noun
absorbent	1 _____
2 _____	ductility
durable	3 _____
4 _____	flexibility
malleable	5 _____
6 _____	non-flammability
rigid	7 _____
8 _____	tolerance

(8 marks)

4 Match the instructions with the words in the box.

> cyclone drought flood forest fire

1 _____ Prevent water from getting into your property and move your possessions upstairs.

2 _____ Don't leave glass bottles on the ground after a picnic as these can act like a magnifying glass.

3 _____ Avoid wasting water, for example, by not washing your car or watering plants.

4 _____ You should clear your property of loose material which could injure people in the storm.

(4 marks)

5 Replace the words in italics with the strong adjectives in the box.

> exceptional massive staggering

1 The vehicle travelled at a *unbelievable* speed of 202.9 kph.

2 We should use this material as it has *very good* torsal strength.

3 The boat hit the bridge with such a *big* force that it caused a lot of damage.

(3 marks)

6 Match 1–4 with a–d to make sentences.

1	This material	a)	highly impact resistant.
2	This material is	b)	extremely heat-resistant material.
3	This material is an	c)	very good resistance to corrosion.
4	This material has	d)	resists abrasions very well.

(4 marks)

7 Complete these sentences using the correct form of the verb *break*.

1 You can _____ it.

2 It can _____ easily by someone.

3 It doesn't _____.

4 It can tolerate a blow without _____.

5 It _____ easily.

(5 marks)

8 Complete these sentences using the correct form of the words in brackets.

1 This material is no good. It's _____ of _____ impact. (incapable / resist)

2 Kevlar has _____ to _____ tears and abrasions. (able / resist)

3 We need to buy a new door which has _____ of _____ fire. (capable / withstand)

(3 marks)

F Quick test PHOTOCOPIABLE

9 Rewrite these sentences so the meaning is the same.

1 We could use these new ski boots.
Let's try _____.

2 I would suggest that you test the compressive strength of the material.
How about _____?

3 What about encouraging staff to cycle to work?
Why don't we _____?

(3 marks)

10 Complete these sentences using the active or passive form of the verbs in the box.

burn down   meet   not melt

1 Glaciers in the Himalayas _____ by 2050.

2 The forest fire is out of control. By this evening, the village _____.

3 It's unlikely that the government _____ its target for renewable energy by 2020.

(3 marks)

11 Find and correct the mistakes in these sentences.

1 This material is similar as Kevlar, except that it costs more.

2 This car is unlike my old one. It uses hydrogen instead from petrol.

3 The building is different from all the others. It resembles like a sail of a boat.

(3 marks)

Part 2: Reading and writing

Reading

Read the text and answer the questions true (T) or false (F). Correct the false sentences.

Mini E

The Mini E looks like the standard Mini Cooper and is just as much fun to drive, except that in the bonnet, instead of a petrol engine, you will find a 150 kilowatt motor. A lithium ion battery, weighing 259 kg, replaces the back seat, making the Mini E a heavy car to drive. There is a plug outlet to charge up the car, where you would normally insert fuel into the tank of a petrol-powered car. The car can be fully charged in 2–3 hours on a fast-charge system and can cover about 150–175 km on a single charge. Just as in the standard Mini, the Mini E has the speedometer in the centre of the dashboard. In front of the driver are the dials with a charge indicator replacing the rev counter and a power gauge instead of a fuel gauge. As the Mini E has only one gear, there is no clutch.

It can accelerate from 0–100 km/h in just 8 seconds. The steering is sharp and the suspension has been tightened, due to the weight of the battery, which makes the car less responsive than standard petrol cars. Another difference is that you don't often need to brake. The Mini E uses regenerative breaking to capture kinetic energy. Once you take your foot off the accelerator, the speed quickly decreases and this switches the motor into a generator to recover the energy to recharge the battery.

Performance trials are currently taking place on the car in the US. It is believed that once in production, and the cost of batteries comes down and there is more infrastructure for charging electric cars, then this car will become very popular with the general public.

1 The electric motor is situated in the front part of the Mini E.

2 The instrument panel inside the Mini E is very similar to a petrol-powered Mini.

3 When you turn the steering wheel, the Mini E reacts quickly.

4 You use the accelerator to slow down.

5 The main reason why you can't buy a Mini E at the moment is because the batteries are too expensive and there are few places to charge up the cars.

(5 marks)

Writing

Look at the table below. Write a short text to describe spandex used in cycle shorts. Talk about comfort, durability and performance.

Sport	Clothing	
cycling	shorts	
Material	**Type**	**Properties**
spandex	synthetic fibre with polymer base	elasticity, flexibility, stretch resistant, moisture absorbent, abrasion resistant wind resistant, lightweight

Spandex is _____
_____
_____
_____
_____
_____
_____
_____
_____

(5 marks)

Word list

Unit 1

activate (verb) **1.2 (p6)**
air-sea rescue (noun phrase) **1.1 (p4)**
allow (verb) **1.3 (p8)**
altitude (noun) **1.2 (p6)**
antenna (noun) **1.3 (p8)**
as a result (phrase) **1.3 (p9)**
automatically (adverb) **1.1 (p5)**
away (adverb) **1.3 (p8)**
base (noun) **1.3 (p8)**
beacon (noun) **1.1 (p4)**
breakable (adjective) **1.3 (p8)**
carry out (phrasal verb) **1.2 (p6)**
check (verb) **1.3 (p9)**
clear (adjective) **1.3 (p9)**
coastguard (noun) **1.1 (p5)**
convert (verb) **1.2 (p6)**
cover (noun) **1.3 (p8)**
crash (verb) **1.2 (p6)**
crew (noun) **1.1 (p5)**
detach (verb) **1.1 (p4)**
eject (verb) **1.3 (p8)**
emergency (adjective) **1.1 (p5)**
emergency (noun) **1.2 (p6)**
ensure (verb) **1.3 (p9)**
fire (a flare) (verb) **1.1 (p4)**
fit (verb) **1.1 (p5)**
flare (noun) **1.1 (p4)**
flat (adjective) **1.3 (p9)**
floating (adjective) **1.1 (p5)**
force (noun) **1.3 (p8)**
forward (verb) **1.1 (p5)**
free (verb) **1.3 (p8)**
free-floating (adjective) **1.1 (p5)**
frequency (noun) **1.2 (p7)**
happen (verb) **1.1 (p5)**
helicopter (noun) **1.1 (p4)**
increase (verb) **1.1 (p5)**
inflate (verb) **1.1 (p4)**
kilometre (noun) **1.1 (p5)**
lever arm (noun) **1.3 (p8)**
life jacket (noun) **1.1 (p4)**

life raft (noun) **1.1 (p4)**
light (noun) **1.3 (p8)**
link (verb) **1.1 (p5)**
locate (verb) **1.1 (p5)**
magnet (noun) **1.3 (p8)**
megahertz (noun) **1.1 (p5)**
membrane (noun) **1.3 (p8)**
method (noun) **1.1 (p5)**
move out of range (phrase) **1.3 (p8)**
out of range of (phrase) **1.3 (p8)**
pick up (a signal) (phrasal verb) **1.2 (p6)**
place (verb) **1.3 (p9)**
pressure (noun) **1.3 (p8)**
prevent (verb) **1.3 (p8)**
process (verb) **1.2 (p6)**
pull (verb) **1.3 (p9)**
push (verb) **1.3 (p9)**
R-clip (noun) **1.3 (p9)**
radio (noun) **1.1 (p4)**
reach (verb) **1.3 (p9)**
receive (verb) **1.1 (p5)**
release (verb) **1.3 (p8)**
remove (verb) **1.3 (p9)**
rescue (verb) **1.1 (p4)**
rescuer (noun) **1.1 (p4)**
rod (noun) **1.3 (p8)**
safety device (noun) **1.1 (p4)**
sailor (noun) **1.1 (p4)**
satellite (noun) **1.1 (p4)**
save (a life) (verb) **1.1 (p5)**
send (a signal) (verb) **1.1 (p4)**
signal (noun) **1.1 (p4)**
sink (verb: sink–sank–sunk) **1.1 (p4)**
slide (verb) **1.3 (p9)**
spring (noun) **1.3 (p8)**
strike (verb: hit; strike–struck–struck) **1.1 (p4)**
submerge (verb) **1.3 (p8)**
surface (noun) **1.1 (p5)**
survivor (noun) **1.1 (p4)**
switch on (phrasal verb) **1.1 (p5)**
take place (phrase) **1.1 (p5)**

tear off (phrasal verb) **1.3 (p9)**
touch (verb) **1.3 (p9)**
transmit (verb) **1.1 (p5)**
view (noun) **1.3 (p9)**
visible (adjective) **1.1 (p5)**
water pressure (noun) **1.3 (p8)**
wavelength (noun) **1.1 (p5)**
winch (noun) **1.1 (p4)**

Unit 2

adjust (verb) **2.2 (p13)**

aerospace engineering (noun) **2.1 (p11)**

air hose (noun) **2.3 (p14)**

angle (noun) **2.3 (p15)**

blowing (noun) **2.3 (p14)**

carbon fibre (noun) **2.1 (p11)**

cavity (noun) **2.2 (p12)**

chamber (noun) **2.3 (p15)**

closure (noun) **2.3 (p14)**

component (noun) **2.3 (p15)**

composite (noun) **2.1 (p11)**

compress (verb) **2.2 (p13)**

cool (verb) **2.2 (p13)**

correct (adjective) **2.2 (p13)**

cylinder (noun) **2.2 (p12)**

design (verb) **2.1 (p10)**

die (noun) **2.3 (p14)**

direction (noun) **2.2 (13)**

eject (verb) **2.2 (p12)**

engine (noun) **2.1 (p11)**

expansion (noun) **2.3 (p14)**

expect (verb) **2.1 (p10)**

extruder (noun) **2.3 (p14)**

extrusion (noun) **2.3 (p14)**

feed (verb: feed–fed–fed) **2.2 (p12)**

fibreglass **2.1 (p10)**

fill (verb) **2.3 (p15)**

flow (verb) **2.2 (p13)**

force (verb) **2.2 (p13)**

form (noun) **2.2 (p13)**

fuselage (noun) **2.1 (p11)**

heater (noun) **2.2 (p12)**

hopper (noun) **2.2 (p12)**

illustrate (verb) **2.3 (p15)**

inject (verb) **2.2 (p12)**

injection moulding (noun) **2.2 (p12)**

ladle (noun) **2.3 (p15)**

melting (noun) **2.3 (p14)**

manufacture (verb) **2.1 (p10)**

metal (noun) **2.2 (p13)**

molten (adjective) **2.3 (p14)**

motor (noun) **2.2 (p12)**

mould (noun) **2.2 (p12)**

movement (noun) **2.3 (p15)**

nozzle (noun) **2.2 (p12)**

oar (noun) **2.1 (p10)**

opposite (adjective) **2.2 (p13)**

packaging (noun) **2.1 (p10)**

parison (noun) **2.3 (p14)**

pellet (noun) **2.2 (p12)**

piston (noun) **2.3 (p15)**

plan (verb) **2.1 (p10)**

plastic (adjective) **2.1 (p10)**

plate (noun) **2.2 (p13)**

polycarbonate (noun) **2.1 (p117)**

polyester (noun) **2.1 (p117)**

process (noun) **2.2 (p12)**

produce (verb) **2.1 (p11)**

propel (verb) **2.2 (p13)**

protective goggles (noun) **2.1 (p10)**

raise (verb) **2.2 (p13)**

ram (noun) **2.2 (p12)**

roller (noun) **2.2 (p13)**

rotate (verb) **2.2 (p13)**

rotating (adjective) **2.2 (p12)**

rowing boat (noun) **2.1 (p10)**

screw (noun) **2.2 (p12)**

shape (noun) **2.2 (p12)**

sheet (metal) (noun) **2.2 (p13)**

show (verb) **2.3 (p15)**

soft (adjective) **2.2 (p12)**

solid (adjective) **2.2 (p12)**

store (verb) **2.2 (p13)**

thin (adjective) **2.2 (p13)**

throw out (phrase) **2.2 (p12)**

transfer (verb) **2.2 (p13)**

volleyball net (noun) **2.1 (p10)**

warm (adjective) **2.2 (p12)**

wing (noun) **2.1 (p11)**

Unit 3

abort engine (noun) **3.2 (p22)**

action (noun) **3.2 (p23)**

aircraft (noun) **3.1 (p21)**

ascend (verb) **3.2 (p23)**

astronaut (noun) **3.1 (p20)**

attach (verb) **3.2 (p23)**

attitude-control engine (noun) **3.2 (p22)**

backpack (noun) **3.3 (p111)**

body (noun) **3.3 (p24)**

build (verb) **3.1 (p21)**

burn (verb) **3.2 (p22)**

burn down (phrasal verb) **3.1 (p20)**

canopy (noun) **3.3 (p24)**

capsule (noun) **3.2 (p20)**

catapult gun (noun) **3.3 (p24)**

catch fire (verb/phrase) **3.1 (p20)**

clear (of sth) (verb) **3.3 (p111)**

cockpit (noun) **3.3 (p24)**

collapse (verb) **3.1 (p20)**

collide (verb) **3.1 (p20)**

crew (noun) **3.2 (p22)**

deploy (verb) **3.3 (p24)**

descend (verb) **3.3 (p24)**

detach (verb) **3.1 (p20)**

detect (verb) **3.2 (p23)**

detonate (verb) **3.2 (p23)**

develop (verb) **3.1 (p21)**

direction (noun) **3.2 (p22)**

disable (verb) **3.2 (p23)**

drogue (noun) **3.3 (p24)**

eject (verb) **3.1 (p21)**

ejection seat (noun) **3.1 (p21)**

ejection system (noun) **3.1 (p21)**

equip (verb) **3.3 (p25)**

escape (verb) **3.1 (p20)**

exhaust (noun) **3.2 (p22)**

experience (verb) **3.2 (p22)**

explode **3.3 (p115)**

explosive bolt (noun) **3.2 (p22)**

fail (verb) **3.1 (p20)**

fault (noun) **3.2 (p23)**

fire (an engine) (verb) **3.2 (p23)**

float down (verb) **3.2 (p23)**

fly (verb: fly-flew-flown) **3.1 (p20)**

focus (verb) **3.1 (p21)**

guide (verb) **3.2 (p23)**

guide rail (noun) **3.3 (p24)**

handle (noun) **3.3 (p24)**

iceberg (noun) **3.1 (p20)**

jettison engine (noun) **3.2 (p22)**

laboratory (noun) **3.1 (p21)**

land (verb) **3.1 (p20)**

launch (verb) **3.1 (p20)**

launch abort system (LAS) (noun) **3.1 (p20)**

length (noun) **3.2 (p22)**

lower (verb) **3.2 (p23)**

main (adjective) **3.3 (p24)**

maximum (adjective) **3.2 (p22)**

obstruction (noun) **3.3 (p25)**

ocean (noun) **3.1 (p20)**

oil rig (noun) **3.1 (p20)**

once (conjunction) **3.2 (p23)**

orient (verb) **3.2 (p22)**

parachute (noun) **3.1 (p21)**

pilot (noun) **3.1 (p21)**

protective cover (noun) **3.2 (p22)**

radar (noun) **3.3 (p25)**

restraint (noun) **3.3 (p24)**

rig (noun) **3.2 (p22)**

rise (verb) **3.3 (p25)**

rocket (noun) **3.1 (p20)**

roller (noun) **3.3 (p24)**

run into (phrasal verb) **3.1 (p20)**

seat (noun) **3.3 (p24)**

sensor (noun) **3.3 (p25)**

separate (verb) **3.2 (p23)**

spacecraft (noun) **3.1 (p21)**

spin around (verb phrase) **3.2 (p23)**

stabilise (verb) **3.2 (p22)**

steady (adjective) **3.3 (p24)**

throw out (phrasal verb) **3.3 (p24)**

thrust away (verb phrase) **3.2 (p23)**

tip (noun) **3.2 (p23)**

touch down (phrasal verb) **3.1 (p20)**

work (function) (verb) **3.2 (p23)**

Unit 4

accuracy (noun) **4.2 (p28)**

advertisement (noun) **4.1 (p27)**

allow (verb) **4.2 (p28)**

apprentice (noun) **4.1 (p26)**

approximately (adverb) **4.2 (p29)**

backwards (adverb) **4.2 (p29)**

barrel (noun) **4.2 (p28)**

benefit (noun) **4.3 (p30)**

blog (noun) **4.1 (p26)**

brain cell (noun) **4.2 (p28)**

brass (noun) **4.2 (p28)**

breakthrough (noun) **4.2 (p28)**

business (noun) **4.1 (p27)**

career (noun) **4.1 (p27)**

certificate (noun) **4.3 (p31)**

client (noun) **4.1 (p27)**

competence (noun) **4.1 (p27)**

cone-shaped (adjective) **4.2 (p28)**

conical (adjective) **4.2 (p28)**

current (adjective) **4.1 (p26)**

curriculum vitae (CV) (noun) **4.1 (p27)**

design (verb) **4.1 (p26)**

degree (noun) **4.1 (p26)**

diameter (noun) **4.2 (p28)**

difference (noun) **4.2 (p28)**

diploma (noun) **4.3 (p30)**

employee (noun) **4.3 (p30)**

employer (noun) **4.1 (p26)**

exact (adjective) **4.2 (p29)**

experience (noun) **4.1 (p27)**

external (adjective) **4.2 (p28)**

extract (verb) **4.2 (p29)**

gene gun (noun) **4.2 (p28)**

genetic (adjective) **4.2 (p28)**

hairdryer (noun) **4.2 (p28)**

hand held (adjective) **4.2 (p28)**

hole (noun) **4.2 (p28)**

honest (adjective) **4.3 (p30)**

human (noun) **4.1 (26)**

inaccurate (adjective) **4.2 (p28)**

increase (verb) **4.2 (p29)**

insert (verb) **4.2 (p28)**

institution (noun) **4.1 (p27)**

job title (noun) **4.1 (p26)**

knowledge (noun) **4.3 (p30)**

laboratory technician (noun) **4.2 (p28)**

major (adjective) **4.2 (p28)**

Masters degree (noun) **4.1 (p26)**

maximum (adjective) **4.2 (p29)**

mechatronics (noun) **4.1 (p27)**

membrane (noun) **4.2 (28)**

minimum (adjective) **4.2 (p28)**

modified (adjective) **4.2 (p28)**

negatively (adverb) **4.3 (p30)**

optimum (adjective) **4.2 (p28)**

organisational (adjective) **4.1 (p27)**

originally (adverb) **4.2 (p28)**

packing line (noun) **4.1 (p26)**

part-time (adjective) **4.3 (p30)**

pharmaceutical (adjective) **4.1 (p27)**

pilot (verb: test) **4.1 (p26)**

position (noun: job) **4.1 (p27)**

positive (adjective) **4.3 (p30)**

post (noun: job title) **4.3 (p30)**

prevent (verb) **4.2 (p28)**

profile (noun) **4.1 (p26)**

project (noun) **4.1 (p27)**

prototype (noun) **4.2 (p28)**

pulse (noun) **4.2 (p28)**

qualification (noun) **4.1 (p27)**

recoil (noun) **4.2 (p28)**

reduce (verb) **4.2 (p28)**

responsibility (noun) **4.1 (p27)**

robot (noun) **4.1 (p26)**

robotics (noun) **4.1 (p26)**

role (noun) **4.1 (p27)**

roughly (adverb) **4.2 (p28)**

salary (noun) **4.3 (p30)**

similarity (noun) **4.2 (p29)**

skill (noun) **4.3 (p30)**

social (adjective) **4.1 (p27)**

spacer (noun) **4.2 (p28)**

spread (verb) **4.2 (p28)**

stainless steel (noun) **4.2 (p28)**

standard (adjective) **4.2 (p28)**

straight (adjective) **4.2 (p28)**

target (noun) **4.2 (p28)**

technician (noun) **4.1 (p27)**

test (verb) **4.1 (p26)**

tissue damage (noun) **4.2 (p28)**

training (noun) **4.1 (p27)**

welcome package (phrase) **4.1 (p27)**

Word list

Unit 5

action (noun) **5.1 (p36)**
add (verb) **5.2 (p39)**
adjust (verb) **5.2 (p39)**
alternatively (adverb) **5.1 (p37)**
altitude (noun) **5.3 (p40)**
anyway (adverb) **5.1 (p37)**
audible (adjective) **5.1 (p36)**
brake (verb) **5.1 (p36)**
brake line (noun) **5.2 (p38)**
brake pad (noun) **5.2 (p38)**
brake pedal (noun) **5.2 (p38)**
breathing equipment (noun) **5.2 (p38)**
by the way (phrase) **5.1 (p37)**
calliper (noun) **5.2 (p38)**
check (verb) **5.1 (p36)**
clean (verb) **5.2 (p38)**
condition (noun) **5.2 (p39)**
continuously (adverb) **5.1 (p36)**
corrective (adjective) **5.1 (p36)**
counter-steer (verb) **5.1 (p36)**
depart (verb) **5.1 (p36)**
detect (verb) **5.1 (p36)**
disc (noun) **5.2 (p38)**
drain (verb) **5.2 (p39)**
drift (verb) **5.1, (p36)**
east (noun) **5.3 (p40)**
empty out (phrase) **5.2 (p39)**
examine (verb) **5.2 (p39)**
exchange (verb) **5.2 (p39)**
extinguish (verb) **5.2 (p38)**
fill up (phrasal verb) **5.2 (p39)**
flashing (adjective) **5.1 (p37)**
fluid (noun) **5.2 (p38)**
for instance (phrase) **5.1 (p36)**
frequently (adverb) **5.2 (p39)**
good working order (phrase) **5.2 (p39)**
hard hat (noun) **5.2 (p38)**
have a point (phrase) **5.1 (p37)**
head (verb) **5.3 (p40)**
helmet (noun) **5.2 (p38)**
hydraulic fluid (noun) **5.2 (p38)**
in lane (phrase) **5.1 (p36)**
in other words (phrase) **5.1 (p37)**
indicator (noun) **5.1 (p36)**
inspect (verb) **5.2 (p39)**
instruction (noun) **5.2 (p38)**
(un)intentionally (adverb) **5.1 (p36)**

intervene (verb) **5.1 (p36)**
lane (noun) **5.1 (p36)**
Lane Keeping Assist (noun) **5.1 (p36)**
level (noun) **5.2 (p39)**
maintain (verb) **5.1 (p36)**
mandatory (adjective) **5.2 (p38)**
master cylinder (noun) **5.2 (p38)**
material (noun) **5.2 (p38)**
mechanic (noun) **5.2 (p38)**
mend (verb) **5.2 (p39)**
modify (verb) **5.2 (p39)**
monitor (verb) **5.1 (p36)**
motion (noun) **5.1 (p36)**
oil (verb) **5.2 (p38)**
on purpose (phrase) **5.1 (p36)**
opposite (adjective) **5.1 (p36)**
out of lane (phrase) **5.1 (p36)**
piston (noun) **5.2 (p38)**
prohibited (adjective) **5.2 (p38)**
refill (verb) **5.2 (p39)**
regain (verb) **5.1 (p36)**
remain (verb) **5.1 (p36)**
repair (verb) **5.2 (p39)**
replace (verb) **5.2 (p39)**
return (verb) **5.1 (p36)**
rule (noun) **5.3 (p40)**
safety (noun) **5.1 (p36)**
safety harness (noun) **5.2 (p38)**
site (noun) **5.2 (p38)**
spongy (adjective) **5.2 (p38)**
stay (verb) **5.1 (p36)**
steer (verb) **5.1 (p36)**
steering wheel (noun) **5.1 (p36)**
switch off (phrasal verb) **5.2 (p38)**
tactile (adjective) **5.1 (p36)**
thickness (noun) **5.2 (p39)**
top up (verb phrase) **5.2 (p39)**
torque (noun) **5.1 (p36)**
twisting (adjective) **5.1 (p36)**
tyre (noun) **5.3 (p41)**
vehicle (noun) **5.1 (p36)**
vibrate (verb) **5.1 (p36)**
visible (adjective) **5.1 (p36)**
warning (noun) **5.1 (p36)**
wear (verb) **5.2 (p38)**
west (noun) **5.3 (p40)**

Unit 6

(un)able (adjective) **6.1 (p43)**

absolutely (adverb) **6.1 (p43)**

addition (noun) **6.2 (p44)**

aim (noun) **6.3 (p47)**

as a result of (phrase) **6.2 (p45)**

at the latest (phrase) **6.1 (p43)**

attraction (noun) **6.2 (p44)**

bring down (phrasal verb) **6.1 (p42)**

calcium carbonate (noun) **6.2 (p44)**

calcium sulphate (noun) **6.2 (44)**

carbon capture (noun) **6.2 (p44)**

carbon dioxide (noun) **6.1 (p42)**

(non-)carbon-based (adjective) **6.1 (p42)**

caused by (phrase) **6.2 (p45)**

(electric) charge (noun) **6.2 (p44)**

chemical reaction (noun) **6.2 (p44)**

coal (noun) **6.2 (p44)**

condense (verb) **6.3 (p46)**

consume (verb) **6.1 (p43)**

consumption (noun) **6.1 (p42)**

cooling water (noun) **6.2 (p44)**

deadline (noun) **6.1 (p42)**

desulphurisation (noun) **6.2 (p44)**

due to (phrase) **6.2 (p44)**

electrode (noun) **6.2 (p44)**

emission (noun) **6.1 (p42)**

emit (verb) **6.2 (p45)**

extraction well (noun) **6.3 (p46)**

finalise (verb) **6.1 (p43)**

fissure (noun) **6.3 (p46)**

flue gas (noun) **6.2 (p44)**

gasification (noun) **6.2 (p45)**

generator (noun) **6.3 (p46)**

go along with sth (phrase) **6.1 (p43)**

greenhouse gas (noun) **6.1 (p42)**

gypsum (noun) **6.2 (p44)**

hand over (phrasal verb) **6.3 (p47)**

humidify (verb) **6.2 (p45)**

in complete agreement (phrase) **6.1 (p43)**

injection well (noun) **6.3 (p46)**

insertion (noun) **6.2 (p44)**

ionisation (noun) **6.2 (p45)**

ionise (verb) **6.2 (p45)**

let's look at (phrase) **6.3 (p47)**

lime wash (noun) **6.2 (p44)**

liquefy (verb) **6.2 (p45)**

methane (noun) **6.1 (p42)**

move on (phrasal verb) **6.3 (p47)**

negative (adjective) **6.2 (p44)**

nitrous oxide (noun) **6.1 (p42)**

no later than (phrase) **6.1 (p43)**

oil (noun) **6.2 (p44)**

oil well (noun) **6.2 (p44)**

owing to (phrase) **6.2 (p45)**

ozone (noun) **6.1 (p42)**

particle (noun) **6.2 (p44)**

positively (adverb) **6.2 (p44)**

power station (noun) **6.2 (p44)**

presence (noun) **6.2 (p44)**

pressure (noun) **6.2 (p44)**

pulverise (verb) **6.2 (p45)**

purification (noun) **6.2 (p44)**

raw (adjective) **6.2 (p44)**

reaction (noun) **6.2 (p44)**

recovery (noun) **6.2 (p44)**

removal (noun) **6.2 (p44)**

(non-)renewable (adjective) **6.1 (p42)**

reservoir (noun) **6.3 (p46)**

rise (noun) **6.2 (p44)**

rock layer (noun) **6.3 (p46)**

rotation (noun) **6.2 (p44)**

saline aquifer (noun) **6.2 (p44)**

set a deadline (phrase) **6.1 (p43)**

solidify (verb) **6.2 (p45)**

steam (noun) **6.3 (p46)**

storage (noun) **6.1 (p42)**

store (verb) **6.2 (p44)**

sulphurise (verb) **6.2 (p45)**

(not) sure about (phrase) **6.1 (p43)**

Unit 7

alarm (noun) **7.1 (p52)**
amplify (verb) **7.2 (p54)**
assure (verb) **7.1 (p53)**
baggage X-ray machine (noun) **7.1 (p52)**
basically (adverb) **7.3 (p57)**
battery (noun) **7.3 (p56)**
beep (verb) **7.1 (p52)**
burst (noun) **7.2 (p54)**
capacitance (noun) **7.3 (p56)**
capacitor (noun) **7.3 (p56)**
CCTV camera (noun) **7.1 (p52)**
cell (noun) **7.3 (p57)**
checkpoint (noun) **7.1 (p52)**
circular (adjective) **7.2 (p55)**
coil (noun) **7.2 (p54)**
concourse (noun) **7.1 (p52)**
conductor (noun) **7.3 (p56)**
confirm (verb) **7.1 (p53)**
create (verb) **7.2 (p54)**
detector (noun) **7.1 (p52)**
dielectric (noun) **7.3 (p56)**
die out (phrasal verb) **7.2 (p54)**
earth (noun) **7.3 (p56)**
electric current (noun) **7.2 (p54)**
evidence (noun) **7.3 (p56)**
expected (adjective) **7.2 (p54)**
explain (verb) **7.1 (p52)**
finger (noun) **7.3 (p56)**
fingerprint scanner (noun) **7.3 (p56)**
flow (verb) **7.2 (p55)**
gantry (noun) **7.1 (p53)**
generate (verb) **7.2 (p54)**
hand-held (adjective) **7.1 (p52)**
harmless (adjective) **7.2 (p54)**
height (noun) **7.2 (p54)**
horizontal (adjective) **7.2 (p54)**
ignore (verb) **7.1 (p52)**
incident (noun) **7.1 (p52)**
increased (adjective) **7.3 (p56)**
inform (verb) **7.1 (p52)**
innocent (adjective) **7.1 (p53)**
inspector (noun) **7.1 (p52)**
instruct (verb) **7.1 (p52)**
interfere (verb) **7.2 (p54)**
inverter amplifier (noun) **7.3 (p56)**
iris (noun) **7.3 (p56)**
jaw (noun) **7.1 (p52)**
magnetic field (noun) **7.2 (p54)**

manage (verb) **7.1 (p52)**
manual (adjective) **7.1 (p52)**
metal detector (noun) **7.1 (p52)**
metal plate (noun) **7.1 (p52)**
microchip (noun) **7.3 (p57)**
non-conductive (adjective) **7.3 (p57)**
official (noun) **7.1 (p52)**
optical (adjective) **7.3 (p56)**
order (verb) **7.1 (p52)**
passenger (noun) **7.1 (p52)**
password (noun) **7.3 (p56)**
pin number (noun) **7.3 (p56)**
pitch (noun) **7.2 (p54)**
procedure (noun) **7.1 (p52)**
produce (verb) **7.2 (p54)**
promise (verb) **7.1 (p53)**
pulse (noun) **7.2 (p54)**
pulse-induction technology (noun) **7.2 (p54)**
raise (verb) **7.1 (p52)**
reflected pulse (noun) **7.2 (p54)**
resistor (noun) **7.2 (p54)**
ridge (noun) **7.3 (p56)**
scanning (noun) **7.3 (p56)**
screen (noun) **7.2 (p54)**
search (verb) **7.1 (p52)**
security (adjective) **7.1 (p52)**
security check (noun) **7.1 (p52)**
sensor (noun) **7.3 (p56)**
separate (adjective) **7.2 (p54)**
spiral (adjective) **7.2 (p55)**
stand aside (phrase) **7.1 (p52)**
step back (phrase) **7.1 (p53)**
supervisor (noun) **7.1 (p52)**
surgery (noun) **7.1 (p52)**
surprise (adjective) **7.1 (p52)**
sound (verb) **7.2 (p54)**
switch (noun) **7.3 (p56)**
take off (clothes) (phrasal verb) **7.2 (p54)**
tell (verb) **7.1 (p53)**
terminal (noun) **7.2 (p55)**
thin (adjective) **7.3 (p56)**
underneath (preposition) **7.1 (p52)**
valley (noun) **7.3 (p56)**
vertical (adjective) **7.2 (p54)**
voice recognition (noun) **7.3 (p56)**
walk-through (adjective) **7.1 (p52)**
wire (noun) **7.2 (p54)**
X-ray machine (noun) **7.2 (p52)**

Unit 8

barrel (noun) **8.1 (p58)**
break (noun) **8.2 (p60)**
by means of/(phrase) **8.2 (p60)**
cable (noun) **8.2 (p60)**
coast (noun) **8.2 (p60)**
combination (noun) **8.2 (p60)**
complete (verb) **8.1 (p59)**
complex (adjective) **8.2 (p60)**
concrete (noun) **8.2 (p60)**
construction (noun) **8.2 (p60)**
continuous (adjective) **8.2 (p60)**
derrick (noun) **8.3 (p62)**
drill (verb) **8.1 (p59)**
drill bit (noun) **8.3 (p62)**
drill collar (noun) **8.3 (p62)**
drill pipe (noun) **8.3 (p62)**
drill string (noun) **8.3 (p62)**
electricity supply (noun) **8.2 (p60)**
elevator (noun) **8.2 (p60)**
enormous (adjective) **8.2 (p60)**
fabric (noun) **8.2 (p60)**
fasten (verb) **8.2 (p61)**
(gas/oil) field (noun) **8.2 (p61)**
fit (verb) **8.1 (p59)**
fix (verb) **8.1 (p59)**
flow (verb) **8.2 (p61)**
hollow (adjective) **8.2 (p60)**
hook (noun) **8.3 (p62)**
hydraulic cylinder (noun) **8.2 (p60)**
in order to (phrase) **8.2 (p61)**
install (verb) **8.1 (p59)**
intense (adjective) **8.2 (p60)**
kelly (noun) **8.3 (p62)**
lay (verb) **8.1 (p59)**
leak (noun) **8.3 (p62)**
lower (verb) **8.1 (p59)**
mainland (noun) **8.2 (p60)**
make up (verb phrase) **8.3 (p63)**
mooring line (noun) **8.1 (p58)**
mud hose (noun) **8.3 (p62)**
mud pump (noun) **8.3 (p62)**

natural gas (noun) **8.2 (p60)**
network (noun) **8.1 (p59)**
offshore (adjective) **8.1 (p58)**
oil field (noun) **8.2 (p60)**
ongoing (adjective) **8.2 (61)**
pipeline (noun) **8.1 (p58)**
platform (noun) **8.1 (p58)**
pour (noun) **8.2 (p60)**
powerful (adjective) **8.2 (p61)**
produce (verb) **8.1 (p59)**
pulley (noun) **8.3 (p62)**
pumping station (noun) **8.1 (p58)**
ream (verb) **8.3 (p63)**
reamer (noun) **8.3 (p63)**
rebar (noun) **8.2 (p61)**
recoverable (adjective) **8.2 (p60)**
reserve (noun) **8.2 (p60)**
reinforced (adjective) **8.2 (p60)**
riser (noun) **8.1 (p58)**
rotary table (noun) **8.3 (p62)**
seabed (noun) **8.1 (p58)**
secure (verb) **8.1 (p59)**
slip (verb) **8.2 (p60)**
slip-forming (noun) **8.2 (p60)**
spar (noun) **8.1 (p58)**
stability (noun) **8.2 (p60)**
structure (noun) **8.2 (p60)**
sub-sea electrical cable (noun) **8.2 (p60)**
sufficient (adverb)) **8.2 (p60)**
swivel (noun) **8.3 (p62)**
tank (noun) **8.2 (p61)**
topside (noun) **8.1 (p58)**
tow (verb) **8.1 (p59)**
transmitter (noun) **8.3 (p63)**
travelling block (noun) **8.3 (p62)**
tree (noun) **8.1 (p58)**
trip in (verb phrase) **8.3 (p63)**
turntable (noun) **8.3 (p62)**
valve (noun) **8.2 (p61)**
winch (noun) **8.3 (p62)**
workforce (noun) **8.2 (p60)**

Word list

Unit 9

a great deal (phrase) **9.1 (p68)**

academic block (noun) **9.3 (p72)**

acceleration (noun) **9.1 (p68)**

adjacent (adjective) **9.3 (p72)**

administration building (noun) **9.3 (p72)**

arch (noun) **9.3 (p73)**

architect (noun) **9.2 (p70)**

architectural (adjective) **9.3 (p73)**

area (noun) **9.2 (p70)**

at an angle (phrase) **9.2 (p70)**

beam (noun) **9.3 (p73)**

beauty (noun) **9.2 (p71)**

bend (noun) **9.1 (p68)**

bill (noun) **9.1 (p69)**

braking power (noun) **9.1 (p68)**

broken (adjective) **9.3 (p73)**

building (noun) **9.2 (p70)**

bulb (noun) **9.1 (p69)**

bulge (verb) **9.2 (p70)**

bumpy (adjective) **9.1 (p68)**

campus ship (noun) **9.3 (p72)**

circular (adjective) **9.2 (p71)**

column (noun) **9.3 (p73)**

comfort (noun) **9.1 (p68)**

compact (adjective) **9.1 (p69)**

conical (adjective) **9.2 (p70)**

consume (verb) **9.1 (p69)**

curved (adjective) **9.2 (p70)**

curvilinear (adjective) **9.2 (p71)**

cylindrical (adjective) **9.2 (p70)**

diagonal (adjective) **9.2 (p70)**

diagrid (adjective) **9.2 (p71)**

doughnut-shaped (adjective) **9.3 (p72)**

ease (noun) **9.1 (p68)**

edge (noun) **9.2 (p70)**

elevation (noun) **9.3 (p73)**

elliptical (adjective) **9.2 (p70)**

excitement (noun) **9.1 (p68)**

extensive (adjective) **9.2 (p71)**

feature (noun) **9.3 (p73)**

floor (noun) **9.2 (p70)**

fluorescent (adjective) **9.1 (p69)**

functionality (noun) **9.2 (p71)**

hatched (adjective) **9.3 (p73)**

height (noun) **9.2 (p70)**

horizontal (adjective) **9.2 (p70)**

incandescent (adjective) **9.1 (p69)**

inclined (adjective) **9.2 (p70)**

indicate (verb) **9.3 (p73)**

innovation (noun) **9.2 (p71)**

input (noun) **9.1 (p69)**

inspire (verb) **9.2 (p71)**

lake (noun) **9.3 (p72)**

leaning (adjective) **9.2 (p70)**

light bulb (noun) **9.1 (p69)**

lumen (noun) **9.1 (p69)**

maritime (adjective) **9.3 (p72)**

output (noun) **9.1 (p69)**

oval (adjective) **9.2 (p70)**

perpendicular (adjective) **9.3 (p73)**

plan (noun) **9.2 (p70)**

pointed (adjective) **9.2 (p71)**

purpose-built (adjective) **9.3 (p73)**

rectangular (adjective) **9.2 (p70)**

represent (verb) **9.3 (p73)**

research centre (noun) **9.3 (p72)**

ring-shaped (adjective) **9.3 (p72)**

rough (adjective) **9.1 (p68)**

safety (noun) **9.1 (p68)**

sail-like (adjective) **9.2 (p71)**

semi-circular (adjective) **9.3 (p72)**

services building (noun) **9.3 (p72)**

set of teeth (phrase) **9.3 (p72)**

slightly (adverb) **9.1 (p68)**

solid (adjective: continuous) **9.3 (p73)**

speed (noun) **9.1 (p68)**

stability (noun) **9.1 (p68)**

staircase (noun) **9.3 (p73)**

storage space (noun) **9.1 (p68)**

storey (noun) **9.2 (p70)**

straight (adjective) **9.2 (p70)**

structural (adjective) **9.2 (p70)**

suspension (noun) **9.1 (68)**

swimming pool (noun) **9.3 (p72)**

tapered (adjective) **9.2 (p70)**

tower (noun) **9.2 (p70)**

turbine (noun) **9.2 (p71)**

turning to (phrase) **9.3 (p73)**

virtually (adverb) **9.2 (p70)**

watt (noun) **9.1 (p69)**

wheel (noun) **9.1 (p68)**

workshop (noun) **9.3 (p72)**

zigzag (adjective) **9.2 (p70)**

Unit 10

abstract (noun) **10.3 (p78)**

annually (adv) **10.2 (p76)**

as indicated (phrase) **10.3 (p78)**

attachment (noun) **10.3 (p78)**

background (noun) **10.3 (p78)**

base (sth on sth) (phrasal verb) **10.3 (p78)**

bearing (noun) **10.1 (p75)**

bomb (noun) **10.1 (p74)**

break away (phrasal verb) **10.1 (p75)**

bridge (noun) **10.1 (p74)**

buckle (verb) **10.1 (p75)**

buckling (noun) **10.1 (p74)**

carry out (phrasal verb) **10.2 (p76)**

catastrophic (adjective) **10.3 (p79)**

collapse (noun) **10.1 (p74)**

compression (noun) **10.1 (p74)**

concentrate (verb) **10.3 (p79)**

conclude (verb) **10.3 (p79)**

conclusion (noun) **10.3 (p78)**

continued (adjective) **10.1 (p75)**

contract (verb) **10.1 (p75)**

corrosion (noun) **10.1 (p74)**

crack (noun) **10.2 (p75)**

cracked (adjective) **10.3 (p79)**

cracking (noun) **10.3 (p79)**

damage (noun) **10.1 (p75)**

death (noun) **10.1 (p74)**

deck (noun) **10.2 (p76)**

disaster (noun) **10.1 (p74)**

disintegration (noun) **10.1 (p75)**

expand (verb) **10.1 (p75)**

fail (verb) **10.3 (p79)**

fatigue (noun) **10.1 (p74)**

finding (noun) **10.3 (p78)**

footage (noun) **10.3 (p78)**

fracture (verb) **10.2 (p77)**

fracture (noun) **10.3 (p79)**

fractured (adjective) **10.2 (p77)**

friction (noun) **10.1 (p75)**

girder (noun) **10.1 (p75)**

gusset plate (noun) **10.2 (p76)**

highway (noun) **10.3 (p79)**

impact (noun) **10.1 (p74)**

inadequate (adjective) **10.3 (p79)**

injury (noun) **10.1 (p74)**

insulating tile (noun) **10.1 (p75)**

introduction (noun) **10.3 (p78)**

investigation (noun) **10.1 (p74)**

loading (noun) **10.1 (p75)**

method (noun) **10.3 (p78)**

near-miss (adjective) **10.3 (p79)**

non-destructive (adjective) **10.3 (p78)**

nose cone (noun) **10.1 (p75)**

overall (adjective) **10.3 (p78)**

physical evidence (noun) **10.3 (p79)**

pier (noun) **10.2 (p76)**

portion (noun) **10.3 (p79)**

present (verb) **10.3 (p78)**

radio mast (noun) **10.1 (p75)**

railway signal (noun) **10.3 (p79)**

reckon (verb) **10.1 (p75)**

recommendation (noun) **10.3 (p78)**

reference (noun) **10.3 (p78)**

reinforcement (noun) **10.2 (p76)**

report (noun) **10.3 (p78)**

rubbing (noun) **10.1 (p75)**

runway (noun) **10.1 (p75)**

rust away (verb) **10.1 (p75)**

seal (noun) **10.1 (p75)**

(space) shuttle (noun) **10.1 (p75)**

snap (verb) **10.1 (p75)**

snap in two (phrase) **10.1 (p75)**

span (noun) **10.3 (p79)**

speculation (noun) **10.1 (p74)**

spreading (noun) **10.2 (p76)**

stretch (verb) **10.2 (p77)**

stretching force (noun) **10.1 (p75)**

strip (noun) **10.1 (p75)**

summarise (verb) **10.3 (p78)**

support strut (noun) **10.2 (p76)**

temporary (adjective) **10.1 (p75)**

tensile force (noun) **10.2 (p77)**

tension (noun) **10.1 (p74)**

thermal shock (noun) **10.1 (p74)**

tile (noun) **10.1 (p75)**

traffic (noun) **10.2 (p76)**

trigger (verb) **10.1 (p75)**

truss (noun) **10.2 (p76)**

undersized (adjective) **10.2 (p76)**

update (verb) **10.3 (p78)**

view (noun) **10.1 (p75)**

wear (noun) **10.1 (p74)**

wear down (phrasal verb) **10.2 (p77)**

wreckage (noun) **10.3 (p78)**

Unit 11

ability (noun) **11.2 (p87)**

abrasion (noun) **11.2 (p87)**

absorbent (adjective) **11.2 (p86)**

application (noun) **11.1 (p84)**

aramid fibre (noun) **11.1 (p84)**

attachment (noun) **11.1 (p84)**

blow (noun: impact) **11.1 (p85)**

break (verb) **11.1 (p85)**

bulletproof (adjective) **11.3 (p89)**

(in)capable (adjective) **11.3 (p89)**

capacity (noun) **11.3 (p89)**

childproof (adjective) **11.3 (p89)**

climbing (noun) **11.1 (p84)**

compressive (adjective) **11.2 (p86)**

corrosion-resistant (adjective) **11.3 (p89)**

covering letter (noun) **11.1 (p84)**

demonstrate (verb) **11.1 (p84)**

ductile (adjective) **11.2 (p86)**

ductility (noun) **11.2 (p86)**

due course (phrase) **11.1 (p84)**

durability (noun) **11.2 (p86)**

durable (adjective) **11.2 (p87)**

effect (noun) **11.1 (p85)**

elastic (adjective) **11.1 (p85)**

elasticity (noun) **11.1 (p84)**

equipment (noun) **11.1 (p84)**

extreme (adjective) **11.2 (p87)**

extremely (adjective/adverb) **11.2 (p86)**

fibre (noun) **11.1 (p84)**

fireproof (adjective) **11.3 (p89)**

fire resistant (adjective) **11.3 (p89)**

firm (adjective) **11.1 (p84)**

flexible (adjective) **11.1 (p85)**

graphite (noun) **11.1 (p84)**

hammer (verb) **11.2 (p86)**

heat tolerant (adjectival phrase) **11.2 (p86)**

high-performance (adjective) **11.2 (p87)**

How about … (phrase) **11.3 (p88)**

hull (noun) **11.3 (p89)**

I would suggest that we … (phrase) **11.3 (p88)**

impact (noun) **11.1 (p85)**

impact absorbent (adjectival phrase) **11.1 (p85)**

impact resistant (adjectival phrase) **11.1 (p85)**

invitation (noun) **11.1 (p84)**

invoice (noun) **11.1 (p84)**

Let's do … (phrase) **11.3 (p88)**

Let's try doing … (phrase) **11.3 (p88)**

lightness (noun) **11.1 (p84)**

lightweight (adjective) **11.1 (p85)**

malleability (adjective) **11.2 (p86)**

non-flammability (noun) **11.2 (p86)**

nylon (noun) **11.1 (p84)**

package (noun) **11.1 (p84)**

padding (noun) **11.1 (p85)**

personal (adjective) **11.1 (p84)**

polyurethane foam (noun) **11.1 (p85)**

presentation (noun) **11.1 (p84)**

property (noun) **11.1 (p86)**

proposal (noun) **11.1 (p84)**

protection (noun) **11.1 (p84)**

protective (adjective) **11.2 (p86)**

quality (noun) **11.2 (p87)**

reduce (verb) **11.1 (p85)**

resist (verb) **11.2 (p86)**

responsive (adjective) **11.2 (p87)**

return (verb) **11.1 (p85)**

rigidity (noun) **11.1 (p84)**

rope (noun) **11.1 (p84)**

severe (adjective) **11.3 (p89)**

shear (adjective) **11.2 (p86)**

shock resistant (adjectival phrase) **11.3 (p89)**

ski pole (noun) **11.1 (p84)**

skiing (noun) **11.1 (p84)**

stain resistant (adjectival phrase) **11.3 (p89)**

strength (noun) **11.1 (p84)**

stud (noun) **11.1 (p84)**

synthetic (adjective) **11.1 (p84)**

thermosplastic polyurethane (TPU) (noun) **11.1 (p85)**

tolerance (noun) **11.2 (p86)**

tough (adjective) **11.1 (p85)**

violent (adjective) **11.1 (p85)**

water resistant (adjectival phrase) **11.3 (p89)**

waterproof (adjective) **11.3 (p89)**

We could … (phrase) **11.3 (p88)**

weigh (verb) **11.1 (p85)**

What / How about doing … (phrase) **11.3 (p88)**

Why don't we do … (phrase) **11.3 (p88)**

withstand (verb) **11.1 (p85)**

Unit 12

achieve (verb) **12.2 (p92)**

aerodynamic (adjective) **12.2 (p92)**

apparent wind (noun) **12.2 (p92)**

Arctic, the (noun) **12.1 (p90)**

atmosphere (noun) **12.1 (p91)**

canvas (noun) **12.2 (p92)**

cockpit (noun) **12.2 (p92)**

completely (adverb) **12.2 (p93)**

composite (noun) **12.2 (p92)**

craft (noun) **12.2 (p92)**

cyclone (noun) **12.1 (p91)**

DC converter (noun) **12.3 (p94)**

DC motor (noun) **12.3 (p94)**

depleted (adjective) **12.3 (p94)**

downward (adverb) **12.2 (p92)**

drag (noun) **12.2 (p92)**

efficient (adjective) **12.2 (p92)**

electron (noun) **12.3 (p95)**

enable (verb) **12.2 (p92)**

environment (noun) **12.3 (p94)**

equal (verb) **12.2 (p92)**

exactly (adverb) **12.2 (p93)**

except that (conjunction) **12.2 (p92)**

exchange (noun) **12.3 (p94)**

flat (battery) (adjective) **12.3 (p94)**

flood (verb) **12.1 (p90)**

flux (noun) **12.3 (p95)**

forest (noun) **12.1 (p90)**

fossil fuel (noun) **12.1 (p90)**

fuel cell (noun) **12.3 (p95)**

fuel tank (noun) **12.3 (p95)**

fusion (noun) **12.2 (p92)**

gearing (noun) **12.3 (p94)**

gigatonne (noun) **12.1 (p90)**

glacier (noun) **12.1 (p91)**

hovercraft (noun) **12.2 (p93)**

hydrogen (noun) **12.3 (p95)**

ice cap (noun) **12.1 (p91)**

instead (adverb) **12.1 (p90)**

in the same way as (phrase) **12.2 (p93)**

inverter (noun) **12.3 (p95)**

invest (verb) **12.1 (p90)**

lift (noun) **12.2 (p92)**

(un)like (preposition) **12.2 (p93)**

low-lying (adjective) **12.1 (p90)**

keel (noun) **12.2 (p92)**

magnetic (adjective) **12.3 (p95)**

massive (adjective) **12.2 (p92)**

maximise (verb) **12.2 (p92)**

minimise (verb) **12.2 (p92)**

miracle (noun) **12.2 (p92)**

non-contact charging (noun) **12.3 (p95)**

oxygen (noun) **12.3 (p95)**

power panel (noun) **12.3 (p95)**

power source (noun) **12.3 (p95)**

power supply (noun) **12.3 (p95)**

prediction (noun) **12.1 (p90)**

primary (adjective) **12.3 (p95)**

propel (verb) **12.2 (p92)**

recharge (verb) **12.3 (p94)**

rectifier (noun) **12.3 (p95)**

refuel (verb) **12.3 (p94)**

renewable energy (noun) **12.1 (p90)**

require (verb) **12.2 (p92)**

resemble (verb) **12.2 (p92)**

sail (noun) **12.2 (p92)**

sailboat (noun) **12.2 (p92)**

(best/worst-case) scenario (phrase) **12.1 (p90)**

secondary (adjective) **12.3 (p95)**

sideways (adverb) **12.2 (p92)**

skate (noun) **12.2 (p92)**

smash (verb) **12.2 (p92)**

society (noun) **12.1 (p90)**

solar panel (noun) **12.1 (p90)**

solar-powered (adjective) **12.3 (p94)**

solution (noun) **12.2 (p92)**

staggering (adjective) **12.2 (p92)**

store (verb) **12.3 (p95)**

submarine (noun) **12.2 (p93)**

supply (verb) **12.3 (p95)**

surfboard (noun) **12.2 (p93)**

system check (noun) **12.3 (p94)**

threat (noun) **12.1 (p90)**

tremendous (adjective) **12.2 (p92)**

tropical (adjective) **12.1 (p91)**

wind (noun) **12.2 (p92)**

world record (noun) **12.2 (p92)**

Word list